PENGUIN BOOKS
BRAVE OLD WORLD

'Charmingly old-fashioned, delightfully eccentric, utterly endearing'
Virginia Ironside, *The Lady*

'One of those enthusiasts whose enthusiasm is hard to resist . . . Bizarre yet always
beguiling' *Daily Mail*

'Demonstrates that a simple life can be immensely satisfying' *NFU Countryside*

'Lovely . . . A laid-back almanac of pleasures' *Saga Magazine*

ABOUT THE AUTHOR

Tom Hodgkinson is the editor of the *Idler* and the author of *How to be Idle, How to be Free* and *The Idle Parent*. In spring 2011 he co-founded the Idler Academy in London: a bookshop, coffee house and cultural centre that hosts literary events and offers courses in academic and practical subjects, from Latin to embroidery.

www.idler.co.uk

Brave Old World

A MONTH-BY-MONTH GUIDE TO HUSBANDRY,

OR THE FINE ART OF

LOOKING AFTER YOURSELF

Tom Hodgkinson

PENGUIN BOOKS

PENGUIN BOOKS

Published by the Penguin Group
Penguin Books Ltd, 80 Strand, London WC2R ORL, England
Penguin Group (USA), Inc., 375 Hudson Street, New York, New York 10014, USA
Penguin Group (Canada), 90 Eglinton Avenue East, Suite 700, Toronto, Ontario, Canada M4P 2Y3
(a division of Pearson Penguin Canada Inc.)
Penguin Ireland, 25 St Stephen's Green, Dublin 2, Ireland
(a division of Penguin Books Ltd)
Penguin Group (Australia), 250 Camberwell Road, Camberwell, Victoria 3124, Australia
(a division of Pearson Australia Group Pty Ltd)
Penguin Books India Pvt Ltd, 11 Community Centre, Panchsheel Park,
New Delhi – 110 017, India
Penguin Group (NZ), 67 Apollo Drive, Rosedale, Auckland 0632, New Zealand
(a division of Pearson New Zealand Ltd)
Penguin Books (South Africa) (Pty) Ltd, 24 Sturdee Avenue, Rosebank, Johannesburg 2196, South Africa

Penguin Books Ltd, Registered Offices: 80 Strand, London WC2R ORL, England

www.penguin.com

First published by Hamish Hamilton 2011
Published in Penguin Books 2012

1

Set in Monotype Poliphilus and Blado
Typeset by Bracketpress
Printed in Great Britain by Clays Ltd, St Ives plc

A CIP catalogue record for this book is available from the British Library

ISBN: 978-0-141-03038-8

www.greenpenguin.co.uk

MIX
Paper from
responsible sources
FSC™ C018179

Penguin Books is committed to a sustainable
future for our business, our readers and our
planet. This book is made from paper certified
by the Forest Stewardship Council.

For Alan and Alan, my husbandry gurus

'We must go back to freedom or forward to slavery'

– G. K. Chesterton

CONTENTS

Introduction

Labor omnia vicit
[Toil conquered everything]
– Virgil

The most important but generally the most neglected of the arts of everyday living are simply these: philosophy, husbandry and merriment. Philosophy is the search for the truth and the study of how to live well. Husbandry is the art of providing for oneself and one's family, and merriment is the important skill of enjoying yourself: feasting, dancing, joking and singing.

All these aspects of life were actively cultivated in the Brave Old World. By 'Brave Old World', I mean the time from the Ancient Greeks to the end of the medieval period so, roughly, the two thousand years from 500 BC to AD 1500. The Old World came to an end in around 1535 with the Reformation, Calvinism, the Renaissance and the looting and smashing up of the monasteries. Philosophy, husbandry and merriment have been cultivated since, to be sure, and still are today by a few brave souls, but since the Industrial Revolution, they have tended to take second place to work – for most of us, wage slavery, i.e. boring work done to enrich someone else, the corporation and its shareholders, or for the good of the bureaucratic, totalitarian state. In the Old World, cultivated leisure was the most important part of life. In the new, the job is the priority.

The art of thinking has been gradually dropped from the school curriculum. And the art of producing one's own food at home has been replaced with the chore of driving to the supermarket and buying it all. And we are the poorer for all this, not the richer.

The purpose of this book, which seeks to combine entertainment with instruction, is to examine the old ways and argue that they were often good ways, and that we could improve our lives immeasurably by adopting them in today's world. It is not for a moment intended as an exercise in whimsical nostalgia. It is clearly impossible to travel back in time; we are stuck in the here and now, and indeed there is much to be celebrated in the modern age. But fear of appearing nostalgic should not prevent us from recognizing and celebrating the good things of the past. As Ovid wrote in the *Fasti* of AD8:

Laudamus veteres, sed nostris utimur annis:
mos tamen est aeque dignus uterque coli.

[We praise past ways, but use the present years, yet both are customs worthy to be kept.]

So, for example, we can sing the praises of those brilliant pieces of technology, the book and the scythe, while also enjoying the iPad or Skype, and all that modern technology which Aldous Huxley called 'nearly miraculous'. (However, ask yourself which of the iPad or the scythe will still be around in a thousand years' time.) *Brave Old World* focuses on husbandry, by which I mean the act of turning your household into a creative and productive entity, rather than just somewhere to watch a gigantic television screen after work. The word 'husband' is derived from the Old English *húsbonda* meaning 'the head of the household', and the word also suggests a careful and thrifty manager. 'Husbandry' means nurturing, that is, nurturing animals, crops, your children, yourself.

To prepare this book, I have read several old texts on husbandry, from the Greek Hesiod to the Romans Columella, Varro and Cato. Virgil's great didactic farming poem, *The Georgics*, as you will see, is a key reference point. In the Middle Ages, there was a wonderful tradition of farming and gardening calendars, particularly in the Flemish area, and I will refer to a number of these throughout the book too. These were perpetual calendars with a special code for working out which day of the week it was, and were illustrated with lovely little pictures of medieval men and women going about their tasks. The farmer would keep one on his wall.

I have learned that books on gardening and farming are themselves a literary form: the didactic farming poem goes back to Hesiod's *Works and Days* of the eighth century BC and probably reached its zenith in Virgil's *Georgics*. This book is a modest contribution to that genre. Like previous examples of the form, I have quoted from the great authorities. There is the lovable Thomas Tusser, author of the Tudor best-seller *Five Hundred Points of Good Husbandry*. I've looked at John Evelyn's seventeenth-century gardening guide-book *Directions for the Gardiner*, and William Cobbett's nineteenth-century *The English Gardener*. Another excellent find has been a medieval translation of Palladius, a Roman writer on farming and gardening who lived in the fourth century AD.

Brave Old World is in no way intended as a complete guide to self-sufficiency. It should be seen as an addition to your shelf of books on gardening and husbandry. It is perhaps more of a literary than a practical guide, though there is plenty of practical stuff in it. We stand on the shoulders of previous titans: Virgil did not feel the need to keep bees himself in order to write about them, and he referred to previous authorities in order to compile *The Georgics*. It is the same with William Cobbett: much of the material for his husbandry guide *Cottage Economy* was gleaned from an old farmer's wife. And one of John Evelyn's great books on gardening was itself a translation of a French best-seller, *Le Jardinier françois* by Nicolas de Bonnefons. Evelyn, a close friend of Charles II, also produced a brilliant gardening calendar, the *Kalendarium Hortense*, with the following typically extravagant seventeenth-century subtitle: 'Or, the Gard'ners Almanac, Directing what he is to do Monthly, throughout the Year; and what Fruits and Flowers are in Prime'.

Gardening books, then, have always offered a mixture of the didactic and the romantic, the practical and the literary. And it is true that the writer of a good book on husbandry does not necessarily need to be a good husbandman himself. Tusser, who was educated at Eton and Trinity Hall, Cambridge, was a notoriously unsuccessful farmer. His own attempts to make money from agriculture ended in disaster. Thomas Fuller, a contemporary of Pepys, who was described by that life-loving diarist as 'the great Tom Fuller', wrote a short entry on Tusser in his *Worthies of England*:

Thus our English Columella might say with the poet:

Monitis sum minor ipse meis

[I fall short of my own precepts]
— Ovid

None being better at the theory, or worse at the practice, of husbandry.

Tusser's skill, then, was communication.

Brave Old World combines nods to such literary authorities with tales of my own experience living on a rented farm in North Devon. And it must be admitted that I am not particularly good at the practice of husbandry either. In fact, *Idler* readers know our place as 'the disastrous smallholding'. I moved here with my family from London in 2002, and since then my wife, Victoria, and I have embarked on various experiments in husbandry. We have grown vegetables, kept pigs and chickens, killed them, cooked them and eaten them. We have inherited a pony, and Victoria has kept and lost bees. We have sent ferrets down rabbit holes and skinned rabbits. We have brewed foul beer and made wonderful elderflower cordial. Victoria makes butter and bread, and it is the best butter and bread you have ever tasted. We have made jams, pickles and marmalades. We have chopped, stacked and dried logs. We have made a thousand fires. We have murdered a thousand slugs. We have made parsnip wine and sold eggs. We have discovered that the simple life is both extremely complicated and very hard. It is studded with disappointments, but the satisfactions are immense. And the end of it is simply this: you save a lot of money and you make much better food. And in the process, you connect with the living world, with nature, the cosmos. You also connect yourself with the ancient tradition of householding, home-making, husbandry, or whatever you want to call it. When you nurture yourself in this way, you disconnect yourself from the world of the supermarkets, with their low, low prices and low, low standards, you become healthy, and whole.

It is neither possible nor particularly desirable to be entirely self-sufficient. Self-sufficiency implies a wilful separation from others, whereas husbandry is all about sharing the work and sharing the knowledge. I love books, but the best advice will come from your neighbour, who has actually done the things that you want to do.

You must get people to help, and if your businesses thrive and you can employ people to help, then all the better. Make things; sell them.

You must accept your own limitations. It is simply impossible to earn a living *and* become a reasonable vegetable gardener, cook, butcher, poultry-keeper, swineherd, woodsman, builder, baker, jam-maker, *charcutier*, haymaker, beekeeper, brewer, dairymaid, carpenter and cleaner overnight, or even over ten years. Start small and keep your aspirations low. In the old days, an apprenticeship lasted a full seven years.

All the above are arts and, as such, must be learned slowly and over many years. You must study carefully, read many books, go on courses and, of course, learn from your own successes and failures, as well as those of other people. There is hard work involved. Don't believe those who tell you that growing vegetables, for instance, is easy: it is immensely complicated. This is my fifth year of growing vegetables, and this year I have abandoned the 'no work' principles of letting nature do all the work. I tried that, and I ended up with a nightmarish wilderness, a horrific mess which I found painful just to think about, let alone actually get out to and work on. This year, I have gone back to traditional methods and used hard toil. I have dug and cultivated and manured and weeded. I have protected crops with eggshells and wire frames. I have even put down organic slug pellets, because I found it too depressing to see my lettuces vanish to the greed of the evil slug in a single night. I have kept the paths trim with the edge of the spade. I have kept the hens out. The result is that the small vegetable garden is a delight to work in and I look forward to my sessions in it, rather than dreading them, as before. Though it pains me slightly as an idler to confess it, gardens need a lot of tending. As Virgil says:

Labor omnia vicit
improbus, et duris urgens in rebus egestas.

[Toil conquered everything, unrelenting toil, and the want that
pinches when life is hard.]

The good news is that this toil is a million times more enjoyable
and satisfying than the daily grind of office work, with its psychically
damaging lack of end product with which to be satisfied. And really,
an hour a day in a small garden or allotment would suffice, with the
occasional two- or three-hour stretch of digging and manuring. So
when we talk about *labor*, it is really just small but regular amounts
that are required, rather than back-breaking toil.

The title of my book is of course a play on Huxley's *Brave New
World*, itself a quote from *The Tempest*. My point here is that the
Old World was indeed braver than ours. In war, the knights and
kings would ride out at the front of the armies. They would not
sit in back rooms and send thousands of young men to their deaths
like our modern-day cowards in the state. When our liberties were
attacked, we fought to defend them. We would ride horses, walk for
miles, chop wood, grow vegetables. We were hardy, free and strong,
but we have become sickly, servile slaves, queuing up at doctors'
surgeries to be handed our American-made pills and panaceas.

But what about the plagues, the pain, the toothache? Well, this
is a point explored by Orwell in *The Road to Wigan Pier*, in which
he attacks 'machine-worship' as dehumanizing. Today, we have
'technology-worship' in its place. Orwell found himself on the
receiving end of attacks when he supported the Brave Old World:

As a matter of fact, most attacks upon the Middle Ages and the
past generally by apologists of the present are beside the point,

because their essential trick is to project a modern man, with his squeamishness and his high standards of comfort, into an age when such things were unheard of . . . explain that you wish to aim at making life simpler and harder instead of softer and more complex, and the Socialist will usually assume that you want to revert to a 'state of nature'.

It would be a mistake, though, to see the Brave Old World as a comfort-free zone. It was actually a more sensual period, and people loved nothing more than a roaring fire, wine and music. There were many pleasures. Perhaps the point is that before air conditioning and shopping malls levelled everything out, we lived a life of contrasts. You would go from being very cold to being very hot. A fast would be followed by a feast. Bitter tears would be followed by merry jests. Life was lived passionately.

To tend your own garden is to reject wholeheartedly the pain-free Brave New World that Huxley describes. In the Brave New World, people are taught to be squeamish and to hate nature, except as something to travel to and gaze at when the weekend comes. The Brave New Worlders, for example, get in helicopters and go for picnics on Exmoor at the weekend. Physical and mental pain have been practically wiped out. When it all gets a bit much, you just take the tranquillizing drug Soma and bliss out for fourteen hours. The mission to destroy pain is certainly a feature of our modern world, with ibuprofen on hand for physical pain and anti-depressants for mental pain. Illegal drugs such as ecstasy are commonly taken in the West, by all age groups and by all social groups: I have been amazed recently to discover that ecstasy-taking is all the rage among the British landed gentry and their courtiers, from age fifteen to eighty. Painkillers are advertised with slogans such as: 'Hit pain where it hurts.' There is even an American movement which envisages the complete end of pain. It's a world of comfort. My mother, your archetypal aspiring grammar-school girl, thinks that this is all marvellous: she read *Brave New World* and didn't realize it was a satire. She just thought it was a good idea. 'You don't have to look after your own children. There's no mess. No nature. What's the point of nature, anyway?' she said to me.

Towards the end of *Brave New World*, the Resident World Controller for Western Europe, Mustapha Mond, debates the new philosophy with the Savage. It's all about removing inconveniences, he says:

> 'But I like the inconveniences.'
>
> 'We don't,' said the Controller. 'We prefer to do things comfortably.'
>
> 'But I don't want comfort. I want God, I want poetry, I want real danger, I want freedom, I want goodness. I want sin.'
>
> 'In fact,' said Mustapha Mond, 'you're claiming the right to be unhappy.'

Truth, beauty, pain, unhappiness: the modern world seeks to abolish these things. But in the Old World, we are faced with them every day. I see them daily in my vegetable patch. Can we really be happy? Do we want to be happy? Today's world has seen an industry spring up that is based around the idea that we can be happy: there are books and seminars out there that promise to reveal the secrets of happiness. There are conferences and seminars on the subject. The English public school Wellington College offers happiness lessons. This phenomenon was predicted by Huxley in his 1946 introduction to *Brave New World*, written ten years after the book was first published. Huxley also reveals the true agenda of the happiness project: 'The most important Manhattan Projects of the future will be vast government-sponsored enquiries into what the politicians and the participating scientists will call "the problem of happiness" — in other words, the problem of making people love their servitude.

Huxley says that, to achieve this aim, we will need a more sophisticated method of conditioning infants. This is indeed happening in primary schools, which are putting the twin curriculum aims of 'wellbeing' and 'ICT' (Information and Communication Technology) at the heart of the curriculum, at the expense of teaching the basics such as times tables or grammar. Children are conditioned from a young age into the idea that they are living in a technological utopia and are very lucky not to be living in the horrible past or in some ghastly famine-struck place such as Africa. They are taught to be happy and cheerful — in other words, not to question the world they are about to enter. For its part, the world of advertising reinforces this message. McDonald's and Tesco are your friends, and they offer up cheerful morons such as Ronald McDonald to prove it, and of course their rather vague slogans: 'Every little helps,' 'Always lower prices' and 'I'm lovin' it.' (*Who* is loving *what*?)

Note also that in *Brave New World*, people go to the 'feelies', an advanced version of the movies. At the feelies, you can actually feel the bearskin rug you see on the screen. Now this is not a million miles away from the modern use of the word 'experience' in advertising copy. Instead of good food, restaurants offer a 'quality dining experience'. Holiday operators also use the word, as do theme parks and other peddlers of fun. I can foresee a time when books will be sold as a 'thrilling reading experience'. Life has been reduced to a series of long periods of boredom in the office punctuated by high-octane 'experiences' which you can rack up on your list of things to do before you die. That is not really living: that is slavery with the occasional circus thrown in.

The science of positive psychology, too, aims to keep the workers happy. This is because, so it is claimed by the adherents of this false creed, happy workers make productive workers. Happiness boosts the bottom line. Therefore management theorists try to keep people cheerful and positive in the workplace. The flipside of this, however, is that if things are going badly then it is your fault. You are not being badly treated. You are not being underpaid. You must not go on strike or grumble. Instead, go and see the company therapist. They should be able to sort you out. They'll cheer you up and send you back into the slave pits feeling grateful. And if counselling doesn't work, there's always Ativan or Prozac. Dose you up on those tranquillizing concoctions and you'll go back meekly and happily into the workplace, your spirit having been chemically or mechanically removed. Meanwhile, the profits of the drugs companies soar. As they say in *Private Eye*, 'Trebles all round!'

* * *

Well, this is the situation from which I hope to break free by celebrating certain aspects of the Brave Old World. In the Old World, we are happy to be unhappy. We snap our fingers at government and corporation. We are unafraid of truth, beauty and pain. The road to liberty is not a smooth and straight one. It is a hard path. But it is worth it. Let me end with this beautiful thought from Chesterton, written in his 1916 introduction to Cobbett's *Cottage Economy*:

We must go back to freedom or forward to slavery. The free man of England, where he still exists, will doubtless find it a colossal enterprise to unwind the coil of three centuries. It is very right that he should consider the danger and pain and heart-rending complication involved in unwinding that coil. But it is also proper that he should consider the alternative; and the alternative is being strangled.

– Tom Hodgkinson, August 2010, North Devon

CHAPTER ONE

January

Chop Wood

Igne levatus hiems

[Winter is eased with fire]

– Ovid

JANUARY is for keeping warm. It is the month for fireside loafing and late-night feasting, for candles, the warmth of the wood-burning stove and the delicious sweet smell of woodsmoke. In the pre-Industrial era, the harsh weather provided a good excuse to stay in and avoid toil.

The word 'January' is derived from the name of the two-faced Roman god Janus, and the medieval calendars show Janus enjoy-ing a slap-up meal at his trestle table, one face looking back at the year just gone and the other looking forward at the year to come. A French poem of the thirteenth century (from *The Penguin Book of French Verse*, vol.1, Penguin Books, 1961) emphasizes the impor-tance of pleasure and comfort during this unfriendly month:

> *Quant je le tens refroidier*
> *Voi, et geler,*
> *Et ces arbres despoillier*
> *Et iverner,*
> *Adone me vueil aisier*
> *Et sejorner*
> *A bon feu, lès le brasier,*
> *Et à vin cler,*
> *En chaude maison,*
> *Por le tens felon.*
> *Je n'ait il pardon*
> *Qui n'aime sa garison!*

[When I see the weather growing cold, and the frost coming, and my trees losing their leaves, and growing wintry, then I want to take my ease and stay in front of a good fire, beside the glowing charcoal, with clear wine, in a warm house, because of the bad weather. May he never forgiven be, who does not care for his own comfort!]

Virgil writes, 'Hiems ignava colono' (Winter is the farmer's lazy time: Georgics, Book I, l.299). A similar scene to that described in the poem above is also to be found in a 1712 letter by Alexander Pope: 'I am just in the reverse of all this Spirit and Life, confin'd to a narrow Closet, lolling on an arm chair, nodding away my days over a fire, like the picture of January in an old Salisbury Primer.'

There is a wonderful illustration for January in Les Très Riches Heures du Duc de Berry, an elaborate calendar produced in 1409 by the Limbourg brothers and commissioned by the enormously wealthy Duc de Berry. In it, we see the duke throwing a party. He is surrounded by courtiers, and everyone is giving and receiving gifts. The scene for February shows a more humble winter scene: two peasants are warming their feet by the fire in their cosy smallholding. They have pulled up their smocks and have their knees wide apart, and it is clear that neither man nor wife is wearing any underwear.

This is the spirit we must bring back to January: lolling, nodding and keeping our stomachs full and our bodies warm. And we must sleep much. In the words of a Scottish medieval poet included in a collection by W. A. Craigie, we should make sure we take nourishing naps and keep our toes toasty warm:

> Ane nap is nowrissand eftir none,
> Ane fyre is fosterand for my feit,
> With dowbill sokkis for my schone
> And mittanis for my handis meit.

[A nap is nourishing after noon, a fire is comforting for my feet, with double socks inside my shoes, and welcome mittens for my hands.]

In January, Victoria and I concentrate on keeping the fires alight and eating well, an approach that is happily in accord with ancient wisdom. At home we have two wood-burning stoves, one in the sitting room and one in my study. Both need to be kept alight virtually non-stop throughout January and February. There is nothing gloomier than a grey hearth on a winter's day; nothing more cheery than a glowing red fire. With skill, it is possible to keep the wood-burners going twenty-four hours a day: last thing at night, we stack the blaze with logs, and then close the air vents at the front of the stove. We also close the vent in the flue that comes out of the back of the burner. Starved of oxygen in this way, the fire should slowly smoulder all night. In the morning, we just open up the vent again, give the fire a little stir with the poker, and up it goes once more. When this happens, you feel deeply satisfied, and you have saved a good deal of labour in lighting the fire anew. This last winter, we were snowed in for nine days, and very enjoyable it was, too: there was no work and no school, just the pleasant tasks of keeping warm, cooking and playing games.

This brings me to the heart of the matter: the tricky art of organizing a good wood supply. You must have plenty of logs, and they must be dry. After eight years of living in the country, I still fail at this most basic task and, come March, our supplies tend to run out. I am then forced to take a humiliating trip to the nursery to buy very expensive orange nets of seasoned wood.

The Need for Dry Wood

The simple rule for a good fire is that your wood must be thoroughly dried out or 'seasoned'. When wood is first cut down, it is saturated with water. This is not water that has fallen on the tree from the sky but moisture it has sucked up from the ground to feed itself. Now, the less water there is in the wood, the more quickly and easily it will burn. A water-soaked log will sit and smoulder in the fire in a most depressing fashion.

How can you tell that your logs are properly dried out? Well, I have looked into this subject deeply. In fact, I became obsessed. When asked by friends what Tom likes to talk about best, Victoria will answer: 'logs'. I even bought a book on the subject, a great read called *The Harrowsmith Country Life Guide to Wood Heat*, by Canadian log man Dirk Thomas. He sets out the following indicators:

Weight: Seasoned wood is much lighter than green wood of the same species.

Smell: Green wood often has a pleasant, sappy aroma. Seasoned wood will smell like wood, but not as strongly.

Loose bark: As wood dries, the bark adheres less tenaciously.

Colour: The wood visible on the sides and split ends fades as wood seasons . . . if your new load is bright and fresh in colour rather than dull and subdued, you'll want to take a closer look.

These are all good indicators, but they will take experience to learn, since they are relative. A foolproof way of testing whether your logs are dry is to invest in a moisture meter. This little gadget will give you the percentage of water content in your log. The logs should be split with an axe and the wood tested in a few places, by sticking the two little pins of the gadget into the wood. An LCD display gives a reading. A very wet and heavy log will have a water content of 70 per cent or more. The ideal is 20 per cent – logs this dry will burn well and your fire will glow beautifully and pump out the heat.

It is important to understand all this because, in general, log merchants claim that their logs are seasoned but, in actual fact, they very rarely are. I know this to be true from harsh experience, from spending cold evenings by the fire trying to stoke up a blaze from logs that I now know were soaking wet inside. How bitterly I have cursed the mendacious log merchants who have sold us piles of wood that simply would not burn! Trying to burn a wet log wastes energy: the heat from the fire will disappear as it attempts to evaporate the water in the log. You will hear a familiar, disheartening hissing sound, and steam rather than smoke will rise from the log. The fire actually seems to be sucking heat out of the room.

On Buying Logs

When it comes to log merchants, my landlady says, 'You've got to get ahead of them.' To be safe, you must assume that log merchants will never deliver seasoned wood and, therefore, you need to order the logs a year or more before you need them. Logs take a long time to dry out. Victoria's cousin Lucy says they should be left for at least two years. And the pioneering organic farmer Guy Watson is a three-year man. I once bought a load of wet logs and piled them up in a stone barn. One year later, some of the bigger pieces still had a 40 per cent moisture content. This sort of forward thinking does not come naturally to city-bred types like me who are accustomed to popping out to the twenty-four-hour supermarket when we run out of some important staple, but I am learning. A good idea is to order two large loads at once. Chop up the larger logs, and stack neatly.

It is possible to dry logs more quickly than the standard year. My friend in this matter is, again, Dirk Thomas, and his advice is to site your log pile in a windy and sunny spot. It should ideally be where the laundry dries. This way, you will harness the sun and the wind, which will help to dry out the logs. We have built what he calls a 'solar log dryer' in the yard. The logs are piled on pallets. This prevents water coming up from the ground and soaking into the logs. On three sides, the logs are open to the elements. They are covered with a roof made of plywood covered in roofing felt so they cook in the sun but most of the rain is kept off them. We have put a gutter on the roof in order to collect the rainwater, and to keep the rain off our heads when we collect logs on a wet day.

My friend Nick tells me that, in Sweden, they make log ricks: the wet logs are stacked in a circle and topped with a sloping log roof, bark facing outwards, which keeps them sheltered from the rain. Again, the wind blows through them and the sun cooks them.

The smaller the log, the quicker it will dry. I therefore cut the larger ones into two or three before stacking them. Do not stack them tightly. When stacking the logs, you should make sure that there is plenty of space between them so that the air can circulate. I have found that logs arranged in this way will dry out in a few months rather than the one or two years it would take if they were left in a damp barn. The Canadian log man claims that a 'solar log dryer' such as the one I describe above has the potential to dry out the logs in a mere two weeks, but my experience suggests that this is wildly optimistic.

This last winter, thanks to my valiant efforts all year round buying, chopping and stacking logs, we had an excellent supply of dry wood. I should add, though, that there is a huge amount of work and thought involved. The log man dumps the logs in the yard. I have to stack them and chop them up. Then, during the winter, I wheelbarrow loads of logs from the pile to the porch, and then carry them from the porch to the fires themselves. Then you need a good supply of dry twigs and kindling to get the fire going; wet twigs will not do it. When the burners are really blazing, they absolutely tear through the logs, so you have to work to replenish the supply. You

will also need to clean the ash out of the fire daily and make sure that
the chimneys are swept annually. The key is to *enjoy* the work. And
while there is nothing I want to do less on a cold, rainy day than go
out to the barn and chop logs, once you are engaged in this sort of
work, it can be a real pleasure. It is also good exercise and it warms
you up. Log chopping – which tends to be the man's job – is
immensely satisfying, too. And it is a physical outlet. Many are the
occasions when I have stormed off to the log barn following a row
with Victoria and laid into a pile of logs with great ferocity.

On Differing Types of Wood

The issue of drying and burning logs is further complicated by the
varying properties of different woods. Some are soft, some are hard,
and all have unique characteristics. Oak, beech and ash pump out a
lot of heat, while softwoods such as pine and birch generate less heat
and burn quickly. As you will see, the log merchant who makes
false claims as to the dryness of his logs is not a new phenomenon.
An anonymous old poem about logs, 'Logs to Burn', complains
about mendacious log merchants:

> Logs to burn, Logs to burn, Logs to burn,
> Logs to save the coal a turn,
> Here's a word to make you wise,
> When you hear the woodman's cries.
>
> Never heed his usual tale,
> That he has good logs for sale,
> But read these lines and really learn,
> The proper kind of logs to burn.

Another rhyming guide to wood types runs thus:

Beechwood fires are bright and clear
If the logs are kept a year,
Chestnut's only good they say,
If for logs 'tis laid away.
Make a fire of elder tree,
Death within your house will be;
But ash new or ash old,
Is fit for a queen with crown of gold.

Birch and fir logs burn too fast
Blaze up bright and do not last,
It is by the Irish said
Hawthorn bakes the sweetest bread.
Elm wood burns like churchyard mould,
E'en the very flames are cold.
But ash green or ash brown
Is fit for a queen with a golden crown.

Poplar gives a bitter smoke,
Fills your eyes and makes you choke,
Apple wood will scent your room
Pear wood smells like flowers in bloom
Oaken logs, if dry and old
Keep away the winter's cold.
But ash wet or ash dry
A king shall warm his slippers by.

'Green' here is used in the sense of 'unseasoned', and it is commonly held that ash will burn well even when green. It is true that it has a lower moisture content than most woods, but it will still benefit from a few months of sun and wind. Fir logs spit and crackle, it is true, but this is not a problem for a wood-burner because you can enclose the fire by shutting the door. In my experience, oak is a good burn but must be very dry, and old, and that will take two years. Beech is now my favourite, since it is easily found, dries more quickly than oak, and burns bright and hot, as the poem suggests.

I suppose the ideal situation would be a nice pile of different sorts of wood cut to different sizes: small bits of pine to get the fire going and then nice big oak logs to plant in there once it is very hot. As for the supposed bitterness of poplar smoke, I am soon to find out. One year ago, I was kindly given a load of timbers from a friend's garden, most about six feet long. Some were poplar. My old neighbour has just come to stay, and she chainsawed them up for me, ready to be chopped by my axe.

The main point to remember is this: you will need far more wood than you think, and you will need to buy it far more in advance than you think. And, when buying an axe, take advice. There are specific axes out there for specific jobs.

On What to Do When Your Logs Run Out

However well we buy and store our wood, it is always likely that, at some point, our supply of dry logs will run out. This will tend to happen in February or March. All the dry logs have gone, so what can you do? Well, I have discovered a few emergency measures:

1. Buy a bag of coal. You can throw a handful of coal on to a log-burning fire or into a wood-burner. The coals will get nice and hot — hot enough perhaps to burn some of the wet logs. The coals will burn on the ashes and you won't necessarily need a

grate. And coal has the advantage that it can be left alone for long periods. However, it is also dirty, and the heat it produces is inferior to that of a wood fire.

2. Dry logs quickly. Chop up your logs very small. Place them on their ends around the fire, or even put them in the oven to dry out. My friend Graham tragically failed to organize a good supply of dry logs for his wood-fired Rayburn and was reduced to cooking the logs with the heat from the previous logs to make them burn.

3. Poach wood. It should be possible to poach large quantities of wood. Pallets burn beautifully, being made of well-seasoned softwood. How do you find old pallets? Well, I have found that far superior to the Internet is the Old World practice known as 'asking around'. In fact, I would go so far as to say that 'asking around' is the new Internet. By asking around, you will instantly plug yourself into a network of at least dozens and possibly hundreds of people in your local area, each with their own local knowledge.

The Internet commodifies asking around. It seeks to make a profit from it. The Internet has elevated the middleman; it is a middleman's fantasy. Find transactions that were taking place anyway, and cream a little bit off the top of each. Hey presto! Vast wealth. Where, once upon a time, we would have asked someone in the pub, or mentioned our need at work, we now spend fruitless hours searching through eBay. Digital networks take the place of real networks. And they take a cut: either directly, as on eBay or PayPal (note the Newspeak nature of the new words), or indirectly through ad-based businesses such as the mighty Facebook. With asking around, there is no middleman, and capitalism is all about the middlemen. Capitalists don't do anything. Just as you are about to hand your money to the stallholder in the market, and he is about to give you the product, the smart-arse capitalist pops up in between you, takes the credit for introducing you to one another and takes 5 per cent. The history of capitalism since 1535 could be called *The Rise of the Middleman*.

Anyway, whenever you see a pallet, take it home. I sing the praises of the humble pallet. They are very useful things, and can be used for building as well as for burning. They make excellent compost-heap structures, and could be used for staging when you put on gigs in your barn. You can also make tables, chairs and benches out of them.

I chat about such matters most mornings with Trevor, the school-bus driver. He gets skiploads of old bits of wood from builders' yards. There is some work in chopping and sawing them up, to be sure, but the wood is free. As well as an axe and a saw, you will need a metal bar for breaking up the pallets. And make sure you get a good axe which is designed for splitting logs: I have realized after eight years that I have been struggling with the wrong axe. Good tools make all the difference. Buy the best you can afford.

4. Poach from woods. My neighbour used to go down into the woods with a van and a chainsaw, saw up fallen logs and cart them back home to her barn, where she chopped them. These fallen logs have already been seasoned *in situ*. By using fallen branches, she argues, she is tidying up the forest. And I am told that some woodland experts now believe that the wood and the forest benefit greatly from man's intervention in the form of wood-clearing. Clearly, though, you'd need to ask permission from the landowner. In the twentieth century, it used to be believed that forests should be left alone, and that fallen boughs should be left to rot back in. But now some woodmen are arguing that forests are healthier for a little tidy-up: the wildflowers, for example, will begin to grow back. When we walk through our local woods, I

will often drag home a couple of boughs or, to use that wonderful word, 'faggots', very dry bits of wood, bigger than a twig, smaller than a log. We also collect twigs: if they are dry, they will snap easily. (A quick way to dry out damp twigs is to put them on the Rayburn for a few days, or near any other heat source.)

5. Poach ash. When desperate for wood, I have sawn off the ash branches that grow from my landlord's hedgerows. I sawed off one particularly thick branch with a handsaw. It took about half an hour. Then the thing took about two or three hours to process. First of all, the twigs and smaller branches must be snapped off by hand or with the loppers, then the main branch chainsawed. (Chainsaws are terrifying and I think best left to the experts.) Then the pieces must be chopped up into logs. Well, that was half a day's work, and the fire lasted perhaps five hours at most. In future, I might be better off paying someone to come round with a chainsaw once a year and saw everything up.

6. Buy seasoned logs from a nursery or garden centre. The logs for sale in orange nets from nurseries are, however, very expensive. And I find it humiliating to buy them. To me, a pile of orange nets is a confession of failure to organize a decent supply of wood. You have run out and now you are throwing money at the problem. Last winter, I bumped into a neighbour at the nursery. He was also buying the orange nets. We looked at each other sheepishly, as if to say, If you don't tell, I won't. Back home, I swiftly emptied the nets on to my log pile to give any visitor the impression that I had chopped them myself two years previously and stored them carefully ever since.

So in order to avoid this sort of pain, you need to think ahead. If you have access to woodland, then cut and chop all year round. If not, you must order two or three loads of logs a year in advance.

You can never have too many logs: logs everywhere, different piles of them, all at different stages of drying out. You can make your weekly rounds with your moisture meter and check their progress.

On Buying a Wood-burner

Firstly, I would say that, although they are perhaps less romantic, wood-burners are far more efficient and easier to run than an open fire. The open fire, it is true, will take a wider range of log sizes. But it is less easy to control. Wood-burners are neater, too, and they heat the room very quickly. And they are equally at home in an urban setting as in a rural one. There was already a wood-burner in the sitting room in our house when we moved in, but my study had no heating and was very cold, so we decided to put a wood-burner in there, too.

I needed to find a cheap second-hand one. So I asked around. First, I asked Alan if he knew anyone with a wood-burner to sell. He put me on to Greg, who had a couple of tatty old burners in his barn. I bought one of them for £50. It is an Efel Kamina, an old Belgian stove, and features a very attractive lion motif. It needed new glass, and to be scrubbed and repainted. Gradually, I managed to restore it, at a cost of around £100. A friend installed it for me, and it goes very well indeed. I also learned during this process not to take advice from the men who work in wood-burning-stove shops. They told me I had made a mistake in buying my Efel Kamina and would be better off buying a new one for £600. But not only are new ones hideously expensive, they are also, in general, horribly twee and tacky in design. There was not one single wood-burner in the shop I liked the look of. But my old Efel Kamina is gorgeous.

On Making a Fire

If possible, I avoid using firelighters. To me, it feels like cheating.
And the same effect – indeed, better – can be obtained very easily
with eight or ten crumpled-up pieces of newspaper, a few strips of
cardboard and an old candle stub. Under this, there should be a
bed of ash on the floor of the wood-burner. Arrange some nice dry
kindling wood in a pyramid over the paper. On top of this, place
three or four small logs or faggots, or chips or bits of pallet. (All
hail the mighty pallet! Free source of seasoned softwood, makeshift
fence and compost-bin wall!) Light with a match then monitor the
fire in the early stages. It may need to be poked, bellowed or blown
at: the fire needs plenty of air circulating around it. Shut the doors
and open all vents. There is nothing better than seeing the goodly
blaze and feeling the room start to warm up. The wood-burner can
heat a room to a high level of cosiness – much warmer than can be
achieved with that soulless, bloodless invention of the weak New
World: central heating. We'll be sitting in T-shirts in midwinter.

Keep piling on the logs and keep poking the fire. They do need
to be tended. They need air. But this is an activity that can fit in
with any home-based work. To stoke the fire and put more logs
into the wood-burner in my study is a welcome break from reading,
writing or emailing. It gives you a little time out. Your hands pick
up an agreeable smell from handling the logs. Sometimes you burn
your fingers, and this makes you feel alive. It is also a test of your
growing stoicism. The wood crackles and spits. The entire process
is a sensual treat. The wood brings an intense pleasure, and this is
partly to do with the contrast to the cold that preceded it. The Old
World is full of extremes and of 'passionate intensity', in the phrase
from Yeats; it was far richer sensually than our own. Our New
World mission, through air-conditioning and central heating, has

flattened everything out to a constant twenty degrees all year round, with no variation from home to car, from office to supermarket to home again. We walk through a techno-utopia and give no thought to the pleasurable art of keeping ourselves warm.

Against Central Heating

Wood is the fuel of the free. In his essay 'Fires', that prolific English essayist of the early twentieth century E. V. Lucas writes that a wood fire is *de natura* an anti-authoritarian statement. It snaps its fingers at big business and government. This is in contrast to heating with unpoetic, unsensual, unvarying gas:

> Who could be witty, who could be humane, before a gas stove? It does so little for the eye and nothing for the imagination; its flame is so artificial and restricted a thing, its glowing heart so shallow and ungenerous. It has no voice, no personality, no surprises; it submits to the control of a gas company, which, in its turn, is controlled by Parliament. Now, a fire proper has nothing to do with Parliament. A fire proper has whims, ambitions and impulses unknown to gas-burners.

Central heating is bland, uniform, stuffy and may even be bad for your health. It should be torn out of every house. We need to fling open the doors and let the air rush in. Central heating is part of the comfortist-capitalist plot. It has no zest, no life in it, no danger, as well as being very expensive to run. The wood fire hisses, crackles, requires attention. It is alive. It is a friend. And, indeed, a wood fire is by nature convivial. When you're alone, the fire is a companion. With the fire you can be an active person, using the bellows and poker, or a passive person, simply gazing at it and losing yourself in melancholic contemplation. It is a great pleasure to stretch out in front of the fire some time after lunch, to lie on your back with your hands together, as depicted on the tombs of saints in Westminster Abbey, and doze in front of the blaze. The dog and the cat will also be attracted by the heat and lie down for a nap, if a human has not got there first. A fire is a feast for the senses: it is heat, and art, and music and smell all in one. It is theatre.

The hearth encourages conversation and story-telling among friends and family:

> I still had hopes my latest hours to crown,
> Amidst these humble bowers to lay me down . . .
> Around my fire an evening group to draw,
> And tell of all I felt, and all I saw.

So says the displaced wanderer in Oliver Goldsmith's 'The Deserted Village'. And here are a few lines from American poet R. H. Messinger that celebrate the sounds and smells of a good wood fire:

> Old wood to burn!
> Ay, bring the hillside beech
> From where the owlets meet and screech,
> And ravens croak;
> The crackling pine, and cedar sweet;
> Bring too a clump of fragrant peat,
> Dug 'neath the fern;
> The knotted oak,
> A faggot, too, perhaps,
> Whose bright flame, dancing, winking,
> Shall light us at our drinking;

> While the oozing sap
> Shall make sweet music to our thinking.

Deep drinking and deep thinking: yes, both are done best by a roaring fire, and the fire described above, rather wonderfully, mixes four different varieties of wood with peat. Most of all, the fire is uniquely our own. This is in strict contrast to oil and gas heating. With oil and gas, we are mere participants in a plan drawn up for us some time ago by the ruling elite. With central heating, we are reduced to powerless little consumers. And we are trapped by it. You cannot grow your own oil. You cannot hunt through skips at night for bits of discarded gas. You cannot find electricity lying by the roadside. It cannot be coppiced. It can only be bought, and you have to buy it from a cartel – there is no other way.

Against Television

It is a commonplace to point out that the television is the modern hearth. But what a poor substitute for the hearth it makes. Instead of a crackling, oozing, spitting fiery mass, we have a Big Brother in the fireplace, broadcasting its propaganda into our homes. Can we not see that the giant plasma televisions they put on their walls are precisely the same as those imagined by Orwell in *Nineteen Eighty-Four*? The television is someone else, whereas the fire is our own. The television is nearly always a waste of time, whereas an hour spent staring at and tending the fire is an hour richly lived, because you will have been thinking during that time. Your imagination will have been flowing.

Unlike the television or the central heating, of course, the fire can be used to cook food as well. At home, we have often reflected on that very sensible Old World strategy of living in one room – the kitchen — whose fire warms, cooks and entertains. It would make more sense and save money, and time, to stay in one room rather than heating other rooms that you may barely use. The splitting up of people was a Victorian innovation. Aldous Huxley writes that the corridor was not invented till the eighteenth century; before that, you walked through one room to get to another, meaning that messy life was shared and observed by others far more than it is today.

Notes for the City Dweller

Those stuck in town, or 'in populous city pent', as Milton had it, may find it difficult to keep a wood fire, though it is not impossible. Wood-burning stoves are neat and elegant and will fit into a city house. Most city laws will allow one, if properly fitted. Smoke-free laws allow clean-burning wood-burners and recommend the use of smoke-free coal.

Victoria's parents live in a house on a Kensington square without central heating. There is a giant coal bunker under the pavement, and Victoria's father lugs bucketfuls of coal up to his study (they are the last house in the square to use the coal bunker). Now that is what I call stylish. And, for all the slimmers out there: being cold can help to keep you thin. Throw out the central heating and you'll no longer need fancy diets and visits to the gymnasium. You'll get a lot of exercise from all the wood-chopping, too, and from the log-carrying and coal-dumping.

The really wood-friendly would go all the way and install some sort of wood-fired range in the kitchen. These wonderful machines may be used to do all the cooking, heat the kitchen and the water and will even run one or two radiators upstairs. The downside is that they use an awful lot of wood, and the wood needs to be extremely dry. I confess that we are grateful sometimes for our oil-fired Rayburn, much as, in some ways, I would prefer to install a wood-burning version.

Holly and ash might save us. Plant a wood of holly and ash everywhere, now! As another Old World wood poem has it:

> Holly, burn it green; holly, burn it dry;
> Of all the trees whatsoever, the critically best is holly.

On Bonfires

If, for now, it is impossible for you to have a fire indoors, then find somewhere to make a fire outdoors. This is always a huge pleasure: there is something deeply satisfying about piles of burning materials. A bonfire is purging, it is beautiful, it creates heat and light. Every few months, we pile up all our cardboard boxes with brushwood that my neighbour has cut down, and we build a fire in the middle of the yard. In the last one we made, we burned all Victoria's school essays and university files. And how to build the fire? We need to follow these instructions about the gypsy technique, the pyramid approach, set out by Victorian nature writer Richard Jefferies:

> Two short sticks were put in the ground, and a third across them like to a triangle. Against this frame a number of the smallest and driest sticks were leaned, so that they made a tiny hut. Outside these there was a second layer of longer sticks, all standing, or rather leaning, against the first. If a stick is placed across, lying horizontally, supposing it catches fire, it just burns through the middle and that is all; the ends go out. If it is stood nearly upright, the flame draws up to it; it is certain to catch, burns longer, and leaves a good ember.

This same principle can be applied to the indoor fire in the wood-burner or open hearth, but some fire makers hold that such a pyramid structure will not make a good heart to the fire, so you may need to push the sticks in and down once it is blazing, and some fire builders will put a larger log at each side of the pyramid to keep the heat in.

January's Lessons

The smallholder's life is not always easy. In fact, when we run Simple Living courses at our home, I tell the participants that the first thing you learn about simple living is how complicated it is. Hence, I suppose, the great proliferation of books on husbandry through the ages. I am comforted by biographer Richard Holmes's account of the young Coleridge's everyday life in his little cottage in Nether Stowey in 1798 with his wife, Sara, and baby son, Hartley: 'The cottage life was not altogether easy, especially in those first cold months . . . The fires in the two tiny ground floor parlours had to be constantly stoked, and Sara had to cook and dry washing over an open hearth in the back kitchen.' Perhaps Sam and Sara should have installed wood-burners.

When I look back over my own diary entries for January over the years, I find the same complaint repeated: the weather is unutterably foul. At one point I muse on Plough Monday, the traditional day for returning to work in the Middle Ages following the long winter's rest. It is the first Monday after the Feast of the Epiphany. 'I had planned to resurrect that medieval custom,' I wrote. 'But when I looked out of the window, I decided to stay in.'

Another common feature of my entries for January is delight in the appearance of snowdrops and primroses. When you look at these wildflowers closely, you realize what Blake meant when he saw

heaven in a wildflower. The snowdrop has little bell-shaped heads
that look down at the ground, like a fancy Victorian lightshade. The
primrose is altogether more open. It has five heart-shaped petals with
a darker yellow star in the centre, and is really exquisite. It is worth
sitting down to sketch wildflowers, not so much for the end result,
which in my case is likely to be pretty disappointing, but for the
experience of really studying them, and looking closely. Sketching is
a kind of meditation, which will fill you with awe and wonder.

In his 1784 poem *The Task*, a sort of Virgilian celebration of
country life, eighteenth-century poet William Cowper wrote the
following lovely lines about the pleasures of winter in the cottage:

> I love thee, all unlovely as thou seem'st,
> And dreaded as thou art! . . .
> I crown thee king of intimate delights,
> Fire-side enjoyments, home-born happiness;
> And all the comforts that the lowly roof
> Of undisturb'd Retirement, and the hours
> Of long uninterrupted evening, know.

So, in January, we stay in and keep warm. Forget about the
garden. There is nothing to do there. You may, if you like, sow a few
seeds indoors. But most of your time should be occupied in playing
cards, parlour games and draughts in front of the fire, and drinking
fine ales.

January's Husbandry

In deference to the non-lazy out there, I have gathered a few pieces
of advice from our panel of Old World husbandry experts. They
seem to be generally agreed: this is the month – if you really want

to do something out there – for a few early sowings of salad-type plants, plus general weeding and tidying up. Palladius recommends various sowings, including barley, tares, vetches and fenugreek. He writes that you should start planting lettuces; dig the ground; put herb seeds in a lump of goat dung that you have hollowed with a nail. Fell timber in this month, as it is less moisture-filled than at other times of year.

Tusser, in *Five Hundred Points of Good Husbandry*, advises of the need to care for your doves (our neighbour keeps doves and very beautiful they are, too):

> Feed Dove (no more killing), old Dove house repair,
> save dove dong [dung] for hop yard, when house ye make faire.

January is also, as Tusser tells us, the time for weeding, a job best delegated, and I can't resist quoting these lines, if only for his gleeful description of annoying roots:

> Let servant be readie, with mattock in hand,
> to stub out the bushes that noyeth the land:
> And cumbersome rootes, so annoying the plough,
> turne upwards their a–s–s [arses] with sorrow enough.

John Evelyn, in the seventeenth century, recommends sowing salad seeds: 'Sow *Chervil, Lettuce, Radish*, and other (more delicate) Salletings, if you will raise in the *Hot-bed*. In over-wet, or hard weather, *cleanse, mend sharpen* and prepare *Garden-tools*.'

The hard-working William Cobbett would have us toiling even when it snows. He has a challenging to-do list:

Even deep snow gives time for cleaning, thrashing, and sorting of seeds, preparing stakes and pea-sticks, tying mats, sorting bulbs, and many similar sorts of employment. Dry frost makes an opportunity of manuring land with ease and neatness, and also of pruning gooseberries, currants, and other hardy shrubs . . . *Sow*, for early use, radishes and carrots on a warm sunny border; peas, beans, round spinage, parsley; small salad in frames, old mint roots on heat under glass will soon give a supply of green mint . . . Turn dunghills and compost heaps. I say it at once for the whole year, destroy vermin wherever you can find them . . . roll, pole, and sweep grass walks, verges and lawns; keep them clear from leaves and rubbish; root out dandelions and docks if there. Plant box edgings.

John Seymour, in the seventies, is a little less ambitious: 'We plant trees in January, and fruit bushes. We prune trees and bushes . . . we cut pea and bean sticks,' he writes in *Self-Sufficiency*.

I would add: order your seeds. Leafing through the seed catalogue by the fire of a winter's evening, and dreaming of your summer crops, is a real joy. Just be careful not to go crazy: I tend to buy more seeds than I sow, because I over-estimate my own level of industry. You should also put your seed potatoes out to start chitting. Chitting is the act of putting your seed potatoes in egg boxes and allowing them to grow little sprouts. This supposedly means that they grow better once planted.

January's Merriment

Medieval Christmas lasted a full twelve days, and one of the key feasts took place on 6 January, or the Feast of the Epiphany. So why not throw a Twelfth Night feast? Old customs persist: for example, a Mummers' play, in which St George fights an evil knight, was performed last year at our local pub during Christmastide. This tradition could easily be carried out at home. Or read short sections from Shakespeare's *Twelfth Night*, in particular the scenes featuring the odious Malvolio and the knavery of the medieval roustabouts. Make costumes: in olden times, we used to dress up and wear antler-topped hats and bells around our ankles. Another custom was the Oranges and Lemons game: one team dressed up in yellow and wore a giant 'L' sewn to the front of their tunics, while the other team dressed in orange and wore an 'O'. It all sounds a bit like something out of a seventies Saturday morning kids TV show.

Another seasonal custom is wassailing. Twelve people go out and find an apple tree, each carrying a tankard containing cider topped with caraway seeds. They form a circle around the tree and chant the following rhyme:

> Hail to thee, old apple tree!
> From every bough
> Give us apples enow;
> Hatsful, capsful,
> Bushel, bushel, sacksful,
> And our arms full, too.

Toast the tree and shout, 'Wassail!' Repeat the rhyme, give a drink to the tree, clank your tankards together and shout, 'Huzzah!' This will ensure a bountiful crop.

January's Calendar

January is sacred to the Roman god Janus, the two-faced one. We find the image in Chaucer's 'Franklin's Tale':

> Janus sit by the fyr, with double berd,
> And drynketh of his bugle horn the wyn.
> Biforn him stant brawen of the tusked swyn,
> And 'Nowel' crieth every lusty man.

Ovid, in his *Fasti*, the great poem about festivals and feast days, writes of 'two-headed Janus, opener of the softly gliding year'. January is the time for drinking and eating and staying warm by the fire, for lusty pleasures, for ale and wine.

1 January: New Year's Day. Kalends of January.

6 January: Feast of the Epiphany, or Twelfth Night, when we commemorate the manifestation of the young Christ to the Magi. Plough Monday. This is the first Monday after Twelfth Night and the traditional start of the labouring year.

11 January: Old New Year's Eve. This would have been New Year's Eve before the calendar reform of 1752, when eleven days were lost. It is still celebrated in some determinedly Old World communities, notably the Scottish village of Burghead.

12 January: St Distaff's Day. The female equivalent of Plough Monday, this was when the women were to start spinning: 'Partly work and partly play, Ye must, on St Distaff's Day,' wrote Robert Herrick.

13 January: Ides of January. Feast day of St Hilary, fourth-century Bishop of Poitiers.

17 January: St Anthony's Day. The long-lived monastic St Anthony (AD 251–356) lived for twenty years in the desert. Another excuse for a feast.

20 January: St Agnes's Eve. Tonight, maids go to bed supperless, as Keats mentions, in the hope of dreaming of their future husband. St Agnes is the patron saint of virgins, having been martyred at the age of twelve or thirteen for refusing to marry.

22 January: St Vincent's Day. He died in Spain in the fourth century AD, after submitting uncomplainingly to various tortures. Have another feast.

24 January: Cornish Tinners' and Seafarers' Day. St Paul's Eve.

25 January: Burns Night. Today we remember the great poet Robert Burns who was born this day in 1759.

30 January: King Charles I was beheaded by Cromwell and the fun-hating Parliamentarians this day in 1649. Until the mid-nineteenth century, this day was celebrated with religious ceremonies, a custom which was attacked by the Republican-minded Keats.

CHAPTER TWO

February

Dig Earth

In terra libertatem quaerimus

[We seek freedom in the earth]
– Tom Hodgkinson

AFTER the feasting, the fires and the fun of January, it is time
to get out of the house and into the vegetable garden. Growing
your own vegetables is rewarding, saves money, and can be a great
joy. But, like any other art, it must be carefully studied over a number
of years, and that means immersing yourself in practical experience,
books and the experience of others, either through conversation or
by taking courses. Growing vegetables is hugely complex: there
are hundreds of co-factors to keep in mind. Every vegetable patch
is different and there is much debate on how to make the earth
fruitful. One thing, though, is agreed: it's all about the soil. Good
soil produces good food. And all the great writers on husbandry
tell us that February is the time to prepare the soil, by manuring it
and digging it. Our favourite Tudor writer, Thomas Tusser, for
example, insists that now is the time to 'laieth on doong' [dung].
And as well as laying on dung, the soil needs to be broken up and
cultivated. Medieval calendar scenes show images of the fields being
ploughed. Ploughing turns over the clods, ready to be broken down
into a fine crumb-like texture with harrow, rake or cultivator, so that
the roots of the seeds will grow unimpeded and with great joy.

The soil must be carefully and lovingly fed, and husbanded. Your
primary aim with soil is to maintain its fertility without recourse to
that New World abomination, artificial fertilizer, which, like many
of man's inventions, appears miraculous at first – crops shoot up –
but is eventually revealed to be harmful. Columella and the other
Latin writers use concepts that are completely familiar to the organic
gardener: crop rotation, maintaining fertility through manure,
including green manures such as mustard, and the importance of
letting fields lie fallow. In *De Re Rustica*, Roman husbandry scribe
Columella writes: '*Licet enim maiorem fructum percipere, si frequenti et
tempestiva et modica stercoratione terra refoveatur*' (We may reap greater
harvests if the earth is quickened again by frequent, timely and
moderate manuring).

Virgil, too, insists on crop rotation and the application of manure:

> *Sed tamen alternis facilis labor, arida tantum*
> *ne saturare fimo pingui pudeat sola neve*
> *effetos cinerem immundum iactare per agros.*

[By rotating crops, the work is made easy, and do not be afraid to saturate the dry earth with rich manure, and scatter ashes over the exhausted fields.]

For John Seymour, too, February is the month for 'carting muck'. The application of manure to the surface of the soil is crucial. It can help turn an unpromising patch of earth into nice fat soil. Here Seymour describes how his wife, Sally, created a fertile garden with easily workable soil:

Sally, every year, barrows in loads of muck [to her garden]. It is immensely heavily manured . . . Sally uses no chemicals in her round garden because there is absolutely no need. She has achieved such high humus states there – the general fertility of the soil is so high – that to shove in 'chemicals' would be like taking coals to Newcastle. That's the soil condition to aim at. I dug down two feet six in Sally's garden yesterday. For the whole of that depth the soil was kindly, friable [easily crumbled], obviously fertile.

Clearly, as your fruit, vegetables and herbs grow, they feed on nutrients in the soil, and so those nutrients need to be constantly replaced. As luck would have it, horses, cows and chickens convert grass into fantastic soil dressing, making it completely unnecessary to buy chemical fertilizers. The desired friability can be achieved by a lot of breaking up: the soil needs to be dug, mattocked and raked.

You can also use a wonderful tool called a hand cultivator, a sort of three-pronged claw at the end of a handle. This is used to loosen soil so that roots can grow more easily. It aerates the soil: like a fire, the soil needs air, and the cultivator is the equivalent of the poker and bellows. A bit of stirring up keeps the soil alive. The cultivator will also help to mix your organic matter into the soil.

The Importance of Digging

As an extremely idle gardener, I was initially delighted to learn of the no-dig system originated by Japanese organic farmer Masanobu Fukuoka and developed by today's permaculture and organic gardeners. The recent custom, upheld by our hard-working grand-fathers, has been to dig deep trenches in the earth and fill them with year-old manure or compost before covering them with soil. The no-dig gardener holds the view that this level of intervention, quite apart from being back-breakingly tiring, actually damages the soil and brings weed seeds to the surface. Instead of digging, you should 'mulch'. Here is Fukuoka:

> Using straw, green manure and a little poultry manure, one can get high yields without adding compost or commercial fertilizer at all. For several decades now, I have been sitting back, observing nature's method of cultivation and fertilization. And while watch-ing, I have reaped bumper crops of vegetables, citrus, rice, and winter grain as a gift, so to speak, from the natural fertility of the earth.

This is the principle, and of course he is right as far as fertilization goes. Poultry manure can be obtained by keeping a couple of hens in the backyard. Green manures are sown just before harvesting your crop, and I confess I've never had much luck with those. Compost, though, which Fukuoka claims is not necessary, is easy to make and is a useful source of soil fertility and of course a good use of your kitchen scraps. There are many books and guides on how to make the perfect compost. It would seem that the ideal is to make your compost heap all at once, layering kitchen waste with straw and grass cuttings. You then put a piece of carpet on top and – hey presto! – the whole thing heats up and you have rich, friable compost in six weeks. Well, maybe I am just extraordinarily stupid and lazy but I've never figured out how to manage this. Instead, I just toss the kitchen waste on the heap and occasionally add the sweepings from the henhouse or the ferret cage. We keep a bucket under the sink and mix in ripped-up cardboard and paper. Sometimes I put the garden fork into the heap to give it a bit of air. After a year or so, you have clumpy black stuff which you can spread on to the soil or dig in.

The main problem with the otherwise attractive no-dig system is that it is actually very difficult, and what Fukuoka calls 'no-work farming' can only be achieved after many, many years of patient observation and experimentation. In your early days, you would be best advised to stick to the traditional methods. The beginner gardener should really dig or even double dig when he or she is first preparing the plot. I find that the mattock is very effective for this job. I dig out a trench about a foot deep with the spade. Then I hack at the bottom of the trench with the mattock, turning over another layer of soil. I then tip in a barrowload of manure which I have hauled up from the dung heap and fill the trench back up with the earth I've dug out earlier. In this way, a patch of dense, wormless soil will be transformed into a light and airy substance full of organic matter. The vegetables will love it.

The importance of cultivation or, in other words, disturbing the soil around and between the plants, was insisted upon by the gardeners in Flora Thompson's wonderful portrait of poor rural life in the late nineteenth century, *Lark Rise to Candleford*, recently the object of a dreadful television adaptation. The men would come home from work and put in an hour or two on the allotment, and make sure they 'tickled' the soil:

> They considered keeping the soil constantly stirred about the roots of growing things the secret of success and used the Dutch hoe a good deal for this purpose. The process was called 'tickling'. 'Tickle up old Mother Earth and make her bear!' they would shout to each other across the plots.

In this, Flora Thompson's men have a lot in common with the Romans, who treated the earth as a mother and a goddess, and called her Ceres. Well, after one good double-digging session, it may only be necessary in future years to cultivate, in the manner described above, and mulch. But my advice to the beginner is: follow the rules at first. As you gain experience, you will develop your own techniques but, at the beginning, you must throw away all pride and reduce yourself to the level of the humble apprentice who knows nothing.

I tried one bed on the no-dig system from the beginning and, frankly, it was a disaster. Instead of digging, I put a layer of straw and manure on the surface of the soil. When I came to plant out my courgettes, they all died within a week. A couple of squash seedlings survived but then produced only two tiny pathetic fruits, which rapidly shrivelled.

Darwin and the Earthworm

Perhaps the greatest friend of all to the gardener and the soil is the humble earthworm, or *lumbricus*. It is the worm that is at the centre of any organic, natural system. The worm digs the soil for you; he is a little ploughman. And for an insight into his habits and industry, we have Charles Darwin to thank for his excellent study, *The Formation of Vegetable Mould through the Action of Worms* ('mould' here being used to mean 'light cultivated topsoil'), first published in 1881. Darwin clearly became obsessed with worms, a hitherto largely unconsidered subject in gardening. Encourage the worm, says Darwin, and you will save yourself a heap of work: 'The plough is one of the most ancient and most valuable of man's inventions; but long before he existed the land was in fact regularly ploughed, and still continues to be thus ploughed by earthworms.' The earthworms, deaf, dumb and blind, continually eat and digest animal and vegetable matter, making casts from which plants then feed. Worms make our food, which is why Darwin exalts the humble earthworm to a position of great importance to civilization: 'It may be doubted whether there are many other animals which have played so important a part in the history of the world.'

Leaves, bones, insect parts, twigs and other bits of organic matter are buried beneath the accumulated castings of the worms. Worms cultivate the soil and enrich it:

> Worms prepare the ground in an excellent manner for the growth of fibrous-rooted plants and for seedlings of all kinds. They periodically expose the mould to the air, and sift it so that no stones larger than the particles which they can swallow are left in it . . . They allow the air to penetrate deeply into the ground. They also greatly facilitate the downward passage of roots of moderate

size; and these will be nourished by the humus with which the burrows are lined.

The word 'humus', I should say, can be defined as 'the organic component of soil', and good soil needs a lot of it. Now Darwin, charmingly, kept pots of worms in his study in order to carry out experiments on them. He tried to discover, for example, whether they were sensitive to light and sound. Darwin would wander into his study and play a succession of musical instruments to the worms and observe their reactions. He records that the worms took no notice 'of the deepest and loudest notes of a bassoon', and he concludes that they are deaf. He was also to be found playing a C on the piano to some worms which he had placed upon it, in order to ascertain if they reacted to vibrations.

Darwin's many and varied worm experiments have provided us with good scientific back-up for their importance in more or less natural gardening systems. *The Formation of Vegetable Mould* . . . has been cited and praised by organic gardeners for many years. My 1945 Faber edition has an introduction by one Sir Albert Howard, who writes:

In directing attention to one of Nature's chief agents for restoring and maintaining the fertility of soils, the publication of this new edition of Darwin's book will do much to establish the truth that Nature is the supreme farmer and gardener, and that the study of her ways will provide us with the one thing we need – sound and reliable direction.

It is perhaps needless to add that Howard, like his contemporary, organic farmer Lady Eve Balfour, was against chemical fertilizers. They kill worms:

Agriculture took the wrong road when artificial manures were introduced to stimulate crop production and when poison sprays became common to check insect and fungus pests. Both these agencies destroy the earthworm and thus deprive the farmer of an important member of his unpaid labour force.

Sadly, the technocrats did not listen and, seduced by their own cleverness and by greed, they have continued to put artificial fertilizers into the soil, thus damaging it. *Do not feed the plants, feed the soil.*

And how to encourage the earthworm? We need to give the soil frequent and generous dressings of organic manure: straw, woodchips, leaves, compost, grass clippings – even dead animals. I buried the entrails of our pig in the garden (although I later found that this is not permitted by the meddling bureaucrats of the New World and that I ought to have paid to have the entrails collected and taken to an approved incineration facility). If you do not see one or two juicy earthworms in each spadeful of soil, then it is time to encourage your little ploughmen by spreading some delicacies over the earth. This sort of mulching is how the forest maintains its fertility: think of that rich, dark, crumbly stuff you see at your feet in the woods. That is the accumulation of years of leaves, animal waste, dead animals, twigs and branches, all composted by the most excellent worm.

Study of the earthworm thus leads us to conclude that we will keep things natural in the garden and do a lot of mulching. But we also recognize that even the most determined and experienced 'do nothing' gardener will accept the need for a bit of digging, raking, hoeing and cultivating.

In this, if you have them, you can also call upon your chickens for aid. Maybe let them into the garden in February. They scratch the soil and manure it, and also eat slugs and slug eggs. The problem is, they will also eat seeds and seedlings, and they will take dust baths in your lovingly prepared soil. Any recently sowed patches or small plants must be protected . . . but more on that in the next chapter.

Let me add a word here about bio-dynamic gardening. This is the technique, or approach, invented by the esoteric German philosopher Rudolf Steiner of filling a cow horn with dung, leaving it buried in the ground for a few months, and then mixing the resulting powder with water. Just a light spray of the mixture over your crops is supposed to have a magical effect. It is described in his *Agriculture Course*, a baffling collection of essays Steiner gave on the subject. I have recently been informed by a group of sensible Germans that Steiner, whom I formerly vaguely revered as a sort of 'natural' philosopher, is in fact a little on the sinister side. My advice would be to strike Steiner from your list of books on husbandry, as he will only confuse you with his ideas. Much better, I would say, to read a hard-headed, practical chap such as William Cobbett. And while we are on the subject of authorities, by far the best contemporary book I have read is *Grow Your Own Vegetables* by the upliftingly named Joy Larkcom. It has an organic approach but is not full of mumbo-jumbo. This year, I followed her advice in our vegetable garden and we have had the best year ever.

Land for All

Clearly, modern society is in danger of losing its connection with the soil. The Brave New World has taken our land away, while telling us every day how fortunate we are to be living in technological paradise, with its Facebook and iPads. Since Henry VIII, the Acts of Enclosure have taken the common land away from the people. Land is far less widely shared today than it was in the Middle Ages, when every villein or cottar, any subject of the manor, had a few acres to call their own. Now, most of the land in the UK is owned by big supermarkets or the Duke of Westminster. The creation of this New World began in the early sixteenth century and split up the old harmony between work and leisure.

The writer H. J. Massingham was a Cobbettesque 'radical traditionalist' who wrote a number of books in the 1940s which championed 'the old ways' and this erstwhile connection with the land. In *The English Countryman*, Massingham starts by quoting from the historian R. H. Tawney, another defender of the peasant system: 'The past has shown us no more excellent social order than that in which the mass of the people were the masters of the holdings which they ploughed, and of the tools with which they worked.' He goes on to describe the medieval period as 'the golden age of the peasant'. The New World, he says, attacked the old, by taking away the land and the fun. And it was the Puritans wot did it:

The Tudor 'inclosiers' made war on the peasant's work by turning husbandmen into beggars; the Puritans upon his leisure partly by direct persecution and partly by raising the prejudice against his music, dancing, poetry, festivals and customs as 'the dregs of Antichrist' – 'Dost thou think that because thou art virtuous there shall be no more cakes and ale?' . . . the Puritan was the first figure in our history to tip the national scales from self-subsistence in the country to business in the town, and his zeal was directed towards making a solitude of that crowded ground between the peasant's work and his religion which was filled with his communal recreations.

The Puritan was a sober businessman to the old-fashioned Christian's boozy peasant. And old-fashioned Christianity had impeded the progress of trade, because it banned usury. One of the first tasks of the Reformation was to lift the ban on charging interest on loans. Out with saints. Out with feast days, incense and colour. In with the freedom to lend money to the poor and charge interest.

As well as bringing back the medieval festivals, we need to bring back access to the land. The earth heals, it brings recreation and sustenance. It can bring freedom from wage slavery. And it brings autonomy. We need to reacquaint ourselves with the gods of the countryside. And we need to oppose the mega-city movement with all our might. Behind the mega-city movement lies the idea that we will soon witness a gigantic, global and final move from the countryside to enormous cities such as the fast-growing Chongqing in China, which has a population of 30 million, and reminds me of Mega-City One, the megalopolis in the comic 2000AD.

Many Old World ideas are returning under the umbrella of the permaculture movement. It is true that this movement is not romantically named. I prefer the old, poetic names for such groups: the Ranters, the Diggers, the Levellers, the Brethren of the Free Spirit; and I suppose my own movement would have to be called the Idlers. Still, while clumsily titled, permaculture is a good thing. In permaculture, groups of low-interference gardeners come together to rent or buy areas of land for play and food.

City-dwellers can very easily cultivate the old ways. First of all, many city houses have gardens. These gardens generally consist of a lawn and some flowerbeds; however, a small area of earth can be used to grow a surprisingly large amount of vegetables, and pots may be placed anywhere. The soil may actually be better in the city, since it has not suffered decades of fertilizers being dumped on it, and there will be far more variety in flora over a small space in the city, with its proliferation of gardens. For this reason, bees can thrive in urban areas. Ironically enough, thanks to the decline in mixed farms and the rise in monoculture in the countryside, there may often be only a very small variety of crops and flowers grown across large rural areas. There are more areas of communal land in the form of parks in the cities, and it is a relatively straightforward matter to get together with a few local residents and plant, for example, an orchard on a piece of wasteland. Our cities are covered in unproductive patches of earth that could easily be brought back to life – just add manure. The worms will love it: after all, they have no prejudice against city living. In fact, they will prefer it, because there is less chance that they will be ground up by a tractor pulling a plough or poisoned by a greedy monoculturist spraying fertilizer or weedkiller on the soil.

Allotments, shared-land schemes, community land purchase: all are gaining in popularity. What they share is the Old World sense of a commons. Land is not a commodity to be bought and sold, traded, speculated and built on. It is a free gift for everyone. It will feed us and heal us. And the memory – mythical or not – of the common ground, is a useful check against tyranny. It is a memory that is shared by Virgil, who writes of a sort of hunter-gatherer, pre-agricultural golden age:

> *Ante Iovem nulli subigebant arva coloni:*
> *ne signare quidem aut partiri limite campum*
> *fas erat; in medium quaerebant, ipsaque tellus*
> *omnia liberius nullo poscente ferebat.*

[Before the reign of Jove no farmers subjugated the land; even to mark possession or to place boundaries on the fields was sacrilege; man made gain for the common good, and Earth of her own accord gave her gifts all the more freely when none demanded them.]

– *Georgics*, Book I, ll. 125–8

The battle for the land, then, is nothing new. It has been at the heart of the liberty project for at least two thousand years, and lately and notably it was prominent in Gerard Winstanley's Diggers movement of 1649. The Diggers wanted to return to an Edenic paradise:

> . . . there had lately appeared to [Winstanley's fellow Digger] Everard a vision, which had bad him arise and dig and plough the earth, and receive the fruits thereof . . . their intent is to restore the Creation to its former condition. That as God promised to make the barren land fruitful, so now what they did was to restore the ancient community of enjoying the fruits of the Earth, and to distribute the benefits thereof to the poor and needy, and to feed the hungry and clothe the naked.

The Diggers even had their own song, which railed against the lawyers and clergy who brainwashed the people and culminated in a chorus of 'Stand up now, diggers all.' I did once entertain the fantasy of starting a band called The Diggers. We would wear smocks on stage and sing the Diggers song, accompanying ourselves with violins, accordions and drums. I excitedly told my friend Marcel about my plan. 'Tommer,' he emailed back, 'it's a terrible idea.' He was right and, can I say, Marcel, thank you for your honesty.

Later, Ruskin makes a plea for us to take back control of the land: 'In the true Utopia, man will rather harness himself, with his oxen, to his plough, than leave the devil to drive it.' Truly, today it is the devil in the driving seat, in the form of men from the ministry and the big supermarkets, and we need to get ourselves back in there. And it needn't be boring: one of the very appealing features of the Old World was the wide variety of work it offered, and the variety in everyday life. You might spend two or three days at the manor, working on the lord's land. You would practise a couple of crafts at home. There would be music and plenty of festivals. And the religious life was far richer and more colourful than post-Reformation religion, as scholar Eamon Duffy conclusively shows in his masterful description of late-medieval religious practice, *The Stripping of the Altars*. One piece of evidence Duffy mentions is the lovely *Kalender of Shepherdes* printed by Wynkyn de Worde, a sixteenth-century best-selling almanac and *vade mecum* which combines a 'jobs for the month' calendar with religious reflection.

For William Morris, a life which combined the practice of a craft with work on the land was a satisfying one. In his essay 'Useful Work Versus Useless Toil' he wrote:

> A man might easily learn and practise at least three crafts, varying sedentary occupation with outdoor – occupation calling for the exercise of strong bodily energy for work in which the mind had more to do. There are few men, for instance, who would not wish to spend part of their lives in the most necessary and pleasant of all work, cultivating the earth.

For my own part, I very much enjoy a mix of intellectual labours and physical ones. In general, I read and write in my study in the morning from nine till one. Then we have lunch of bread and cheese, and sometimes soup. I try to have a quick nap after lunch, and then, weather permitting, I will work in the garden for an hour or two. If the weather does not permit, then I admit I feel a slight sense of relief, and stay indoors.

So put down your guns and pick up your spades. Life on the land may not be exactly easy, but it is satisfying, as Virgil attests towards the end of Book II (ll. 493–4) of the *Georgics*:

Fortunatus et ille, deos qui novit agrestis
Panaque Silvanumque senem Nymphasque sorores.

[And lucky is he who knows the gods of the countryside: Pan, and old Silvanus, and the sisterhood of the nymphs.]

And particularly those nymphs.

February's Husbandry

For Hesiod, February is the time to get warm: 'Defend yourself against the evil days Lenaion brings,' he counsels. He then goes on to give some practical clothing tips, clearly written before the days of Gore-Tex®:

> Then put your body in a shelter too:
> A fleecy coat and tunic to the ground,
> Woven with thicker woof than warp; do this
> So that your body's hair lies still and does
> Not shudder and stand up all over. Next,
> Bind on your feet the fitted oxhide boots,
> Lined with thick felt. And when the chilly time
> Approaches, stitch the hides of newborn kids
> With sinews from an ox, into a cape
> To keep the rain from falling on your back.

Cultivate, says Columella. Get the mattock out, '*Neque enim aliud est colere quam resolvere et fermentare terram*' (For cultivation is nothing else than the loosening and breaking up of the ground). Palladius also recommends manuring for poor land, and says that you should do it at the rise of the moon:

And fede hem that be lene at poire astate
With dung, as Luna gynneth wex and wynne.

Palladius recommends the sowing of hemp, another Old World crop which is being rediscovered by progressive gardeners. He says you should plough, harrow and clear stones and, in the nursery, dig around the plants:

Eke in the seminary sholde
The plantes now be mylged everichone.

Dear Tusser, again, recommends manuring and ploughing:

Who laieth on doong er he laieth on plow,
such husbandrie useth as thrift doth alow
One month er you spred it, so still let it stand,
er ever to plow it, ye take it in hand.

You can also, he says, get some peas and beans into the ground:

Sowe peason and beanes in the wane of the Moone,
who soweth them sooner, he soweth too soone.
That they with the planet may rest and arise
and flourish with bearing most plentifull wise.

Also, harrow after ploughing. The same effect can be achieved by raking and cultivating after you have dug. Put sticks out for your peas:

Stick plentie of bows among runcivall pease
to climber thereon, and to branch at their ease.

Evelyn is out there sowing in February. He tells us to sow beans, peas, radish, parsnip, carrots, onions, garlic and asparagus. 'You may plant forth your *Cabbage-plants*,' he adds. And Cobbett has a very busy February. He tells us to sow beans and peas, and radish, but with a covering of straw:

> *Sow* savoys for early planting, leeks, cabbages if wanted, spinage, parsnips, parsley, carrots, Dutch turnips under litter, cauliflowers on heat. Many of these sowings must depend on the nature of your soil and the weather. *Plant* cabbages, garlick, rocambole, onions for seed, shalots, chives, horse-radish crowns. Get what hoeing you can done in dry days . . . and prepare for the busy month of March.

Toil, endless toil – that is the only way, my idle friends! Cobbett is right, I should add, about the importance of hoeing. After one season of following the no-work-farming advice and taking a laid-back attitude to weeds, my patch turned into a hellish mess of dandelions, couch grass and docks. Crops were choked. Truly, the weeds must be removed!

Every year since I started gardening, I must admit, I have done practically nothing during February beyond sowing broad-bean seeds. The farm is on high ground and we have had long, cold winters, so we have been at least a month behind everywhere else, and this has suited a lazy, procrastinating gardener like me very well. But do not follow my example: do as I say, not as I do. You must stay on top of the vegetable patch.

John Seymour reminds us to buy our early seed potatoes in February, that's if you have not done so in January:

We set the First Early potato seed in trays to sprout. They don't want heat – just light. They don't want frost, though! We sow parsnips on deeply dug unmanured land. As the seed takes such a long time to come up we sow radish with it. The radish will come up quickly and show us where not to hoe, and when it has done its job, we will eat the radish. Radish then we will go on sowing, every week, or fortnight, in tiny odd corners. Turnip lovers (which we are not) can drill early turnips. We plant shallots. Plant rhubarb, God bless it.

February's Merriment

The principal festival of February was of course Shrovetide. The word derives from 'shrive' (to confess), and the idea was that you would enter Lent with a clear conscience, having thoroughly 'fessed up. This was a movable feast that began on Shrove Sunday, the seventh Sunday before Easter. It went on for three days, ending on Shrove Tuesday. Today, we feebly remember it as Pancake Day, the day on which to use up the last of the eggs before the fast of Lent begins. But in olden times, Shrovetide was the occasion of wild merriment, a sort of cathartic release before the privations of Lent began. Writes the great contemporary historian Ronald Hutton, 'Payments for food, drink, and entertainment at this time rank only behind those at Christmas . . . Sixteenth-century accounts for the English and Scottish royal revels show regular and heavy expenditure upon plays, music, and masquerades for Shrove Tuesday.' Hutton also writes that cock-fighting and football were traditional Shrovetide occupations. Apprentices would throw stones at cocks in the street. The mistreatment of poultry, I'm afraid to say, seems to be a common feature of the Old World. Perhaps this is because the results are so comical: just throw a crust of bread at a chicken and it will flap and fuss in the most absurd fashion. The justification for killing the chickens was that they would be no use over Lent. Tusser writes:

> At Shroftide go shroving, go threshe the fat hen,
> if blindfold can kill her, then give it thie men.

Football was another outlet for sadistic impulses, and for this reason Shrove Tuesday football was frequently the object of bans by reforming authorities. The Protestant reformer Philip Stubbs called football 'a devilish pastime . . . a bloody and murdering practice . . . sometime the noses gush out with blood, sometime their eyes start out'.

The great thing about Shrove Tuesday was that it was decidedly a day off. Again, Hutton:

> [T]he undoubted leisure and liberty on Shrove Tuesday was an informal matter for employees, schoolmasters, and whole communities to grant according to long custom. In many places, by the seventeenth century, it was announced . . . by the ringing of a 'pancake bell' near noon . . . at Eton the boys waited until the school clock struck nine upon Shrove Tuesday morning, and then shouted, stamped, thumped sticks, and ran out for a day of leisure.

At my own school, Westminster, the tradition of this combination of violence and freedom at Shrovetide persists in the strange custom of the Greaze. In the Greaze, a giant pancake is cooked and flung by the school cook over a horizontal bar in the main hall. A gang of boys then leaps on the falling pancake. Out of the ensuing scrum, a victor emerges, he who holds the largest slice of the pancake. Following this brutal bundle, the dean 'begs a play' – in other words, grants the school a half-day holiday.

The other major feast for February is of course the gentler St Valentine's Day. This should be the occasion of much eating, drinking and playing of games. One such game is Lady Anne. One player is elected to be the Lover, and he or she stands in the middle of a ring of chairs. The other guests take their seats. They pass a ball around and the Lover must guess who ends up holding the ball. He or she chants:

> Here we come a-piping
> First in February, then in May.
> My lady [*or* my good sir] sits upon the throne
> Bright as a jewel I call my own.
> Here is a glove to cover the hand
> Of the best Valentine in all the land.
> I choose but one, I choose from all,
> I pray dear lady [*or* dear sir], yield me the ball!

If he or she has chosen wrongly, the chosen person says:

> The ball is mine and none of thine
> And so, good morrow, Valentine!

The 'wrong' person gets up and takes the place of the Lover. The scene repeats itself, but if the Lover guesses correctly, the Beloved replies:

> This ball is your and none of mine.
> I choose you as my Valentine!

And so on until everyone is paired up.

And here are some more handy tips for a stylish medieval St Valentine's Day.

Love Lanterns: Love lanterns, a kind of vegetable candle-holder, give a soft, gentle light. Resembling Hallowe'en jack-o-lanterns, the Valentine lights are large hollowed-out turnips (or similarly firm vegetables or fruits).

Love Music – The Chivaree: The guests file into the banquet hall to the sound of stimulating music. The melodies and rhythms are designed to lift the spirits and create the mood for love.

The Surveyor's Wassail and the Valentine Cup: The guests are seated to the sound of the chivaree, a rousing piece of music with horns and drums. The Surveyor, or MC, performs a wassail; the Butler fills a large tankard and places it in a most visible position on the high table. Then the Butler makes an elegant bow, not only to the honoured guests, but to the cup itself. This is the Valentine cup. It is meant for the spirit of love, which everyone wants to welcome into the hall. The guests rise, holding high their own glasses. The surveyor shouts, 'To love! *Amor vincit omnia!*' (I don't need to tell the cultivated reader that '*Amor vincit omnia*' means 'Love conquers all'. It is from line 69 of the tenth *Eclogue* by Virgil, and is a sentiment that endures today: what, after all, is Lennon's 'All You Need is Love' other than a restating of this Virgilian maxim? Combine it with '*Labor omnia vicit*' and you have something of the paradox of good living.) The audience repeats this tribute. All then are seated.

February's Calendar

1 February: Kalends of February. Festival of Imbolc, Celtic start of spring.

2 February: Candlemas, feast of the Purification of the Virgin, and also the Roman feast of Juno Februa, the goddess after whom the month is named.

3 February: Feast day of St Blaise, patron saint of woolcombers.

6 February: St Dorothea's Day.

10 February: Feast of St Scholastica, sister of St Benedict.

13 February: Ides of February. Feast of St Matthias, the apostle who replaced Judas Iscariot.

14 February: St Valentine's Day.

21 February: Feralia, Roman festival of the dead.

28 February: Feast day of St Oswald.

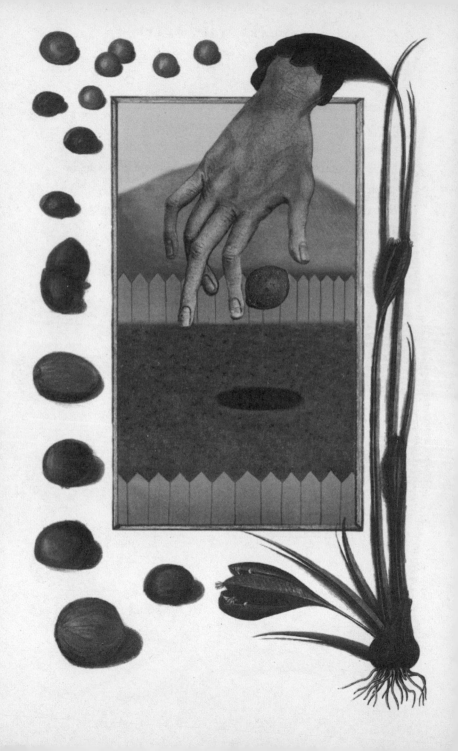

CHAPTER THREE

March

Sow Seeds

In March and in April, from morning to night,
In sowing and setting, good huswives delight:
To have in a garden, or other like plot,
to trim up their house, and to furnish their pot.

– Tusser

O NCE the soil has been prepared, it is time to sow your seeds in the garden. Medieval gardens, at least the European ones, seemed to work on a raised-bed system, one bed for each crop, and often with a little tree in the middle.

The garden was used to grow a wide range of herbs. Tusser's long list of 'seedes and herbes for the kitchen' – he mentions over forty – tends to prove that Tudor and late-medieval cookery must have been intensely flavourful. Tusser gives equally lengthy lists of 'flowers, for windows and pots' (the list includes the delightful Tudor word for daffodils, 'Daffadondillies'), and his list of 'necessarie Herbes to Growe in the garden for physick' includes exotics such as cumin. In the Old World, your garden provided medicine and food, and indeed the separation between the two was not drawn anything like as sharply as it is today.

The Importance of Defence

Once your seedlings have started to grow, Tusser warns that you will need to defend them against enemies such as wind, cat and chicken:

> Things graffed or planted, the greatest and least,
> defend against tempest, the bird and the beast.
> Defended shall prosper, the tother is lost,
> the thing with the labour, the time and the cost.

Oh Tusser, how I wish I'd read these words of wisdom at an earlier stage in my vegetable-growing career! How many times have I cursed my lack of foresight when I have left my work undefended and lost it all? Last year, the gate to the garden fell down. The pony strolled in and ate everything, including all my half-grown lettuce and cabbage plants. Then she wrecked the raised beds, deposited two piles of steaming, unrotted manure and walked out again. It was heartbreaking. I have also had problems with the wind knocking over the beans and tall peas. Through laziness, I didn't bother with any sort of windbreak. This is silly, because it is well known that wind-battered plants will be less bountiful. Last year also, I failed to protect my young seedlings, and the hens pecked their way into the vegetable patch and ate them. Cats will stretch out in newly dug earth and wreck everything. So much lost, and all for the lack of a little foresight.

This year, I have left hawthorn twigs to deter cats; netting to deter hens; a little wire fence around the broad beans to keep everything away from them; and little windbreaks around the cabbages and lettuces. I have put down organic slug pellets and I am also planning to companion plant, i.e. put rocket and parsley in a ring around my lettuces to form a barrier against slugs. I may also dig a shallow trench all the way around the patch and fill it with salt to deter them further. I also plan to leave saucers of beer for them to drown in at night, and I will visit the patch in the evenings armed with a pair of scissors to destroy any I find. Slugs are truly the most loathsome and vile creatures in the galaxy, and I challenge even the most determined vegan Buddhist to show any affection or solicitude towards them.

Keep Your Garden Neat

In her book *Medieval Gardens*, Sylvia Lansberg points out that the gardens of old combined utility and pleasure. In calendar drawings of the time, pairs of lovers are to be seen strolling past neat vegetable patches, peacocks sitting on the fence. The month of March in *Les Très Riches Heures du Duc de Berry*, that fantastically elaborate Book of Hours from the early fifteenth century, shows ploughing, planting and sowing with oxen all going on at the same time. All the gardens in medieval images are extremely well kept and very beautiful.

This year, I have tried to keep things in my garden looking neat. The more messy it is, I have found, the less likely you are to want to go and work in it, and so you become caught in a vicious circle. I used a piece of string, stretched between two sticks, as a planting guide, so the vegetables are in neat rows rather than wobbly ones, as previously. One hopes things will stay nice and 'trim', a lovely word that was used in Tudor times, as Tusser's charming couplet shows:

> Through cunning with dible [dibber], rake, mattock and spade,
> by line and by leavell, trim garden is made.

The old authorities all agree that you must study your own unique patch of earth to determine what will and what won't grow there. The soil, the position, the exposure to wind, what has grown before and what is growing nearby, the local weather conditions: all these will affect what you sow and plant – and when. Writes Tusser:

> Apt time and the season so divers to hit
> let aier and laier help practise and wit.

By 'aier', he means air (the weather and the situation) and by 'laier', he means the nature of the soil, its type and composition. Every position is different; soil types vary wildly, as do weather conditions. What works in one garden will fail in another. This is also a point insisted upon by Virgil in the *Georgics*:

> *Ac prius ignotum ferro quam scindimus aequor,*
> *ventos et varium caeli praediscere morem*

cura sit ac patrios cultusque habitusque locorum,
et quid quaeque ferat regio et quid quaeque recuseto
hic segetes, illic veniunt felicius uvae.

[And ere our iron cleaves an unknown plane, be it first our care to learn the winds and the wavering moods of the sky, the wanted tillage and nature of the ground, what each clime yields and what each discounts. Here corn, there grapes spring more luxuriously.]

   – *Georgics*, Book I, ll. 50–54

Virgil warns that you must work constantly on the garden:

Quod nisi et adsiduis herbam insectabere rastris
et sonitu terrebis aves et ruris opaci
falce premes umbras votisque vocaveris imbrem,
heu magnum alterius frustra spectabis acervum.

[Unless you harry the weeds with unrelenting mattock and scare the birds with noise, and with your billhook cut back the branches overshadowing your ground, and pray to the gods for rain, alas too late will you eye your neighbour's ample store.]

   – *Georgics*, Book I, ll. 155–8

The Golden Age

Hesiod, in *Works and Days*, like Virgil recalls life in a work-free Golden Age set in the mythical past, a sort of Greek version of the famous hobo song 'Big Rock Candy Mountain', a pagan Garden of Eden:

> . . . all good things
> Were theirs; ungrudgingly, the fertile land
> Gave up her fruits unasked.

Well, this would suggest that we have been trying to get back into that garden for at least 2,700 years, but life still seems to be dominated by unremitting toil, envy and want, despite all man's ingenuity in the area of technological advance. The answer, I think, is to enjoy your work in the garden, and to work there little and often. One or two hours a day should be enough to create your own little productive patch of paradise. There is a deep satisfaction in seeing and tasting the fruits of your labours in the form of something edible. Pleasure follows work. At the end of the toil, there is a feast.

Your garden is a retreat. The small farm is praised by Virgil as an escape from the troubles of the town:

> *Quos rami fructus, quos ipsa volentia rura*
> *sponte tulere sua, carpsit.*

> [The fruits his boughs, the crops his fields, produce willingly of
> their own accord, he gathers.]

The troubles of the world recede into the distance and seem unimportant alongside me, here, now, with this mattock, the sun on my back and the earth under my fingernails. It is surely very possible to create this Epicurean sense of 'undisturbedness' (one of Virgil's strongest influences was his teacher the Epicurean philosopher Siro). You can be an Epicurean today: simply unplug the television and the broadband and cancel the papers. We are told repeatedly by the hubristic self-congratulating technocrats that we are lucky to live in an age of lightning-fast electronic communication because, it is said, 'information' is good – but information is not the same as knowledge, as David Hockney put it when I went to interview him, and it is true that we hear less about *quality* of information. I would submit that the quality of the information that emerges the television is almost always extremely poor and not to be trusted. It disappoints. I feel depressed after watching television. But gardening really does work: it is therapeutic, useful and beautiful. It nourishes mind, body and spirit. To create your own garden is the most sublime of all pleasures. The conclusion of *Candide* is that '*Il faut cultiver notre jardin.*' We may have been thrown out of the Garden of Eden, but at least we have the potential to create our own paradise.

Practical Notes

The kitchen garden must be sited as near to the kitchen door as possible. The closer the plants are situated to the kitchen, the more likely it is that they will be well looked after. Seeds can be sown in trays or plugs on the windowsill or in the greenhouse and the seedlings planted out when they are big enough. Or you can buy little plants in the market. There is no shame in this. Many real gardeners buy seedlings from the experts rather than going to the trouble of growing everything from seed themselves. Last week, I bought twenty-four little lettuces from a cheery small supplier in the market, and they were ready to plant out immediately. What a lot of work that saved. I sow rocket and chervil everywhere, in pots and in the earth outside. Salads are easy to grow, as long as the slugs are kept away. (I have found that the only measure that seems to work is to put a thick layer of eggshells around the stem of your growing plants.)

It makes a lot of sense for the thrifty householder to grow salad, because it is expensive to buy. This contrasts with the potato, which takes up a lot of space in the vegetable patch, can be surprisingly worrying, as it seems so susceptible to disease, and involves quite a bit of thought and work: chitting, planting, manuring, earthing up, protecting from disease. When you dig the potatoes up, they often seem to be peppered with slug holes. And they are very cheap to buy, so the whole palaver can seem a little pointless. It is true, though, that the process of actually digging them up is hugely enjoyable, and new potatoes, particularly, taste far better than anything you can buy. Now I tend to plant a load of First Earlies, light salad potatoes, and leave it at that.

You could make the same argument against growing onions: you need a lot in the kitchen, they take up a lot of space in your patch and they are cheap to buy. But could you tell the difference between an onion bought in the shop and a home-grown allium? Probably not. But peas, beans, salad crops, herbs: these really are much better than anything available in the shops. Next on the list would come root vegetables such as parsnips, turnips, beetroot and carrots. Then kale, cabbage and broccoli.

One popular vegetable which I am not currently bothering with is tomatoes. Again, here we have an extremely labour-intensive crop, vulnerable to disease and in need of a great deal of warmth and attention. I have consistently failed to produce good tomato crops over the years, despite staking, tying, feeding, pinching out . . . and I don't even like tomatoes very much. Better to leave them to the experts, I think, especially when you are starting out. The temptation as a beginner is to try and grow a huge range of veg when the sensible thing would be to limit yourself to perhaps ten packets of seeds.

Broad beans are very easy to grow and good ones cannot be bought in the shops. They freeze well, too. Last year, we had forty plants, and this year, I have about eighty. Peas, too, are an absolute joy. There is a huge range of varieties out there, from the towering Alderman or Telephone to the humble Kelvedon Wonder. They should be sown every two or three weeks and can be grown quite early. This year, I waited until the first week of April, because the weather was so cold. Sweet and delicious straight from the pod, they barely need any cooking and will go with anything. Kids love them because they are, after all, nature's own M & M s.

Radishes are easy: they grow fast and anywhere. I keep a bowl of them on the kitchen table, in water, for constant snacking. I also tried growing something called French Blend, a mix of salad leaves such as mustard, chervil and rocket, but I don't recommend it, as one leaf tends to take over. This year, I let three of the radish plants go to seed, and they produced beautiful flowers on a large spreading plant. They then formed seed pods shaped rather like a cutlass. I collected the seeds and next year will sow them.

Sow every week! Keep sowing! Keep your seeds in a biscuit tin. Sow beetroot, sea kale, chard. Read gardening books in the evening. There are plenty out there. In 1563, one Thomas Hyll observed, 'to the makying of bookes of gardenyng there is noe ende,' and this is very true today. The titles are not always very imaginative: my favourite guide used to be *Grow Your Own Fruit and Vegetables* by Lawrence D. Hills, the great organic gardener, but my new favourite is the aforementioned *Grow Your Own Vegetables* by Joy Larkcom.

Lastly, can I recommend nasturtiums? They grow anywhere, look pretty and you can eat the leaves and the flowers in salads. And you can collect their seeds: put them in a jam jar, cover them with good vinegar and, a few months later, you will have a very passable caper substitute.

A Cautionary Note Concerning the Potato

Potatoes, as I mentioned earlier, come with a whole heap of troubles, and indeed Cobbett was no fan. He preferred good home-made bread and writes:

> [M]any labourers, especially in the west of England, use potatoes instead of bread to a very great extent. And I find . . . that it is the custom to allot the labourers 'a potato ground' in part payment of their wages! This has a tendency to bring English labourers down to the state of the Irish, whose mode of living, as to food, is but one remove from that of the pig, and an ill-fed pig, too.

Here Cobbett is remarking on the way the Irish had been, in his view scandalously, encouraged to live on potatoes by the authorities. The Irish Potato Famine of 1845–7 occurred about twenty years after the publication of his *Cottage Economy*, from which we take the above passage. First, the plan to feed a nation on potatoes went disastrously wrong because the potato crops failed three years out of four, and then the grasping landlords evicted their poor and starving tenants. Hundreds of thousands of Irish suffered in this manner. Nearly a million went to the US; others went to Liverpool and Glasgow. One emigrant to the US was Patrick Kennedy, whose great-grandson John Kennedy was elected the first Irish Catholic president in 1960. The potato, says Cobbett, is 'the root also of slovenliness, filth, misery, and slavery'. Far better, he says, to revert to bread and beer for a healthy life, a subject we'll come back to shortly.

The Importance of Sharing

You will find that gardeners nearby will often have an excess of plants and that they will be happy to give them away, thereby saving much labour. March is a good time to gather seedlings from others and plant them. I am planning to start a gardeners' group in my area called the Heddon Valley Diggers. We will meet at the local pub once a month over a few pints of real ale and swap tips and seeds. Seed swapping is an excellent idea: you simply exchange your excess seeds for other people's, and everyone is happy. Again, this idea dates back centuries and is mentioned in Tusser:

> Good neighbours in deede
> change seede for seede.

And:

> One seede for another, to make an exchange,
> with fellowlie neighbourhood seemeth not strange.

This spirit of 'fellowlie neighbourhood' leads to a deeply satisfying connection with a nurturing agricultural tradition and also to a delightful sense of one's disconnection from the world of capitalism. Remove money from transactions and all goes swimmingly and with great joy. No one gets the advantage; no one is ripped off. It is also fairly easy to find small seed companies which encourage you to save seed and can give you advice on how to do so. They produce varieties that are intended for small gardens, whereas some of the large seed companies put their commercial seeds in small packets for the home grower. The problem with this is that the seeds may, for example, all crop at exactly the same moment. And the big seed companies peddle something called F1 hybrids, which are supposed to grow well but produce infertile seed. Of course, if your seeds fail, you are forced to buy more.

Do not be too ambitious. When I began to cultivate my patch, I built raised beds. I had in mind a sort of elegant French *potager* but, unless you have a full-time gardener or a team of experts and workers at your fingertips, this idea is ridiculously ambitious. I ended up with a disastrous mess. This year, I threw out the raised beds and went back to a simpler system, as recommended to me by celebrated gardener Kirsty Knight-Bruce. I now simply have two beds, each measuring about seven feet by thirty-six, separated by a central grass path. Here and there are planks so I can walk around the beds. That is all. In doing this, I have increased my growing area and, in actual fact, it looks much neater. Kirsty explained that raised beds tend to be used when you are working with poor soil: they will hold a big heap of enriching dung. But as my soil is good, there is not much need for them.

I reject the ugly polytunnel. It seems to have the very formidable disadvantage that it is not open to the elements and therefore you have to water it all the time. By contrast, grow your crops outdoors, and you need only water very little. My patch gets so much rain I think I only watered it once last year. They say that polytunnels allow you to grow veg at different times of the year, and crops start earlier, and so on. But who wants to grow veg at odd times of the year and bring some of their produce forward? I was very happy to start late this year; it meant I had another month of not working. And eating seasonally makes sense: parsnips suit the winter and peas suit the summer. That is all there is to it.

In my fantasy world, I would like to have a three-acre garden with shaded walks, orchards, flowery arbours and, in the words of Francis Bacon in his essay 'Of Gardens', 'fair alleys', for solitary contemplation. But I have to work within my limitations and, over the years, I have discovered that I have many. In fact, living in the country has gradually revealed to me a whole new set of things that I am hopeless at, from putting up shelves to keeping the garden tidy to clearing out the shed. So now I accept that the veg garden is more or less purely utilitarian and I no longer aspire to make it into a sweet-smelling bower suitable for Eleanor of Aquitaine to receive Bertran de Born and the merry troubadours of Occitania.

There are frequent disappointments in keeping a garden. Many are the times I have wondered why on earth I bother. However much work I do there, Victoria still buys huge amounts of vegetables. I remember one year when I exploded with rage because she came home with four punnets of strawberries. I had planted twenty-four strawberry plants earlier in the year: 'Have you not seen me planting and tending all those strawberry plants?' I hollered. At other times, I have proudly brought back a trugful of courgettes, only to throw them, unused and rotten, on the compost heap, two weeks later. There are skills to be learned at all stages of the process: keeping the soil in good shape; sowing carefully and at the right times; protecting the growing plants; harvesting the crop; and then making sure that the crop is used. None of these is straightforward.

Therefore it is essential that you enjoy the process and, also, in the early stages, that you do not expect too much from it. Keep it simple, and keep experimenting. Sow seeds in three different places: in pots, and in two different locations outdoors. See which technique works. Last year, I failed initially with the lovely purple climbing bean Blauhilde. I sowed twelve or so on the windowsill. In the warmth, they germinated quickly and started shooting up. So I planted them outside. They all withered and died. So I sowed some more inside. When they had grown a little, I left them in the front porch to get used to the cold. Finally, they started to grow well.

Cosmic Gardening or Not?

We all understand the role of the sun in growing plants. But there is widespread disagreement about the part the moon plays. Planting by the stars and by the moon was a well-established practice in Virgil's time and, again, we see the concept treated as quite normal in medieval husbandry guides, and in Tusser, who writes:

> Sow pease (good trull)
> the Moone past full.
> Fine seedes then sowe
> whilst Moone doth growe.

But an eighteenth-century commentator on Tusser is sceptical about the effect of the moon on plants, commenting that 'planetary influence, especially that of the moon, has commonly very much attributed to it in rural affairs, perhaps sometimes too much.' And for his part, the practical Cobbett dismissed cosmic gardening as fanciful in *The English Gardener*: 'I do hope, that it is unnecessary for me to say, that sowing according to the moon is wholly absurd and ridiculous; and that it arose solely out of the circumstance, that our forefathers, who could not read, had neither almanack nor calendar to guide them, and counted by moons and festivals, instead of by months, and days of months.' The sky, then was our calendar. Virgil's *Georgics* opens with the lines:

> *Quid faciat laetas segetes, quo sidere terram*
> *vertere, Maecenas, ulmisque adiungere vites*
> *conveniat, quae cura boum, qui cultus habendo*
> *sit pecori, apibus quanta experientia parcis,*
> *hinc canere incipiam.*

[What makes the corncrops glad, under which star to turn the soil, Maecenas, and wed your vines to elms, the care of cattle, keeping of flocks, all the experience thrifty bees demand – such are the themes of my song.]

– *Georgics*, Book I, ll. 1 – 5

If we were to embrace cosmic gardening, I suppose at the very least we would become more aware of the phases of the moon and the movements of the stars. We enjoy contemplating the earth; why not contemplate the sky as well?

Sinister old Rudolf Steiner maintains that planting and sowing at the right time help the quality of the plant. Even firewood, he says, benefits from coming from a tree that was planted sensitively:

Assume for instance that we take, as firewood, wood that is derived from trees which were planted in the Earth without understanding cosmic rhythms. It will not provide the same health-giving warmth as firewood from trees that were planted intelligently. These things enter especially into the more intimate relationships of daily life, and here they show their greatest significance. Alas! The life of people has become almost entirely thoughtless nowadays. They are only too glad if they do not need to think of such things. They think it must all go on like any machine. You have all the necessary contrivances; turn on the switch, and it goes. So do they conceive, materialistically, the working of all nature.

This sort of stuff sounds appealing for a few seconds but, on further reflection, it must surely reveal itself to be poppycock, mumbo-jumbo and silly nonsense. I think that, overall, we have enough to worry about as it is without ensuring that our firewood comes from trees that have been planted in the earth with a sensitive understanding of cosmic rhythms, and I certainly cannot imagine putting such a query to the log merchant: 'Yes, my good man, now tell me. Does this firewood come from trees that were planted by someone with a deep understanding of cosmic rhythms? Otherwise, I'm afraid you'll have to take it back. It simply does not provide the right level of health‑giving warmth.' Let us also add that there is something unpleasantly self‑hating in this way of thinking. It is almost anti‑human. I think we should celebrate humanity and all our wonderful achievements. The alternative is to descend into a confusing mess of guilt about man's impact on the planet. So my advice would be not to bother with the cosmic stuff, unless, as Cobbett says, you are simply using the moon and the stars as a calendar. It's just too confusing.

March's Husbandry

While the unromantic Hesiod recommends a striving attitude when it comes to estate management:

> If in your heart you pray for riches, do
> These things: pile work on work, and still more work.

. . . Virgil, on the other hand, is more poetic. He loves the spring. It's when the earth becomes motherly:

> *Parturit almus ager Zephyrique tepentibus auris*
> *laxant arva sinus; superat tener omnibus umor.*

[The bounteous earth prepares to give birth, and the meadows

ungirdle to the zephyr's balmy breeze; the tender moisture avails
for all.]

— *Georgics*, Book II, ll. 330–31

As far as practical advice goes, Virgil, like the good folk of Lark
Rise, recommends constant cultivation:

> *Seminibus positis superest diducere terram*
> *saepius ad capita et duros iactare bidentis.*

[When the sets are planted, it remains for you to break up the soil
oft-times, at the roots, and to swing the ponderous hoe.]

— *Georgics*, Book II, ll. 354–5

Columella's list of vegetables to grow, as described in *De Re
Rustica*, is almost familiar:

Though there are very many kinds of pulse or legumes, those
observed to be the most pleasing and useful to man are the bean,
the lentil, the pea, the cow-pea, the chick-pea, hemp, millet, panic
grass, sesame, lupine . . . panic and millet require a light, loose
soil . . . they cannot be sown before spring, for they are fond of
warm weather above all; but they are entrusted to the earth to best
advantage in the latter part of March.

He would have you sow beans by the moon but, if you miss it, he
says, don't sweat it:

We must take care that the quantity allotted for seed be broadcast
on the fifteenth day of the moon . . . the lentil is properly sown only

from the time of the half-moon up to the twelfth day, in ground
that is lean and loose, or fat, but above all in a place that is dry;
for when in flower it is easily damaged by rankness and moisture
. . . Hemp demands a rich, manured, well-watered soil, or one
that is level, moist and deeply worked. Six grains of this seed to
the square foot are planted at the rising of Arcturus, which means
toward the end of February, about the sixth or fifth day before the
Kalends of March; and yet no harm will be done in planting it up
to the spring equinox if the weather is rainy.

Palladius also tells us to get sowing:

> Now holyhocke is sowe and armorace [wild radish],
> Or arborace that wilde raves are,
> And origon nowe plante him in his place;
> Now lekes, betes, letuce, and capare [capers],
> Savery, colcase, and cresses; noo man spare
> This goldes outher rabes forto sowe;
> And bless it; trust in God that alle shal growe.

Tusser says that March is the time, as I hardly need to remind you,
to kill those pesky rooks and magpies:

> Kill crowe, pie and cadow [jackdaw],
>   rooke, buzard and raven,
> or else go desire them to seeke a new haven.
> In scaling the yoongest, to pluck off his beck,
> beware how ye climber, for breaking your neck.

Evelyn's *Kalendarium Hortense* has a long list of what to sow this
month:

Sow in the beginning *Endive, Succory, Leeks, Radish, Beets, Chard-Beet, Scorzonera* [black salsify], *Parsnips, Skirrets* [an old vegetable], *Parsley, Sorrel, Bugloss, Borrage, Chervils, Sellery, Smalladge!, Alisanders* [horse parsley], &c. Several of which continue many years without renewing, and most of them to be blanch'd by laying them under littier and earthing up.

Sow *also Lettuce, Onions, Garlick, Orach, Purslan, Turneps* (to have early) monethly *Pease* &c. these annually.

Sow also *Carrots, Cabbages, Cresses, Fennel, Majoran, Basil, Tobacco* &c. and transplant any sort of *Medicinal Herbs.*

Now tobacco: there's something to try in the garden.

Cobbett is sowing like crazy. He recommends the following in *The English Gardener*:

Sow artichokes, Windsor beans [broad beans], cauliflowers to come in the autumn; celery, capsicums, love-apples, marjorum [*sic*] and basil, on gentle heat; lettuces, marigold, blue, Prussian, and other peas in succession; onions for a principal crop, but do not sow them till the ground works well and fine; parsley, radishes, borage, savoys, small salading in succession as wanted; asparagus in seed beds, beets, salsafy, scorzenera, skirrets, fennel, cabbages red and white, turnips, nasturtiums, early purple brocoli, thyme, and all sorts of herbs that are raised from seed, Brussels sprouts, parsnips, round spinage, leeks, carrots for a main crop, chervil, coriander, French beans at the close of the month in a warm soil; *plant* out cauliflowers, hops in clumps for their tops, small onions of last year's sowing, for early heading, old onions for seed, lettuces, perennial herbs by slips or parting the roots, asparagus, artichokes from suckers, potatoes for a main crop, cabbages white and red, Jerusalem artichokes, chives, potato-onions, &c.

Why he feels the need to put '&c', as if this is only a partial list, God knows. But Cobbett, as we know, was not exactly slack in his habits. I wonder what he would have thought of Fukuoka.

Seymour is pretty busy, too, in March:

Drill early peas. To do this we scoop out a little trench with a hoe and sprinkle the peas in pretty thickly [generally about two inches apart]. If the land is poor you need to dig a trench first, fill it with muck, compost or leaf mould, bury it and put your peas on that. Soak your pea seed in paraffin if you don't like mice, or if your mice do like peas. You can't have enough peas. Plant one row of early chitted spuds at the beginning of the month and another at the end.

Sow leeks in a seed bed.

Sow lettuce and radish. Plant globe artichoke suckers.

In flower this month, writes Francis Bacon, are 'violets, specially the single blue, which are the earliest; the yellow daffodil; the daisy; the almond-tree in blossom; the peach-tree in blossom; the cornelian-tree in blossom; sweet briar'.

March's Merriment

March was named after the Roman god Mars. Lent, and often the movable feast and blow-out of Easter which follows it, occurs in this month. In the old days, Lent usually meant giving up meat, but medieval manorial records show that a good deal of fish was consumed, so the season was perhaps not as onerously ascetic as you might have thought. And it doesn't seem to have occurred to anyone to give up alcohol.

One thing was for sure: it was a nice long holiday. Alfred the

Great decreed that there was no need to toil during the fortnight either side of Easter. The fortnight before would be taken up with religious observance, and that after with feasting and merriment. The Jacobean poet Nicholas Breton wrote that the season was for 'nothing but play and mirth'. All households would stock up for a major feast on Easter Sunday. This would be followed by sports and fairs on Easter Monday. Remarks Hutton, 'All across England and Ireland in the same century smaller communities engaged in dancing, athletics, racing of horses and dogs, feasting, and a variety of local games. The tradition persists to the present day in the scheduling of fun-fairs and professional sports.' But something has been lost, he adds. 'What has perished is any sense of a celebration of communal identity.' It is also worth remarking that fun nowadays has been commodified: instead of doing it for ourselves, we pay others to organize it for us, whether it be a football match or a funfair.

Merriment at Easter includes Morris dancing, which takes its name from the Moorish dancers of Spain, and it is also the time to put on a mystery play. And, by the way, can we continue to call the festival Easter? One recent horror of the Brave New World was our local primary school's Easter play. Rather than just sticking with two thousand years of tradition, though, and calling it an Easter play, they felt the need to 'keep up with the times', and they renamed it – really, I can hardly bear to type this out – 'The E Factor'. Can you believe it? Well, in the old days, after the feast on Easter Day, which is accompanied by juggling, miming and music, a play which tells the story of Noah's flood begins. It is called 'The Deluge', originates from the town of Chester, and explores the Easter themes of rebirth and renewal after a period of death. A white-haired character enters the room and declares:

I, God, that all this world has wrought,
Heaven and earth, and all of nought,
I see my people, in deed and thought,
Are set foul in sin . . .
When that I made will I destroy!

Old Eastertide was rich and complex, consisting not just of a single day's feasting, as today, but of a whole cycle of special days: Quinquagesima, Shrove Tuesday, Ash Wednesday, Mothering Sunday, Carling Sunday, Palm Sunday, Maundy Thursday, Good Friday, Rogation Sunday, Ascension, Pentecost and Whit Monday.

March's Calendar

1 March: Kalends of March. Roman New Year. Feast of St David. Today is the day to wear a leek or a daffodil in your buttonhole. If your neighbour has not finished his ploughing by today, it is the custom to go and help him out.

2 March: Feast day of St Chad, Bishop of Mercia at Lichfield and patron saint of mineral springs.

11 March: Day of the Luddites. On this day in 1811, a group of Nottinghamshire knitters destroyed the new frames, and further rioting ensued. The rebellion was brutally squashed by the state. I suggest that all liberty seekers remember this day.

15 March: The Ides of March. Caesar was assassinated on this day in 44BC. It is a holy day for Rhea, Greek goddess of the earth.

17 March: Feast of St Patrick, fifth-century Christian monk. On this day, the Lenten restrictions are temporarily lifted, and you can make merry with a clear conscience.

19 March: Feast day of St Joseph, patron saint of dads and carpenters.

24 March, or thereabouts: Equinox.

25 March, or thereabouts: Feast of the Annunciation, or *Festum Incarnationis*. Today, the angel Gabriel appeared and told Mary that she was going to bring forth a son called Jesus. It is also known as Lady Day.

31 March: Roman festival of Luna, goddess of the full moon.

CHAPTER FOUR

April

Tend Fowl

And here I here [hear] the fowlis synge

— Medieval poem of the months

THE MEDIEVAL calendars do not agree on a specific task for April. The most common image appears to be a boy or a girl holding a tree in each hand, symbolizing the renewal of growth associated with spring. Other calendars and church carvings show peasants grafting trees and vines. The month is often associated with the goddess Flora, and is said to be 'full of flowers'. One carving from 1196 in the Parma Baptistery in northern Italy shows 'the king of spring', a crowned figure holding a tree in one hand and a fleur-de-lys in the other. For their part, Virgil and Columella go into great detail about the care of vines at this time of year.

The month is also associated with love. A Flemish calendar from the 1540s shows two pairs of courting lovers chatting in a neat, enclosed garden of rectangular beds. One of the gentlemen sports an impressive codpiece. Another Book of Hours shows a servant girl planting in the enclosed garden as her mistress looks on. In *Les Très Riches Heures du Duc de Berry*, a noble gentleman and gentlewoman appear to be exchanging rings while two ladies gather flowers. There are vineyards in the distance.

Contrary to its characterization by the gloomy modernist T. S. Eliot as 'the cruellest month', April has traditionally been a joyful period of green shoots and hope. This is the month when we hear the birds sing again, and when the swallows start to arrive. It is the month when, Chaucer tells us in his prologue to *The Canterbury Tales*, we want to get out of the house: 'longen folk to goon on pilgrimages', and indeed, this April, I walked with a group of five friends for two days to Canterbury along the old pilgrims' route. Aries is the first month of the year in the old scheme of things, and it is the month of my own birthday. So there is a lot to celebrate.

As a result of this focus on love, renewal, growth and the singing of the birds, I have decided, for the purposes of this book, to make April the month of the hen, and so this chapter will largely focus on poultry husbandry.

My Hen Story

A few hens in the garden will bring a plentiful supply of eggs; hens are very little work and a great joy to watch. To perform the duty of *gallinarius*, or poultry manager, is a pleasure and a privilege. We currently have a brood of six brown hens and one cockerel.

Our experiences in keeping poultry began when we adopted a group of bantams – a beautiful cockerel and four hens – from some friends who were moving house. We liked the idea of bantams because they are self-managing: they will find their own roosting spots in trees, spend the night there and keep out of harm's way while remaining free to roam where they like during the day. But the problem comes in finding their eggs. Like all hens, their instinct is to find a protected and secluded spot to make a little nest. So you may think you are getting no eggs, but in fact the hen is laying her eggs in a secret place in a hedge. Many were the times when we would stumble across a pile of fourteen eggs in a hidden corner somewhere. Ideally, you would put a wire-tap on each bird, and a CCTV camera, and watch their movements during the morning, which is when hens lay their eggs, to discover their secret spots. But this kind of New World investment in cutting-edge surveillance technology is not really in the spirit of things.

And there is another downside to all this freedom. After a few months, we noticed we had just three, and then two, bantams. We assumed that they were being picked off in the fields by the fox. (Note that, in the country, it is always 'the' fox and never 'a' fox. It is also the custom around here to refer to inanimate objects as 'he'. For example, the Rayburn, our oven and heating system: 'You want to make sure he's got plenty of oil, Tom.') After a couple of weeks, they had all disappeared. In any case, the bantams had annoyed our landlord because they roosted high up in his big barn and left their noxious droppings all over the straw bales piled up below. His wife didn't relish going to grab a straw bale and finding her hands covered in chickenshit. 'No more bantams,' our landlord said to me one day. So it was time for a rethink.

Our second plan was to buy what are called 'point-of-lay' hens. These are young hens just about to enter their most productive egg-laying period. We bought six of them for £6 each: Warrens – a boring but productive breed. This is probably the most expensive way of doing it. We assigned them an outbuilding and put some straw bales into it. We had hens again! But our problems were only just beginning. When I showed the man who delivered the hens where they were to be quartered, he pointed to the three-inch gap under the door and said, 'The fox'll be in under that.' I thought, Yeah, yeah, whatever, and gave him the £36. I shut the hens in the barn.

Two days later, when I went to inspect them, I found a scene reminiscent of *Reservoir Dogs*. Two hens were lying dead on the floor. In the corner behind an old kitchen unit there was one live hen. It was hiding behind the corpse of one of its fellows. It must have got itself just out of reach of the fox. What horrors had it witnessed? Later, I found another live hen cowering underneath the oil tank. So two had survived the massacre; two had been carried away; two had been left behind. Older, sadder and wiser, and twenty-four quid down, I got out a plank and a hammer and nails and set about boarding up the gap below the door.

We restocked, but later in the summer lost the whole lot. This time, the culprit was a badger. We had gone away for the weekend and had asked our neighbour to let the hens in and out. When she came to open their door in the morning, a badger popped out, and inside were six dead chickens. Having your hens wiped out by a wily predator produces all sorts of unpleasant emotions. First off, you feel like a failure, a bad husbandman. Then there is the waste of money to consider: we had lost £60 worth of hens, and the whole point of the operation had been that they were supposed to save us money on eggs. (I have never considered any of our smallholding attempts to be indulgences but always a way to save money.) Second off, you are left with a real loathing for the fox (or, in this case, badger). Suddenly you feel like asking the local hunt to come round and chase him down.

So the *gallinarius* must be vigilant about locking up his or her chickens at night. As I write, we have just lost two more hens. Some visitors needed to get their dog out of the way, and put him in a cage in the henhouse overnight. They felt he'd be safe in there as the door can be closed. But it was a ridiculous idea. The presence of the dog scared the hens, and they dispersed around the farm at dusk and roosted elsewhere. The rooster and one hen were gone by the morning. The fox, ever alert, had taken them in the night.

A couple of months ago, I had to leave the house early and was spending a few nights away. It was four o'clock. I herded the hens into the henhouse as best I could. But a couple refused to go in. So I locked the door and figured that they'd be all right left out just for one night. Wrong. Our housesitter arrived the following morning to find a bloodbath. She left a note on the kitchen table which read: 'Blood and feathers in stable.' To lose your chickens in this way is a painful experience.

As well as the hens, we also bought a Dorking cockerel. Dorking is a nice old Roman bird, a five-toed bird of a kind mentioned by Columella. It is supposed to be a good cross-purpose breed: in other words, they are fairly productive egg-wise but their offspring will also make good eating. We bought four hens from a neighbour, too. We then locked them all in their henhouse, where I had set up a perch and a few nesting boxes in the form of old Lloyd Loom laundry boxes placed on their sides ('Never spend any money' is our constant motto). But after a few weeks, the fox started picking them off in the afternoon as they roamed the fields. One day I was awoken from my afternoon nap by a terrific clucking sound. I looked out of the bedroom window. There was a fox up on the grassy bank, ambling along with a hen in its mouth. Curse you, Roald Dahl! Excuse me, sir! Mr Fox is not fantastic, he's a killer! Over the next few days, one hen after another disappeared. Finally, we were left with just a poor young cockerel who had been born on the farm a few months previously. Deprived of the company of his mother and half-sisters, he spent his days sitting on the gate to the pigs' enclosure chatting to them (we often notice that animals of different species socialize with each other in this way). Then, one day, he disappeared as well.

We decided to take a break from poultry farming until the following spring. But buying eggs from the shop after eating your own free-range ones is a real comedown. Not only do you have to pay for them, but the quality – even of the best rare-breed organic free-range eggs on the market, the ones that come with a lengthy description of the farm where the hens are kept, the caring credentials of the farmer, the niceties of their diet, the results of their wellbeing classes – is nothing like as high as that of the ones that come from the backyard. The eggs we had been getting from our own chickens were absolutely superb, the yolks a dark orange rather than yellow, and the white would stand up like a jelly when you cracked one into the pan, whereas that of inferior eggs is runny. To make matters worse, we heard that a mum at the local school, who had started keeping chickens after we did, had been so successful in this undertaking that she was *selling her surplus eggs*! This piece of information filled me with gloom.

Then, the following spring, Victoria saw an ad in the local paper for 'organic hens', £1 each. She went to investigate and found that, although strictly organic, these were in fact battery hens that had passed their most productive egg-laying period. She brought home fifteen of these poor birds. What a sorry sight they were. Clearly, they had never benefited from the services of a self-esteem counsellor. They were scrawny, shy and covered with bald patches. We put them into their henhouse. The following morning, we found three dead. We presumed that they had died from the cold, something new to them, as battery hens are kept in very high temperatures. We kept them all locked in their barn for three days in order to accustom them to their new lodgings. After the three days, we were given a new Dorking cockerel by friends and let him into the henhouse. For a moment, total silence descended while this splendid creature entered. Remember: they had never seen a male before. Imagine George Harrison walking into a room full of fifteen-year-old schoolgirls in 1964. Following this silence, they began contentedly clucking again, and started to enjoy their new sex life.

As the weeks went on, the hens grew their feathers back and became gradually more confident. There was one problem: no eggs. We fed the birds, watered them, locked them in, let them out, spoke in soothing tones to them, built up their confidence. And there were plenty of nesting boxes in their house. I can see now, though, that this was a low point in our country-living experiment from a diary entry I wrote in March 2008 (I suspect following a domestic row):

> *Sometimes I wonder why I bother . . . Brave New World has conquered. I have lost. Goodbye.*

Sometimes the life of a city wage slave looks tremendously appealing.

Curse of the Rat

Well, two months later and the hens were still not laying. 'They need light,' said one neighbour. 'I think you were sold a duff one there,' said another. (It's quite astonishing how much pleasure country locals derive from repeating this phrase to recently relocated townies. Practically anything you buy – car, hens, wood, lawnmower – will be a poor bargain. And this phrase is guaranteed to make you feel like a gullible, over-civilized idiot.) My advisor in countryside matters, Alan, thought there may have been a clever rat stealing the eggs. It's true I had seen an artful rat coming out into the yard to steal chicken food when he thought my back was turned. And when I used to open the door to the henhouse in the morning, a little group of animals would glance up and disperse. We had a white rabbit living in the henhouse at the time, and the rabbit, the hens and the rat all appeared to be in some sort of conference. It was like a scene from *Animal Farm*. The other problem might have been that the hens had made a nest in a hedge somewhere. Alan suggested that we keep them locked in till lunchtime.

I kept visiting the henhouse during the morning, to deter Ratty. By noon, we had two eggs. That afternoon I hid round a corner with my air rifle and waited for the cheeky rat to come out into the yard. It took an hour of stalking but, eventually, I shot him.

Rats can be a real enemy. At one stage, I foolishly left a plastic bin full of chicken food in the chicken house. It had a lid on it but, during a cold spell, a hungry rat gnawed through the lid, creating a sort of foul lacework pattern. He had also eaten right through the bin itself to get at the food within. On another occasion, I opened the bin to find a squeaking rat trapped in there. He was leaping up and down but could not get a grip on the sloping sides of the bin. I shot him with pleasure.

Eggs Galore

We continued to keep the hens locked in till noon or later and, sure enough, the eggs started coming. Some days we would have ten.

Over the summer, we averaged seven or eight eggs a day and, joy of joys, sold some of the surplus. We still have the same basic flock two years later, although the numbers are greatly reduced. We now have four hens and a cockerel, and we get three eggs a day. The obsession with the number of eggs the hens produce each day is clearly common among we *gallinarii*. Here is an extract from George Orwell's diary from 1938:

    22.11.38: Two eggs.
    23.11.38: One egg.
    25.11.38: Two eggs.
    28.11.38: One egg.
    29.11.38: Two eggs.
    30.11.38: One egg.

Each year, one of our hens has gone broody. In the first year, we let the hen find her own nest and left her alone. Soon six little yellow chicks were born. Then I did something extremely stupid. I left a child's bucket filled with water near the brood, thinking that they must be thirsty. The following morning, there were five drowned chicks in the bucket. This was a real disaster: each of those chicks could have grown into either a laying hen or a delicious cockerel. Clearly, I should have left well alone. Chicks are terribly vulnerable. We'd lost some from a previous brood because the children had decided to 'give them a bath'.

The surviving chick grew fast. It went with its mother everywhere and really did go 'cheep cheep' all day long. After a while, we realized that he was growing a fine crest and that he was a cockerel. On the day he uttered his first croaky 'cock-a-doodle-doo', his mother rejoined the main flock, and he was alone.

The problem is what to do now. You can only have one cockerel. Otherwise, they will start to fight. I saw this happen once. Our neighbour came home one day with a load of hens and a cockerel, which she had named Helleborus. One day, Helleborus wandered into our yard and started fighting with Blaziken, our cockerel (named after a Pókemon character). It was a stunning spectacle to watch, especially when you consider that neither had ever had a fight before and therefore every one of their graceful and athletic moves came from pure instinct. They danced around each other and fluttered into the air, and then one played dead while the other trampled over it. It was a like a dance, and beautiful to watch. My daughter Delilah (then aged six) and I stood transfixed. I wondered if I should try to separate them. Isn't cock-fighting illegal? In the event, we carried on watching. It really was very medieval, I thought later. In fact, a bit more medieval than I had planned when we embarked on our pre-Industrial experiment.

So, you have to give away your spare cock, or kill him and eat him. We decided to eat him. We separated him from the others and put him in a cage for two weeks so we could feed him a lot of protein. Then one day (I think when he was around five or six months old – Hugh Fearnley-Whittingstall advises killing them at around eighteen weeks, so we were perhaps a little late), we locked the others in the henhouse so they wouldn't witness the slaughter. Victoria got the HFW book out. (I give thanks to Hugh for the very inspiring, useful, although not always thorough *River Cottage Cookbook*, which has been a great help over the last eight years.) She read out the chicken-killing instructions. I held the cockerel upside down by his feet and held his head in my other hand, my fingers around his warm little neck. I could feel him gulping. I then wrenched his head down sharply, and it worked: he died instantly. (The following year, a local smallholder called Simon Dawson came to kill another spare cockerel, and he showed us what is actually an easier method, involving a broom handle. Book learning is one thing, but it is far, far better to learn from somebody who knows what they are doing.) We hung him up (the cockerel, not Simon) and Victoria slit his throat to bleed him, although this is not actually necessary. I spent about two hours plucking him. (When Simon did it the following year, he did the same job in about five minutes.) This year, I used the broom-handle method, but was a little too vigorous. The cockerel's head came clean off, and the children watched goggle-eyed as the headless bird dashed about in the barn, blood pouring from his neck.

This time, we hung the cockerel upside down in the dairy for twenty-four hours. I cut his feet and wings off with the garden loppers (again, there are better ways of doing this: look them up). I got the guts out of him, which is called 'drawing', and this takes a bit of doing (Andrew Singer's *Backyard Poultry Book* is the best I have found on this). We took him up to London and made a *coq au vin* with him with our friends Stu and George. It was absolutely delicious, a nice 3kg organic chicken that would have cost £12 from the farm shop. We are told that we should buy a load of day-old chicks and feed them up into eaters, and this may well be our next stage in poultry-keeping: growing birds for meat and not just keeping them for eggs.

When I think of all the smallholding pursuits, keeping hens is the easiest and most cost effective. To get £5 to £10 worth of top-quality eggs each week is not difficult. With larger flocks, we have produced forty-two eggs a week or more and, on top of that, you have the possibility of producing some really good eating birds.

Some folk invest in an incubator, which can lead to limitless chicks. You do not need a cockerel for hens to lay eggs, but you do of course need one if you want the eggs to turn into chicks.

You can buy chicks to rear for meat. This year, we bought ten young birds and kept them for two or three months. This, in theory, is a very cheap way of getting a top-quality free-range organic chicken. In actual fact, the exercise was a total disaster. We ate two of the birds while they were still quite young, but the others all met grisly deaths: six were taken by the fox one afternoon, and two more, which we'd put in a cage to fatten them up (it was a big cage), were found dead one morning with their eyes pecked out. We assume that rats were responsible. A money-saving exercise therefore turned into a very costly waste of money and caused a lot of extra worry and work to boot. ('Don't they always?' said our farmer friend Jackie.)

I tend to feed the chickens once in the morning and once in the evening, on bought chicken food, although for more advice on feeding, which is an art in itself, see 'On Feeding Hens'. The rest of the time, they peck at grass and insects and waddle around in the sun. They hate bad weather, and will stay in if there is a hint of rain or snow. They love dustbaths and take a nap after lunch. The cockerel keeps the females in order, and he is a true gent: at feeding time, he waits until all the hens are taking their fill before he has his first peck. When you go out to feed them, the chickens run towards you at great speed. Children can easily be delegated to feed the hens, to let them out and to collect the eggs, and ours have sometimes taken on the job of selling the surplus. The hens make delightful little purring clucking noises and, of course, the cock's crowing is a delight to hear. Keep the doors to the house shut, though: our chickens seem to have taken a vow to get into the house as often as possible. If you leave the back door open, you are sure to find a hen or two clucking around the hall or the kitchen. And although their manure is counted among the very best for your kitchen garden by Columella, it is not appealing in its raw state. My mother, on a rare visit, was particularly horrified when a hen came into the kitchen and pooed on the floor. 'Why have you got all these animals?' she said. 'You can't even cope with your own children.'

On Buying Hens

There are all sorts of fancy breeds of chicken out there. Some are very pretty, some are good layers, some make good eating. I do not pretend to be an expert and, clearly, if you have the funds, you can buy some lovely-looking hens. But the Brave Old World is not about spending a fortune on chicken-keeping as an indulgent hobby. It is about spending as little as possible and getting the most out of it. A cheap way to start is to get a few ex-battery hens and rehabilitate them. There is great pleasure in seeing them come back to life again and gradually learning how to be free. They may never lay intensively, but our six remaining battery hens are doing very well: one egg a day, or every other day. John Seymour's wife, Sally, went for battery hens:

Before their first year is out battery hens are sick, like to die, and cannot be kept alive in the wire cages any longer. They are therefore sold for 'scrap' at prices often as low as ten new pennies [this is 1974]. Sally has bought them thus for half a crown, brought them home in the van, and turned them loose. Always some fail to survive the journey. It takes them two or three days to learn to *walk* – at first you have to carry them about. Within a week they have learned to do something they have never done before, that is, scrap, or scratch about for food. Within a month they are new hens. The feathers grow back on their chafed and naked necks (they had worn their old feathers off on the wire), the sores and calluses on their breasts have healed, they learn to flap their wings, run, chase earwigs, and it does the heart good to see them.

This is precisely our experience. Seymour goes on to say that the downside with these battery hens is that they are unlikely to go broody, but each year one of ours has. I'm not even sure what breed ours are: they are just brown hens. My friend Chris has no idea what breed his chickens are either: his brood is the result of years of mixing up various birds he has picked up for free. This is a good tactic: do not spend money but live like a king. We need to return to the Old World principle of using what's lying around. The expert natural poultry-keeper Matt Holland of Lower Shaw Farm is a fan of mixing stock. Birds of different parentage, born on the farm, will be the hardiest and happiest of all. He says by all means get some battery hens, but mix them with nice breeds such as Black Rock or Leghorn. So we think we may splash out and buy two good-quality hens. Battery hens, says Matt, are not really built for free-range life.

On Housing Hens

There are lots of henhouses for sale out there. All seem pretty costly to me and, to save money, you'd be better off making your own. We were lucky to have a barn to put the hens in. The thing to understand is that, at night, chickens need to be locked in and kept safe from the fox, and they like somewhere to perch, as they sleep on their feet but above the ground, away from predators. Some poultry owners keep the hens in a run all day, sometimes a movable one, so that it can be relocated to a new part of the garden when the chickens have pecked the grass away.

During the day, hens need to peck, scratch, lie around in dust for their post-prandial nap, eat grass, have sex if a cockerel is to hand, and generally go on little constitutionals. They lay their eggs in the morning. Their nesting boxes, which ideally would be about a foot square and perhaps eighteen inches deep, should be raised off the ground by at least two feet so that there is at least a little protection against egg-stealing rats. The idea is to give the hen a little privacy, too, as they like to lay in secret places. You will need a lot of straw in their house and in their nesting boxes, and this manure-covered straw can then be put on the compost heap and dug into the garden.

John Seymour describes the system used by Lady Eve Balfour:

In her garden in Suffolk she kept her hens under the following arrangement. The hens lived in a henhouse. The house was surrounded by a wire fence, and inside the wire fence much straw or other litter was put. Lady Eve claimed that each hen made with this litter a ton of manure to go on her garden. Next to the straw pen were two small pens planted with grass and clover. Lady Eve used to let the hens into one of these two pens every day for a fortnight. She would then close that pen and let the hens into the other pen for a fortnight. Thus the grass and clover got a chance to rest and recover.

So, free eggs and the best manure in return for about ten minutes of very enjoyable work a day – if that. It makes sense. Just remember to clean out the house regularly.

On Feeding Hens

Hens thrive on a varied diet: protein for egg-laying, but also starches. Seymour tells us to throw them a handful of corn in the morning

and a handful of bought-in protein food – called layer's mash –
before dusk. Matt Holland recommends precisely the reverse: pellets
in the morning and a bit of corn two hours before dusk. He also says
that you should tend to underfeed them in order to encourage them
to eat grass and walk around the farm pecking at things. In this way,
they self-medicate and will stay healthy. A 25kg sack of chickenfeed
is the same price as two or three beers and could keep you going
for two months, depending on how many birds you have and
how much other food they get. As for amounts, the wartime book
Keeping Poultry and Rabbits on Scraps by Goodchild and Thompson
recommends that they eat two ounces of carefully prepared nutritious
scraps twice a day. I weighed out two ounces of layer's mash, and
it is indeed a goodly handful, or a 'manuple', as it was called in the
seventeenth century. A small handful – 'as much as you can take up
with the tops of your fingers 3, with ye thumb', as John Evelyn puts
it in *Kalendarium Hortense* – was called a pugill.

We buy sacks of corn and layer's mash and supplement these
with kitchen scraps, though beware: in some countries, you are not
allowed to feed the hens anything that has been in your kitchen. This
seems a silly rule, but there you go. Whereas in 1946, for example,
Britons worked hard to make sure that scraps were used produc-
tively – in other words, to make eggs, chicken meat and manure –
these days, our leaders have the opposite view and do their best to
make sure that nothing is kept and everything is wasted. I suppose
the pendulum will swing back the other way. However, if your hens
are allowed to roam then they will find their own worms, insects
and bits of grass. Goodchild advises to underfeed them slightly in
the morning and overfeed them in the evening. This will ensure that
the hens are not lethargic when they start their day, and also that they
sleep well at the end of their labours. If your hens are completely free
range during the day, then they should be encouraged to eat grass,

which is not only free but produces the best eggs. They will also find insects for themselves. One neighbour of mine does not feed her hens anything at all in the morning.

I have suffered greatly as a result of allowing the chickens into my vegetable garden. They will peck at seedlings and make craters in patches of bare earth. They will destroy lettuces, and they make a grand mess of the compost heap (though they do seem to keep away from broad beans). If you can't keep the hens out of the garden, or don't want to (some gardeners actually like to have hens wandering about because they fertilize the soil and peck at pests), then you will have to protect your young plants. I have learned to put spiky twigs or green netting over patches of newly sown seeds. I have also stuck small bits of chicken wire around newly sown patches, and that keeps the chickens out. They are capable of flying over it, but they don't bother. Cloches or plastic tunnels will keep them off as well, of course. This also keeps other birds away from your newly sown seeds, and while we delight to hear birds singing, we do not want them to steal our food. Really we should keep our poultry in their own yard, with a net over it. This is what the Roman husbandry writer Varro advises. But I like seeing the chickens clucking about the place and wandering where they will in their little procession.

Columella, Pliny, Varro and the rest keep chickens away from the kitchen garden, in special enclosures. They all agree on the high quality of the manure produced. Here is Columella: 'There are, then, mainly, three kinds of manure: that produced by birds, by humankind, and by cattle. Of bird-dung that is considered first which is gathered from dove-cotes, and next is that which comes from hens or other fowl.' As to the manner of spreading, he suggests: 'Scatter over the grainfield the pulverized droppings from the birdhouse in the manner of one casting seed . . . This produces luxuriant crops.'

This is also very similar to Fukuoka's advice. John Evelyn warns, though, against using poultry manure in its unrotted state: 'dung of poultry is excellent when cold, and well tempered and rotted with mould. Use it at the beginning of winter, especially for Asparagus and Strawberries: but being applied to anything, being hot and newly made, it burns and kills all it touches.'

April's Husbandry

Tusser would have us cut down hazel sticks for the peas to climb up. And collect stones:

> Make servant come home with a stone in his hand.
> By dailie so doing, have plentie yee shall,
> both handsome for paving and good for a wall.

I have found this to be true: it is handy to have piles of stones lying about. You can make paths with them.

Tusser writes that this is the time for the 'huswife' to get busy in the dairy:

> Man cow provides
> wife dairie guides.

I have hopefully mentioned these lines to Victoria a few times. For many years, they had no effect. Tusser has strict words for she who neglects this duty:

> Ill huswife unskilful to make hir own cheese
> through trusting of others hath this for hir fees.

Her milke pan and creame pot, so slabbered and sost,
that butter is wanting and cheese is half lost.

However, Victoria does now make butter. It turns out that, to
achieve this, you only need to put cream into the Kenwood for a
while. Victoria bought two wooden paddles from eBay. These are
used to pat the butter and squeeze out the buttermilk, itself a useful
product that can be used to make scones. As if this weren't enough,
she came home yesterday with a smart Italian metal cheese press, of
the Ferrari brand. This is an old-school piece of equipment that
consists of a giant screw which forces a round plate into a container.
The juice is squeezed out through holes and out of a tap, while the
solid product is left behind. As well as cheese-making, this excellent
device can be used for squeezing apples or, indeed, squeezing pretty
much anything.

It would be lovely to have a cow for proper dairy products. I love
the idea of watching Victoria milking it. And we could train up
Delilah in the duties of the dairymaid. And the milk would be so
rich: the milk you buy in the shops has had much of the richness
taken out of it by homogenization and pasteurization. A cow was
an important feature of most households in the Brave Old World.
When the new factory owners tried to seduce the countrypeople into
the towns in the early days of the Industrial Revolution, they would
offer a free cow with every dwelling. About fifty years ago, and
before, the house I now live in had a cow and she supplied the local
area with dairy products. Recently, a lady visited whose aunt had
lived here in the fifties. 'Never bought a pint a milk,' she said of her
relation. 'Never bought a pound a butter.' We are only one or two
generations away from a much more self-sufficient way of life.

In April, Evelyn has yet another long list of sowing to be done:
'Sow Sweet *Marjoran*, *Hyssop*, *Basil*, *Thyme*, *Winter-Savoury*,

Scurvey-grass . . . Sow Lettuce, Purslan, Caully-flower, Radish &c. Set *French beans*, &c, and sow *Turnips* to have them early . . . Towards the middle of this Moneth begin to plant forth your *Melons* and *Cucumbers*.'

Cobbett's list is even longer: ' . . . beans, peas, kidney beans, scarlets, beets, brocoli, purple, white and brimstone . . . savoys, cabbages, green-cale, brown cale . . . Leeks, turnips, spinage, caraway, basil . . . Plant potatoes . . . weeding and hoeing must be done to promote growth . . . Finish planting trees and shrubs.'

Cobbett also recommends growing cucumbers and melons. Over the years, wonderful technologies have been developed to create artificially heated forcing grounds, or methods of getting an earlier crop of cucumbers or salads than would be the case if the process were left to nature – not that I bother with such things. I think now we would tend to stick with the polytunnel and the cold frame. Or you can create mini greenhouses by placing a plate of glass on top of some bricks or stones. I confess that my attempts to grow melons and cucumbers have all failed thus far. I think these crops require a team of gardeners or an exceptionally hard-working smallholder. You can't do everything! Remember that Cobbett and Evelyn were giving directions for gardens that had many men working in them. In fact, the typical head gardener of the nineteenth century had so many people below him that he never had to pick up a spade or push a wheelbarrow.

Seymour tells us to establish an asparagus bed. Also: 'Sow carrots. Peas. Sweet corn. Cucumbers. Plant out leeks.'

I would add a note on nettles. In the garden, you will start to see nettles growing. Do not be afraid! Here is a newspaper cutting on nettles that an impecunious George Orwell cut out and stuck in his diary in 1940:

IN THE KITCHEN:
NETTLES HAVE THEIR USES

NETTLES, unwanted in the orchard or yard, can with great benefit be transferred to the kitchen, where they provide nature's remedy for removing winter spots and blemishes from the skin.

AS A VEGETABLE: Choose only young nettles; these should be thoroughly washed, then boiled, strained and chopped like spinach. They are a good vegetable and excellent blood purifier.

NETTLE BEER: Thoroughly wash a peck of nettle tops and boil them with one ounce of bruised ginger in a gallon of water for half an hour. Cut up a lemon in slices and put in a big bowl with 1lb. of brown sugar, and strain over them the gallon of water from the nettles. Stir well, and when the sugar is dissolved and the mixture lukewarm add a cupful of barm [liquid yeast] and let it work for eight hours. Then skim and bottle.

DANDELION AND NETTLE BEER: Boil fresh nettle tops, 1oz. crushed ginger, 1oz. dandelion root, 2 sliced lemons and 1lb. of sugar in 1 gallon of water for 20 minutes. Strain into an earthenware bowl and when it is lukewarm add 1oz. of yeast on a square of toast and let it work for a few hours. Skim and bottle. It is ready to drink next day.

As far as flowers go, writes Francis Bacon, the following should be blooming:

the double white violet; the wall-flower; the stock-gillyflower; the cowslip; flower-delices, and lilies of all natures; rosemary flowers; the tulippa; the double piony; the pale daffadil; the French honeysuckle; the cherry-tree in blossom; the dammasin and plum-trees in blossom; the white-thorn in leaf; the lilac tree.

April's Merriment

On April Fools' Day we celebrate the ridiculous and play tricks on each other in the morning. At the All Fools' Day feast, the chair of honour at the high table is reserved for the fool, or 'Lord of Misrule'. Today, the natural order of things is turned upside down. Adults play with toys and are bossed around by the children.

April is also the month of St George's Day. St George, the embodiment of chivalric ideals, has been a popular figure in England since the thirteenth century. His festival day was officially established in 1222, and Robert Chambers in his *Book of Days*, first published in 1864, records: 'In the first year of the reign of Henry V, a council held in London decreed, at the instance of the king himself, that henceforth the feast of St George should be observed by a double service; and for many years the festival was kept with great splendour at Windsor and other towns.'

Mummers' plays emerged which re-enacted the slaying of the dragon and, although the cult of the saint took a beating during the Reformation, St George has proved persistent and, to this day, pubs and schools across the country put on plays about him. The British gold sovereign coin shows St George slaying the dragon. We should celebrate St George's Day with a day off and much feasting. Instead, the day passes unremarked by officialdom, as Hutton sadly noted in 1996: 'It seems . . . to have gone into a quiet decline, leaving England in the curious position of having a day which honours the nation upon which everybody works, virtually no religious services are held, and the government itself does not pause for the slightest celebration.'

April's Calendar

1 April: April Fools' Day.

10 April: My birthday.

11 April: Feast day of the hermit St Guthlac.

13 April: Ides of April. This is the Roman festival of Libertas, the goddess of Liberty, and I think would be an excellent candidate for a new Old World feast day or holiday.

16 April: Feast day of St Bernadette of Lourdes.

23 April: St George's Day.

28 April: The three-day Roman festival of Floralia, commemorating the goddess Flora. Beans and seeds were thrown into the crowds, and little medallions depicting scenes of sexual congress were distributed in order to help get revellers into the mood.

CHAPTER FIVE

May

Bake Bread

Without bread, all is misery

– Cobbett

LIKE keeping chickens, baking your own bread both saves money and provides you with a top-quality product. Anyone can do it, whether in a tower block in Rochdale or on a smallholding in Wales. It is enormously satisfying, too, and the result is always delicious and far more nutritious than the stuff commonly available in the shops. Even your less successful loaves are better than the bought stuff. And to bake bread is to feed your soul.

Cobbett, in *Cottage Economy*, poured scorn on anyone who bought bread rather than making it: 'how wasteful then, and indeed how shameful, for a labourer's wife to go to the baker's shop; and how negligent, how criminally careless of the welfare of his family must the labourer be, who permits so scandalous a use of the proceeds of his labour!' Yes, Mr Cobbett. I rage against the machine as well. If Victoria comes back to the house carrying plastic bags bearing the Tesco corporate logo, then I will fly into a rage. What a criminally careless use of my wages that is!

The home baker is far from being criminally careless. He or she makes the best bread from the best ingredients and feeds the family well. Yes, I know that children prefer the white stuff from the supermarket, but that is because they are children and very susceptible to marketing. Do not give in to the seductions of the trolley! We occasionally do buy some hideous white confection, I'm sorry to admit, just for a quiet life. We always regret it. Eating it depresses us.

Old World Bread *versus* New World Bread

You should never, ever, buy bread from a supermarket. Andrew Whitley, the author of *Bread Matters*, started a village bakery in 1976, still bakes and so has over thirty years' experience in the subject. It is Whitley's view that factory bread – supermarket bread – actually makes people ill. He says that New World bread is not really bread at all. It is the result of a hideous invention developed in order to increase profits. In 1961, the boffins at the British Baking Industries Research Association in Chorleywood, Hertfordshire, came up with a high-speed and highly profitable method of creating bread. It is called the Chorleywood Bread Process. It uses low-protein wheat, a selection of additives, and high-speed mixing. In CBP, says the honest Whitley, various horrors are added: a flour treatment agent is used to increase the amount of air in the bread; emulsifiers play a similar role; potentially carcinogenic preservatives are used; enzymes are added to keep bread soft longer after baking, to make the dough more plastic, and to delay the rate at which the bread will go stale. Whitley says that enzymes can be harmful and complains that manufacturers are not required to declare their use on the list of ingredients.

The nutritional content of this sort of factory-made non-bread is roughly 70 per cent that of real bread, according to Whitley. I remember as a student eating vast quantities of New World bread: we would eat ten or twelve slices of toast at a sitting in a desperate attempt to fill ourselves up. But I find just one or two slices of one of Victoria's loaves to be tremendously sustaining. This means that cheap bread is not actually cheap, because you tend to buy far more of it. And to produce our loaves costs around 60 pence, one quarter of the price of the equivalent artisanal loaf.

In addition to the nutrition-zapping Chorleywood Bread Process, modern methods of growing wheat, which involve the addition of chemical fertilizers and weedkillers, have reduced the nutritional value of the flour itself. Then you have the fact that wheat is ground in the modern fashion, with steel cylinders rather than stones, which, says Whitley, further reduces its nutritional value. All in all, you end up with a loaf that contains a fraction of the nutrients of the simple bread that Cobbett describes. This is why you need to look out for good stoneground flour.

Rising time, says Whitley, is another issue, and my friend the critic James Parker, who worked in a proper bakery for some years, concurs that the key to a good loaf is time: it would take him twenty-four hours to produce bread in the bakery, from the initial mixing of the ingredients to the two risings and the final baking. Time in the New World is a commodity: 'time is money', as New World avatar Benjamin Franklin declared; it is expensive. The quicker you can make your bread, the more money you will make. The CBP made bread-baking almost instantaneous. Bread made by the white-coated Chorleywood scientists needed no fermentation. But this is a disaster, says the good Whitley:

> Fermenting dough for six hours as opposed to thirty minutes removes around eighty per cent of a potentially carcinogenic substance called acrymalide that is found in bread crusts, and long yeast fermentations conserve the highest levels of B vitamins in dough (48 per cent of vitamin B1 is lost in rapidly made white bread).

The result of the Chorleywood Bread Process is indigestible pap which, at best, is nutritionally insignificant and, at worst, may even be carcinogenic. It also tastes terrible and sticks to your mouth. So we all need to forget Chorleywood bread – for ever.

The Politics of the Mill

We must take back control of our bread. Bread-baking, like practically every other aspect of providing for ourselves, has been stolen from the cottage by the factory and the multimillionaire CEO and his greedy gang of shareholders. The New World has stolen our bread and sold a pale travesty of it back to us – while telling us all the time that this is freedom! It is time to end its reign.

Control of the mill has long been a political issue. The owner of the mill has a lot of power, because he makes the bread. A common feature of the Middle Ages was the communal water mill. The people harnessed the power of running water – and, of course, of wind – to run their mills. The classical world, too, used water power, and Antipater of Thessalonica, the Greek epigrammatist who flourished around 15 BC, wrote the following lines (quoted by Jean Gimpel in *The Medieval Machine*) in praise of the mechanized mill:

Hold back your hands from the mill, O maids of the grindstones;
 slumber
Longer, e'en though the crowing of cocks announces the morning
Demeter's ordered her nymphs to perform your hands' former labours.
Down on the top of the wheel, the spirits of the water are leaping,
Turning the axle and with it the spokes of the wheel that is whirling
Therewith spinning the heavy and hollow Nisyrian millstones.

Antipater here makes a common mistake when it comes to technology: we are told that a new machine will help us to 'slumber longer', but in fact this rarely turns out to be the case – certainly in our industrial system, anyway. Instead of being used to shorten the working day, machines are used to make greater profits for their owners, and the working day remains the same length – or, indeed, grows longer. We know also that there were water mills in the second century BC. In Provence, in the first century BC, a gigantic water mill was constructed in order to make flour for a local population of eighty thousand people. It could produce twenty-eight tons of flour in a ten-hour day.

Water mills grew in popularity in the Middle Ages, partly

because slavery was on the decline and therefore there was less free labour. Machines took the place of slaves. The Christian Church gradually outlawed slavery (it had of course been a common feature of the pagan world). In 1086 there were a total of 5,624 water mills, according to a survey commissioned by William the Conqueror. The population at the time was around 1.4 million, so that's one mill for every 248 people, or roughly one for every 50 households.

In the later Middle Ages, the communal system turned into a monopoly system. Households were prohibited from grinding their own flour and were forced to pay the lord's mill or the monastery's mill to do it for them. (Interesting to note that the name of one of the popular brands of so-called 'bread' in the UK is Kingsmill, that is, the mill is owned by the king, and not by the individual. We need to bring back Peasantsmill or Yourmill bread.) Woe betide the peasant who was caught using a hand mill at home.

This ban led to anger and resentment and, in 1326, the people of St Albans twice besieged the monastery as a protest against its monopoly on grinding. In 1331, the abbot retaliated by seizing all the millstones from people's homes and paving the abbey's courtyard with them. This was intended to serve as a constant humiliation and a reminder not to mess with the monks. When the Peasants' Revolt broke out in 1381, one of the first acts of the rioting citizens of St Albans was to smash up the stones that symbolized their oppression.

The owners of the mills would often rent out their mill to a tenant miller, who would be charged a high rent and therefore be tempted to pass on the cost to his customers in the form of exorbitant prices. As a result, millers had a reputation for being dishonest. So it is for Symkyn the miller in Chaucer's 'Reeve's Tale':

> Greet sokene [toll] hath this millere, out of doute,
> With whete and malte of al the land aboute.

In Chaucer's tale, one of the proud and haughty miller's clients is a Cambridge College called Soler Hall. When the manciple (steward) of the college falls ill, the miller sees a chance to increase his profits still further. And whereas previously he had stolen with an attempt at subtlety, now his efforts become more brazen:

> For which this millere stal both mele and corn
> An hundred time moore than biforn;
> For therbiforn he stal but curteisly,
> But now he was a theef outrageously.

Most of us now buy our bread from the biggest and most outrageous thieves of all: the supermarkets. These are indeed today's mill owners. The difference between the unscrupulous mill owners of the past and the supermarkets of today is that the supermarkets present themselves as the people's friend through sophisticated marketing campaigns.

Now, if you really wanted to take back control of your bread from the usurious agents of New World philosophy, you would not only bake your own but invest in a hand mill, that medieval symbol of liberty. Not only would this be a further step towards freedom, but it also makes sense from the point of view of nutrition. According to Whitley, 50 per cent of the nutrients of the grain are lost while the flour is stored. So if you grind your own grain and use the results immediately, your bread, as well as being tasty, will be very nutritious. There is also a huge cost saving to be made: a 25kg sack of grain costs £30 to £40 and from this you will get around two hundred loaves, giving you a flour cost of about 20p a loaf. Add 5p for salt and yeast and heat, and you have a 25p loaf.

And when is all this hand-milling to be done? Surely there is a lot of extra toil involved? Well, the Brave Old Worlder has chucked away that evil time-waster called television, with the result that he or she is flooded with time in the evenings, time to do useful things such as talk, drink, sharpen knives and grind corn. Grinding is also a job that can be given to children, in return for small amounts of money or perhaps time on a computer game. With a hand grinder, unlike a noisy electric one, you can continue to chat or listen to music while you do it. Indeed, you could easily educate yourself while grinding by playing a 'learn French' CD or a talking book. Recently, I have been listening with great pleasure to a BBC collection of radio interviews with writers, from Conan Doyle and G.K. Chesterton to Nancy Mitford and Joe Orton.

Throwing out the telly not only brings huge amounts of time back into your life, it saves money, too. In the old days, we used to sing and dance. Now, we watch other people singing and dancing on various talent shows. We also used to read to each other, and this is a nice activity: the other evening, for example, I read Columella's advice on beekeeping to Victoria as she did some sewing. Bread-making is also of course a good evening activity, as it can be easily combined with drinking beer, chatting and listening to music.

How to Make Bread

Like all our experiments in husbandry, our attempts to bake bread at home have been punctuated by failure and disappointment. But when the whole thing goes well, you create the most wonderfully satisfying treat for the senses. To take a well-baked loaf out of the oven is to glimpse paradise. The crust is golden brown and the bread has swollen up deliciously. The smell of the bread hits you, as does the heat of the oven.

Now let us look at how to make bread. Take a very large bowl – Cobbett would use a huge trencher – and half fill it with flour. Stir in a handful of yeast and a handful of salt. Then make a well in the middle and gradually pour in luke-warm water, stirring all the time with a wooden spoon, until you have a nice slush, about the consistency of porridge. Add a spoonful of olive oil, which helps to keep the bread moist. Stir the slush for two minutes. Scatter a handful of flour very thinly over the top then cover the bowl with a tea towel. It will start to bubble and froth. If it is in a warm place, this first rising will happen quickly; and if in a cool place, it will happen slowly. Sometimes we leave it in the fridge overnight; sometimes we wait just four hours.

Now pour out a load of flour on to the kitchen table and tip the slush on to it. You are going to mix the flour with the slush to make a nice, stretchy dough. Keep turning the dough round. Stretch it, fold it, pull it, hit it – get the air in there. Do this for ten or fifteen minutes. Cobbett recommends using a whole bushel of flour (about 55 lbs, or 25 kgs). We tend to use around a kilo of flour in total, and that will make four or five delicious loaves. Break the dough into lumps and place on a sheet or in tins. Scatter a little flour over the top and make deep cuts with a knife. Cover again to keep warm and conserve moisture. Leave to rise until they have roughly doubled in size. They can be left somewhere warm, where, as before, they will rise quickly, or somewhere cool, where they will rise slowly. You can adapt the timings to fit your schedule. The oven should be very hot, at least 250°C. The baking should take twenty minutes to half an hour, depending on the temperature of the oven.

You can easily individualize your bread. You can add practically anything to the mix. Honey can produce a good flavour, or some like to add lard or milk. You can bung in some porridge oats, or cooked peas, or raisins. You could very easily invent your own unique bread which no one else has ever made. And this is the other very appealing feature of home-made bread: every loaf is different. Because of the large number of co-factors in baking – rising times, water quality and quantity, types and mixes of flour, heat of the oven, type of salt, and so on – you will never get the same loaf twice. So you always have individual bread as opposed to the uniform product that emerges from the dark satanic bread factories of the Brave New World.

By learning to make your own bread, you will create the best bread you have ever tasted at a fraction of the cost of buying a loaf of similar quality. And, as Cobbett observes:

And, pray what can be pleasanter to behold? Talk indeed of your pantomime and gaudy shows, your processions and installations and coronations! Give me for a beautiful sight, a neat and smart woman, heating her oven and setting her bread! . . . And what is the result? Why, good, wholesome food, sufficient for a considerable family for a week, prepared in three or four hours.

It is certainly true that when the bread bin is full, peace and harmony reign. Whatever else you have run out of, you will always have delicious bread. We've also noticed that the opposite is the case: when we have run out of our own home-baked bread through laziness, the kitchen feels gloomier. Something is amiss.

Like all aspects of husbandry, bread-baking is an art and takes many years to master. But right from the beginning, you can make something far better than factory bread. In the early days, my bread used to be very heavy. 'Very dense, Tom, very dense,' commented my baking friend James Parker when he inspected one of my loaves. But even this heavy bread was good – especially when toasted. And I learned that a longer rising time and more vigorous kneading helped. You make mistakes, you learn, you improve. Recently, to my delight, Victoria has taken over the bread-baking, and she does an infinitely better job than I ever did. Our only problem is that the children complain: they want factory pap like their friends. Well, they ain't gonna get it.

Our other common mistake is to bake the bread for too long. It should be blasted for twenty minutes in a very hot oven. We sometimes forget about it, a common problem with the virtually odourless Rayburn oven. Another frequent problem is that the bread gets stuck inside the tin. I used to spend an age cursing at the bread while trying to prise it out with a knife. Bits would tear off and we would end up with a ripped-up loaf (it still tastes better than factory pap, I would assure myself), but this problem can be avoided by giving the tin a thorough coating of flour.

Sometimes you want bread quickly, and when this is the case, you can make Roman bread. It is even simpler, and unleavened. Try this recipe from Marcus Cato's *De Agricultura*: 'Recipe for kneaded bread: wash your hands and a bowl thoroughly. Pour meal into the bowl, add water gradually, and knead thoroughly. When it is well kneaded, roll out and bake under a crock.'

NOTE: I have just returned from the kitchen, where I attempted to make Cato's bread, and I'm afraid it was not a great success. It is a trifle on the biscuity side. However, it is better than no bread at all, and I shall try again. Let us call it emergency bread. It is essentially a sort of pitta. (Another sort of emergency bread that Victoria makes is a simple oatcake: sprinkle a layer of oats on a baking tray, cover in water and put in a hot oven for about half an hour.)

The superb Jocasta Innes in her essential book *The Country Kitchen* (such a good book, with so much useful material in it that you could live very well if you just bought this and no other) gives the following chapatti recipe:

8oz wholemeal flour
8oz strong plain bread flour

1 teaspoon salt
1 ½ pt water

Mix the flour and the salt. Heat the water and gradually stir in
to make a stiff dough. Knead thoroughly till pliable, adding a
drop more water if necessary. Cover with a damp cloth and leave
for an hour or two. Knead again. Pinch off egg-sized lumps, roll
between palms into round balls, flatten on a floured surface and
roll out very thinly to about the size of a side plate. Heat a heavy
cast-iron pan over a moderate flame, put in a chapatti, and cook
for a minute until brown spots appear underneath. Turn over and
repeat, pressing it gently with a cloth to make it puff up. As each
chapatti is done, put into a clean cloth, wrapping them up to keep
them hot and soft.

One useful task might be to build an outdoor bread oven. I often
see features on this sort of thing in the *Permaculture Magazine*, and
plan to do it but never get round to it. Perhaps I should run a bread-
oven-making course, and get other people to do the job for me. An
outdoor bread oven could be used for a weekly bake-up, and you
could also offer its use to your neighbours. Everyone would make
up their own loaves at home and then bring them round for the
final baking. This was the economical system used in the medieval
village: an oven would be shared in order to maximize the return
from the heat it generated. And it is a system still used in rural
Greece today. It makes a huge amount of sense: compare it with the
silly wastefulness of so many private ovens all cooking away, using
up electricity, gas or oil. Or I could get *really* old school and use one
of those enormous flat bread-pan things you see in pizza restaurants.

The true self-sufficiency expert and proper farmer would want to
grow his own grain, and Columella and the rest have much advice

on how to grow wheat successfully. I understand that wheat will grow pretty much anywhere. But then we would need to harvest it, thresh it and collect the grain. It's a huge undertaking. Liberty needs to be grabbed back in small steps. The first step is to make our own bread from good flour. Then we can think about grinding our own flour. And, finally, we can make the move to total liberty and grow our own wheat. Truly, we need to seize both the tools and the ingredients of production.

May's Husbandry

May is the most wonderful month in the garden. The weather is finally heating up after the disappointments of April. In May, our authorities are all busy. Palladius gives a range of tasks: Sow millet, plough to kill weeds, dig seed beds, sow melons, leeks, parsley, coriander; castrate little bulls with a cleft cane; make cream cheese; make pesto; make bricks and rose water. Pesto can be made with the wild garlic that grows everywhere in May. And cream cheese can be made with a lemon, some butter and a cheese press.

The Old World had no objection to using children as free labour, as Tusser writes:

> Let children be hired, to lay to their bones,
> from fallow as needeth to gather up stones.

This is an excellent scheme. I would add that children can also be employed as slug-killers, and here is my attempt at a bit of didactic Tudor doggerel:

> Let children be hired to killen ye slugges
> for payment give pennies and kisses and hugges.

Tusser is also insistent on the importance of weeding:

Who weeding slacketh,
good husbandrie lacketh.

The job is made easier if you do little and often, and also if you keep cultivating the soil, to make it friable. Then the weeds pull out with great ease.

Evelyn reminds us to put some nice new earth in our flower-pots, and to keep sowing salad and herbs: 'Sow *Marjoran, Basil, Thyme* . . . *Lettuce, Cabbage*, beans . . . look carefully to your *Mellons* . . . set your *Bees* at full *Liberty*, expect *Swarms* . . . Give now also all your hous'd plants . . . fresh Earth at the surface, in place of some of the old Earth (a hand-depth or so).'

Cobbett has a huge list of jobs to be done, and here is a selection:

Sow kidney beans, brocoli (for spring), cauliflowers for December, cress, cucumbers in frames and in open ground, radishes, spinach, salsify, skirrets, squash, nasturtiums, herbs, endive, cabbages, savoys, lettuces, coleworts [kale]. Prick out and plant celery, lettuces, capsicums, basil, marjoram. Finish planting potatoes. Stick peas. Top broad beans when in blossom. Hoe and thin out the crops of onions, carrots, lettuces, parsnips; hoe and earth up beans, potatoes . . . destroy weeds *everywhere*. Tie up lettuces and cabbages . . . *caterpillars will now be hatching* . . . if troubled with insects, spray fruit with tobacco water. In the greenhouse, water abundantly . . . remove the more hardy plants out into their summer stations.

Seymour also continues his sowing programme: 'Sow spinach, lettuce, radishes, peas. Sow runner and French beans, marrow and other squashes on muck heaps or very rich land. Plant out tomatoes, sow sweet corn, plant sweet corn plants. More peas. You can never have enough peas.'

May's Merriment

May has always had the reputation of being the merry month. It is the time when hope springs in the breast: we have the summer to look forward to, and the winter has at last retreated. The birds are courting, and flowers and vegetables push through the earth and strain towards the sun. As far as agriculture goes, it is not a busy time of year, which may explain why it was always a festive month: there was simply more time for partying. The days are longer, and there are delicious smells in the air. At home, the buttercups and red campion are out in full force. Victoria makes risotto with nettles and wild garlic. We start pulling up the first radishes, and everything in the garden thrusts forth with great vigour.

Our May Day rituals are said by anthropologists of the Sir James Frazer school to be a relic of the pagan era, when we would try to hasten the progress of spring by making one hell of a racket.

Some of the maypoles in medieval Europe could stand ninety feet high and were anchored in all year round. It was only on May Day, though, that they would be decorated, with flowers, ribbons and streamers. Maypole dancing was a sort of fertility ritual, carried out by grown men and women. It was later that it became a kiddies' dance rather than a sexually charged ritual designed to work both men and women into a fever of desire. The sexual nature of the maypole dance was the main reason the Puritans banned it. Today, it is legal again. So why not try it at home? First repeat the following traditional rhyme:

Here we go round the maypole
The merry maypole, the merry maypole,
Here we go round the merry maypole
On a cold and frosty morning!

After working yourselves up into an ecstasy of passion, you all troop off into the woods to 'collect the May', i.e. evergreen boughs of ivy and wildflowers. These are used to decorate the hall (or the kitchen, since that is where most of us do our feasting these days). Writes Chambers in *The Book of Days*:

In the sixteenth century it was still customary for the middle and humbler classes to go forth at an early hour of the morning, in order to gather flowers and hawthorn branches, which they brought home about sunrise, with accompaniments of horn and tabor, and all possible signs of joy and merriment. With these spoils they would decorate every door and window in the village.

So go out there and cut down the hawthorn branches and the flowers and bedeck the house. The more greenery there is indoors, the merrier you will be.

The most important feast of May was Pentecost, nicknamed Whitsun, which falls on the seventh Sunday after Easter. This annual feast, which commemorates the inspiration of Christ's apostles by the Holy Ghost, was being celebrated right back in the fourth century. In the later medieval period, the Church organized local communal celebrations known as Whitsun ales, when pursuits such as dances, cards and summer games could be carried out with licence. There would be a feast, generally consisting of beer, milk, cream, bread, eggs, honey, spices, veal and mutton. Dancing was common, and pipers and drummers were often hired. Another popular May tradition dating back to the twelfth century was the custom of the Robin Hood play. Morris dancing was also popular.

Another merry pastime for May is to try to make a green-themed feast. Make bread green with parsley and slice it up to use as plates. Make a green salad with lettuce, spinach, peas, endive, fennel and greengage plums. Wash it down with a light apple cider. Make green peppermint rice, and whipped cream with green mint. After dessert, try making Jack-in-the-Green. This is a large gingerbread man with green lime icing and sprigs of parsley—an edible green man.

Backgammon and chess were popular Old World pastimes, as was billiards. We bought a cheap pool table for home use, and I see pool as a good New World equivalent of the old games. I could happily play pool all day, and I am encouraging my children to practise, as I see it as an important life skill. Another favourite was Nine Men's Morris, dating from Roman times. Take nine counters each. These can be stones or wooden balls. The game is played on a board on which have been drawn intersecting lines with circles at the intersections. Take turns in placing your counters on the circles and try to get three in a row. You can also play outdoors, using people as counters.

May's Calendar

May is named after the chief of the Pleiades, the Greek Seven Sisters. Her sacred plant is the hawthorn. Indeed, Arcite in Chaucer's 'Knight's Tale' uses the plant on May Day:

> To maken him a garland of the greves,
> Were it of woodbine or on hawthorn leaves.

Old English names for May include 'Thrimilcmonath' or thrice milk month, so-called because the cows were milked three times a day, and 'sproutkale'. May is when the mother goddess appears on the earth, whether in the form of a May Queen or Maid Marian.

1 May: May Day. Robin Hood's Day. Kalends of May. Beltane.

4 May: Veneration of the thorn. The hawthorn tree is honoured on this day.

8 May: The Helston Furry Dance. On this day, the residents of this Cornish town of Helston get dressed up and parade through the streets.

16 May: Feast day of St Brendan the navigator, an Irish Celtic priest.

19 May: St Dunstan's Day. Dunstan became abbot of Glastonbury Abbey in 945. He is the patron saint of goldsmiths, and was a keen brewer.

23 May: Rosalia, the Roman rose festival.

25 May: Feast of St Edmund. King Edmund I was stabbed on this day in AD949.

28 May: Feast day of St Bernard, patron saint of mountaineers.

29 May: Oak Apple Day or Royal Oak Day. In the seventeenth century, the state introduced Oak Apple Day to commemorate the Restoration and the day King Charles II hid in an oak tree to escape the pursuit of Commonwealth soldiers. Everyone would be expected to wear oak leaves on this day. The day enjoyed some success although its popularity waned when the Restoration honeymoon wore off.

30 May: Feast day of Joan of Arc, burnt at the stake on this day in Rouen in 1431.

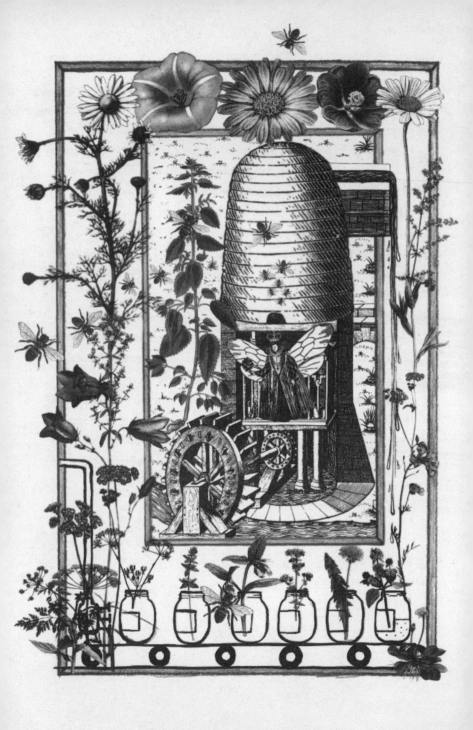

CHAPTER SIX

June

Mind Bees

Protinus aerii mellis caelestia dona
exsequar

[Next I will discourse of heaven's gift,
honey from the skies]
– *Georgics*, Book IV, ll. 1–2

THERE is nothing more joyful, fascinating and useful than keeping bees. Bees bring sweetness and light to the household; they produce honey and wax. They can be kept in the city as effectively as in the countryside. They are an almost essential element of the smallholding. And the world needs bees: like the humble earthworm, the bee plays an essential role in the production of food and therefore in the survival of man. Bees pollinate something like 85 per cent of the world's fruit and vegetables.

But beekeeping is difficult and should not be undertaken lightly. In 2007, American beekeepers reported that they were mysteriously losing their bees in a phenomenon that became known as colony collapse disorder. In Europe, too, beekeepers have reported 30 per cent losses. The Brave New World might well be to blame for the decline in the bee population. Due to their navigation systems, bees are extremely sensitive to magnetic forces, and some scientists claim that mobile phones and wireless technologies confuse them. The enormous quantity of beekeeping books out there dating back millennia is testimony to the endlessly complex nature of beekeeping.

Like other aspects of husbandry, it is enormously satisfying when it goes right. However, as Victoria and I know from painful experience, it can easily go very wrong.

Bees in the Ancient World

Virgil's father was a beekeeper, and indeed the whole of the fourth book of Virgil's *Georgics* is devoted to bees. A medieval illustration for the poem shows a neat row of four beehives in an open-sided hut close to the house. A few comically oversized bees are buzzing about, while a rather attractive female beekeeper and her male companion,

who has a bee sitting on his broad-brimmed hat, bang gongs. This
is because Virgil writes that, to attract a swarm, you should:

> *Tinnitusque cie et Matris quate cymbala circum.*
> *ipsae consident medicatis sedibus, ipsae*
> *intima more suo sese in cunabula condent.*

[Raise a tinkling sound, and shake the mighty mother's cymbals
round about. Of themselves will they settle on the scented resting
places; of themselves, after their wont, will hide far within their
cradling cells.]
  – *Georgics*, Book IV, ll.64–6

Making an almighty racket with cymbals is not considered by
contemporary beekeepers to be a terrific idea. Another mistake most
of the ancients made was to call the queen bee a king. The only
writer who got the gender right was Aristotle.

Both Virgil and Columella warn that bees can get very angry
indeed if you're not careful. Victoria, who at the time of writing
has been keeping bees for two years, can testify to this. She has
been badly stung. Both authorities recommend calming the bees
with a smoker, a device that puffs smoke into the hive, and this is
a technique which is still used today. Columella, in his section of
beekeeping advice, also remarks that 'bees are often overtaken by
diseases'. Again, the phenomenon of colony collapse, which has
been in the news lately, is clearly nothing new, and to avoid it, very
careful stewardship is required.

Once you have found a windless spot for your hives, write Virgil
and Columella, you should plant all around it with clumps of
thyme and marjoram. Columella counsels that bees like ivy, oak,

rosemary, all fruit trees, acanthus, narcissus, white lilies, turnip, poppy, radish, parsnip and the *staphylinos*, or carrot. He does add, though, that the poorest honey is 'the farmhouse honey which comes from vegetables'.

The bee area, or apiary, writes Columella, should be situated a good distance away from 'the foul odours which come from the latrines, the dunghills and the bathroom', so do not site your hives near the composting loo. Virgil writes:

> *Palmaque vestibulum autingens oleaster inumbret.*

[And let a palm or huge wild olive shade the porch.]

This is in order for the bees to have 'retreat from midday heat'.

Ever-flowing water – *perennis aqua* – should ideally be nearby, so the bees can drink. Put some stones in the water:

> *Pontibus ut orebris possint consistere et alas*
> *pandere ad aestivum solem.*

[That they may have many bridges whereupon to halt and spread their wings to the summer sun.]

As for the hives, they are best made of wood. Virgil condemns earthenware hives, as they are hot in summer and cold in winter. Do not build them out of dung either, as they are liable to catch fire. Brick-built hives may be all right: 'The fronts of the hives . . . should slope down more than their backs, so that the rain may not flow in.'

When you buy your bees, affirms Columella, make sure you buy them locally, 'since they are usually irritated by change of climate'.

Be wary of gifts of bees, as 'inferior bees should not be mixed with those of a high quality, since they bring discredit upon them.' Columella then devotes a few pages to the art of capturing a swarm. He notes that, prior to the bees swarming from their hive, there will arise a terrific buzzing. Virgil has something to say on the same subject:

> *Et vox*
> *auditur fractos sonitus imitata tubarum.*

[And a sound is heard that is like a broken trumpet blast.]

When a second queen (called a prince or king by the ancients) is born, she must be killed:

> *Dede neci, melior vacua sine regnet in aula.*

[Give them to death, and let the better prince rule in the empty hall.]
— *Georgics*, Book IV, l.90

Then, as now, the bees were sometimes given extra food in the winter. We call it a fondant, a sort of sugar syrup, and they called it 'sweet liquid' (*dulci liqore*).

Columella also writes of disease. It seems that Roman bees, like ours, suffered from diarrhoea: 'They die from a flux of the belly, unless help is quickly given.' One theory went that, if you found a load of dead bees under your hive, you should wait for a sunny day and bring them out into the sunshine then cover them with wood ashes. The heat will apparently bring them back to life within two hours. Columella recommends a medicine made from pomegranate seeds and wine – lucky bees – although another idea is to place oxen or human urine near the hives. Columella notes that, when illness strikes, the healthy bees will remove bee corpses from the hive, while other live bees inside the hive become lethargic, *ut in publico luctu* (as if in mourning). Other bits of sensible advice include the removal of diseased combs and the introduction of new bees to ailing populations.

As for what to do when, we can summarize Columella's advice as follows: between 24 March, the first equinox (or thereabouts), until the rising of the Pleiades forty-eight days later, open up and clean all the hives. The bees should then be smoked with the fumes of ox-dung. Break off any little worms that are attached to the honeycombs. It is very important that the man who feeds the bees has not had sex the day before. Also, he must not be drunk or have recently eaten strongly flavoured foods such as pickled fish, garlic or onions.

From then until the solstice at the end of June, the hives swarm, i.e. a breakaway group of bees led by the queen leaves the hive for new pastures. Left behind are queen cells and a colony of caretaker bees. Then, between the solstice and the rising of the Dogstar (about thirty days), the bees will go harvesting. Then, for fifty days, they make honey, and this can be gathered by the beekeeper in August. From 24 September, for forty days, the bees make honey for their winter food, and, writes Columella, 'Of this nothing must be extracted, lest the bees, disheartened by continual ill-treatment and, as it were, in despair, should take to flight.' Then you must clean the hives again before shutting them up for winter. The hives must have stalks and leaves heaped upon them to protect them from the cold; this can also be achieved by leaving the intestines of a small bird in the hive (the idea being that these innards give off a gentle heat, like a storage heater). Dried figs pounded with water can also be given to the bees to eat. And as for the administration of the *dulci liqore*, 'it is best to pour sweet liquids through the entrance of the porch by means of small pipes and thus support them during the temporary scarcity until *Arcturi ortus et hirundinis adventus* (the rising of Arcturus and the coming of the swallow).'

As for the extraction of the honey, this task should be carried out in the morning, well before the arrival of the *aestu medio*, the noon-time heat. Columella describes two iron instruments which are needed for scraping the honey from the combs. Do not take all the honey, as the bees themselves need some. Also, ensure that you take the wax for candle-making.

Our Trials with Bees

When a friend offered us a free beehive, an unwanted gift, Victoria leapt at the opportunity. She joined her local beekeeping group and threw herself into a conscientious study of the subject. She bought what is called a 'nucleus', a small colony of bees, to get started, at a cost of £100. She read books and consulted websites. She attended meetings almost weekly. She bought a smoker and two sets of protective clothing. Helpful beekeepers came to visit and give advice. Victoria caught a swarm, and set up a second beehive, which we called beehive number two. She had a fence built around beehive number one so the farmer's cows would not knock it over. She bought a mouse guard, a little piece of wood that slides into the front porch of the hive. It has holes that are big enough to let bees in and out but, obviously enough, not mice. Victoria researched the varroa mite, thought to be responsible for much disease, and subscribed to beekeeping magazines. In the evenings, I was roped in to help nail wooden frames together to fit into the hive.

She followed the news about the bees and went up to London

with the British Beekeeping Association, put on her beekeeping outfit and joined a group outside the Houses of Parliament to protest against the lack of funding for bee research. She even talked to our local MP about it.

I loved seeing the hives in the garden and watching the bees buzzing about in their purposeful way. It is true that, if angered, they will try to attack you, making every effort to find a gap in your clothing through which to crawl in order to sting you. And I have been attacked: three bees chased me away from the hive. Luckily, I was well protected, but they made sure I was a long way from the hive before they finally stopped trying to sting me. The beekeeper is like a capitalist, and as in human communities, bees do not like to be interfered with by an outside power looking to make a profit. They do not want the produce of their labour to be stolen. It is for this reason that the beekeeper has learned to pacify them by smoking them. This again is like the capitalist or, rather, the bureaucrat of the state, who mollifies the workers with large televisions, alcohol and holidays so he can steal from their stores, through tax.

Victoria was a conscientious beekeeper, even to the point of not collecting their honey. She didn't want to steal it; they needed it, she said, to eat during the winter. She would not collect a drop of it, despite my frequent complaints. What exactly is the point of all this? I asked. It just seems to be a lot of work, a lot of headaches, a lot of stress and all for nothing. Eventually, I only had to say 'honey' and I would be glowered at, so I learned not to use the 'H' word in her presence.

Things did not always run smoothly in the beekeeping world either. Political infighting disturbed our local group. There were two rival factions – modernizers and traditionalists – who grew to loathe each other. Angry emails went back and forth, and Victoria felt caught in the crossfire. Both groups attempted to bring her on to their side. She resisted and, as a result, both groups stopped helping her. She was on her own. And then she got scared. On one occasion, she was severely stung by the bees. She had opened up the hive to check their general health. They were greatly incensed and buzzed at her in a rage. They managed to get under her gloves and crawled up her arms. They stung her on her neck. She decided to close up the hive and get out of there as quickly as possible. But the furious bees chased her half a mile around the farm. She also became scared that she might fall prey to anaphylactic shock, a severe allergic reaction where your throat swells up, your heart races and a heart attack can ensue.

Lonely and afraid, Victoria then rather neglected the bees. She did not treat them properly for varroa at the end of the summer. And she should have combined her small colony with her first colony and over-wintered them together. Instead, the two colonies were each left alone all winter. It snowed. It was cold. And when Victoria went to feed the bees with sugar syrup in March, she found every single bee dead. There were brown streaks over the roof of the second hive, indicating that they had suffered from what Columella called 'flux of the belly'. We don't really know why they died, but Victoria suspects that a combination of varroa and the cold winter weakened their immune systems and they became sick.

The lesson she has learned is: do not do it alone. You need to find a mentor or a partner, someone who is going to help you. This year, she has bought a new load of bees for her two hives. So far, they seem to have settled in well. But we won't get any honey this year either.

Let It Be. Or Not

As the bees hate to be disturbed, there has sprung up a *wu wei* school
of beekeepers who adhere to the Taoist principle of minimum interference, rather as Fukuoka does with crop growing. However, other
beekeepers insist that interference is necessary in order to control
pests and diseases, of which the most recent example is the varroa
mite. Today, minimum interference – and there is an excellent
book on this approach called *The Barefoot Beekeeper* – I suspect is,
paradoxically, an approach suited to a very experienced beekeeper
with a lot of time on his hands. After many years of experience, you
learn a light touch. Only the master butcher can cut meat without
effort. The general principle holds true for beekeeping as well as for
other crafts. But I believe that the apprentice should do exactly what
he is told by his masters in the local beekeeping group. He should
not make his own decisions, based on a few half-understood nuggets
of theory picked up from websites. Only later, many years later, can
you start to make your own decisions.

Not so long ago, John Seymour could write, appealingly, in
Self-Sufficiency: 'A day a year is really all you have to devote to your
bees.' This is really not true or, at least, it might be true for a master
beekeeper but it is certainly not true for the beginner. Seymour was a
fan of the let-them-get-on-with-it approach: he is against the feeding
of sugar in wintertime: 'We have not so much kept bees as had bees
around for the last sixteen years, and most years we have got honey
from them, and we have never fed them on any sugar. We merely
abstain from robbing them too severely in the autumn.'

Ah, you say, but times have changed. John Seymour did not have
to worry about colony collapse and the varroa mite. And it is clearly
not really as easy as he makes out, or the Virgils and Columellas
of ages long gone would not have devoted so much space to bee-

keeping. Be wary of the Seymour approach: while I respect him immensely and love his books, he does have a tendency to make it all sound much easier than it really is.

One local man, Cliff, started keeping bees in the way suggested in *The Barefoot Beekeeper*, in a simple arrangement called the top bar hive. This is the most 'natural' and low-impact way of keeping bees. Everything was going well until, one day, the bees all flew away. 'Buggered off, didn't they? Went down the neighbour's chimney,' Cliff said. 'Lost the lot of them.' I wouldn't worry about making everything totally natural: the very fact that you are keeping bees in the backyard and not on some enormous monoculture honey factory is in itself good – and it is important that you do manage to *keep* the bees.

There are three main types of hives in use today:

The WBC
The WBC is named after its inventor, William Broughton Carr. This is the most expensive hive you can buy, but it is extremely weatherproof, since the bees are protected by the wooden walls of the inner boxes and by an outer wall. We have two WBCs at home: the first was a gift, and the second we bought. They are fine-looking hives, to be sure.

The National
This is a cheaper way of starting out. The hives look less charming but are simpler to set up and maintain. This is the most common type of hive used in the UK and, for that reason, probably the one I would recommend to the beginner.

The Top Bar Hive
This is the system recommended by beekeepers who practise non-

interference. With this method, there is no need to buy a hive or the ready-made wax frames you need for the other two types of hive. The bees make their combs in a sort of manger. This, it is claimed, is a very easy and cheap way to keep bees. It should, in theory, make for a healthier and happier bee population. It is also less work for the beekeeper (but take note of the caveats above).

A Note on Honey

While it was clearly a tragedy that every one of Victoria's twenty thousand or so bees died, the collapse did at least mean that we were able to extract the honey, and it has to be said that this was the most delicious honey I had ever tasted. Honey is pure magic; it is sweetness from the skies. To press the honey from the combs, we used our Ferrari cheese press. You simply place the combs inside the basket and twist down the giant screw. The honey slowly trickles from the tap into a jar, and you watch. When the trickle slows down, you turn the screw again. There is a satisfying cracking sound, and the golden nectar trickles out again. In this way, we collected six jars of honey.

Now, I know that, at first sight, the economics of the thing don't look good. I said to Victoria, rather unkindly, that this had to be the most expensive honey ever made. When you added together the cost of the hive, the smoker, the frames, the bees, the syrup, the trips to the bee meetings, the protective clothing, the books and the treatments, we had to be talking about well over £1,000 in all. That gives a unit cost of over £200 per jar, about £197 more than the commercial stuff. However, scoff not: the kit is a one-off cost. And, in future years, we will create more honey. Victoria is going to persist, and she will without doubt improve her beekeeping skills. *Labor omnia vicit*; we shall overcome, some day.

June's Husbandry

Virgil writes that, for planting vines, the 17th of the month is lucky.
He also suggests that you place hawthorn above your windows, an
idea that persisted into the Middle Ages, and anoint the front-door
hinges. He reminds us also that it is true to plant cabbages, and that
'*Cato brassicae miras canit laudes*' (Cato sings wonderful praises of the
brassicas, or cabbage).

If you live in a cold climate, writes Palladius, this may also be the
time to catch up on May's jobs:

> In coldest lande thing left undoon in May
> May now be doon.

Tusser says you should build a 'hovell' to store peas and also to
house fattening piglets later in the year: 'to shut up thy porklings
thou mindest to Fat'.

Well, again and again, the emphasis, as in a modern organic-
gardening guidebook, is on keeping your soil well manured and
well dug. Tusser argues that hops are an excellent crop to grow, for
many reasons:

> The hop for his profit I thus do exalt,
>   it strengtheneth drink, and it flavoureth malt.

Evelyn says that you must sow lettuce, chervil, and radish for
your salads. Gather herbs and dry them in the shade, not in the sun.
Check the bees and control pests: 'Look to your *Bees* for swarms
. . . and begin to destroy *Insects* with *Hoofs* [sheep hooves placed
on sticks as an earwig trap], *Canes*, and tempting baits, &c. gather
Snails after Rain &c.' Again, this is similar to the pest-control

advice you would find in a contemporary organic-gardening book. An equivalent earwig trap is made by stuffing some honey-soaked grass in a plastic cup and placing the cup upside down on a stick.

Cobbett, in *The English Gardener*, is characteristically industrious in June (although it would be well to remember that he is giving directions to his team of gardeners, and I don't think would attempt all this on his own): '*Sow* kidney-beans, pumpkins, tomatoes, coleworts [kale] for a supply of young winter greens.' I have found kale to be easy to grow. But you will need quite a few plants – I would say twenty-four, perhaps of different varieties. Cobbett goes on:

> *Sow* black Spanish radishes for autumn and winter use, other radishes if wanted, endive, principal sowing late in the month. Lettuces, the hardy-cosses are now the best to sow, celery for late, turnips, peas, cardoons. *Plant* cucumbers and gourds, pumpkins, nasturtiums, and in general similar articles not planted out last month, leeks, celery, cauliflowers, brocoli, borecole, and green-cole, savoys, and other articles of autumn and winter use . . . cut mint and other herbs for drying; a general rule for cutting herbs for drying, is, to cut them when in full flower.

If you have forgotten to raise leeks, celery, cauliflowers, broccoli, and so on, then go to the market and buy a load of plants. This is not cheating: you are still saving a huge amount of money. Plus you will not waste seed, and you can buy a wide range of varieties. The plants will have been well grown and, if bought in the market, they should suit your local climate.

Seymour advises:

Plant out your celery plants in the previously prepared trenches, after mid-month. As they grow you will need to earth them up [that is, heap earth around the stems] . . . there is nothing to beat the old-fashioned *earthing up* . . . Plant out more French beans, runners and dwarf beans. Sow lettuces and radishes.

It seems then that our authorities are pretty much in agreement: keep sowing, and plant out the brassicas and the leeks.

June's Merriment

The main festival in June is of course Midsummer's Eve. In the Middle Ages, this was the time to walk in a candlelit procession and chant the following riddle (try it on your friends and family):

> Green is gold.
> Fire is wet.
> Future's told.
> Dragon's met.

When is green gold? In midsummer, we celebrate the earth's new leaves and grasses and, in their early stages, these have a golden hue. Therefore, green is gold. In midsummer, it was the custom to float lighted candles on water. Push your candle across the pond on a little boat. If it reaches the other side, then your wish will come true. So the future is told, and fire is wet. It is also the case that St John's Wort, commonly believed to be a fortune-telling plant, is associated with this time of year, because St John the Baptist's birthday is on Midsummer's Day. Now for the dragon. It was the medieval custom for one midsummer reveller to slay the dragon, and the dragon generally took the form of a dragon-shaped kite or a giant pastry dragon (the medievals were very creative and playful cooks).

Midsummer was also the time to build and enjoy outdoor bonfires. Upon entering the area of the fire, walk around it in a clock-wise direction, to mimic the passage of the sun rising in the east and setting in the west. Wear a wreath of birch on your head, or a sprig of green leaves pinned over your heart.

The following is a good song to learn:

> Summer is a-coming in,
> Loudly sing, cuckoo!
> The seed grows,
> The meadow blows,
> And the woods spring anew.
> Sing cuckoo!
> Ewe bleats after lamb,
> Cow leaps after calf,
> Bullock leaps,
> Buck starts.
> Merrily sing, cuckoo!
> Cuckoo! Cuckoo!
> Well do you sing cuckoo!
> Never cease singing now.

At first sight, this lyric may appear a little twee and hey nonny-nonny. But persist. One year, at a festival, I watched as a group of E-ed up ravers went mental to this song at one in the morning as it was played on stage by early-music group the Princes in the Tower.

One point to make here is that medieval Christianity was very much more in tune with nature than the reformed version of Christianity which followed it. And, indeed, it was a deliberate decision on the part of Pope Gregory and St Augustine to let the people continue to practise their age-old pagan customs, which were generally related to the turning of the seasons and the natural world.

Midsummer was also, like April, the time for a Mummers' play, starring the kind king, the beautiful princess, the Red Dragon, noble St George and the old doctor. I won't reproduce the entire text here, as it is easy to find elsewhere. I'll just say that, helped by the doctor's pills, St George saves the princess and indeed the whole kingdom from the terrible dragon. It is interesting that science, in the shape of the doctor, should make an appearance – perhaps the Old World was not as anti-science as we are led to believe by the prophets of futurism. In actual fact, one of the primary characteristics of the medieval world was its fascination with reason and science: just take a look at the clock in Exeter cathedral if you don't believe me. And read *The Medieval Machine* by Jean Gimpel, which shows that, far from being superstitious and uncultivated, the medievals produced some fantastic machines.

June's Calendar

June is named after the Roman great mother goddess Juno (Hera, in Greek). This is the time of maximum light and minimum darkness. Chambers remarks in *The Book of Days*: 'We never enjoy reading portions of Spenser's *Faerie Queene* so much as when among the great green trees in summer' – although I have read portions of it to Henry very enjoyably during the darker months, by the fire. It's a wonderful tale, positively Narnian.

A reminder of the movable feasts: forty days after Easter comes Ascension Day, or Holy Thursday. Ten days after this comes Whitsuntide. Then Trinity Sunday, with Corpus Christi on the first Thursday after Trinity Sunday. Corpus Christi was invented in 1317. The intention was to draw attention to the sanctity of the Eucharist. It was a day for a grand procession, but also for drama, and the craft guilds would band together to put on some sort of pageant based on biblical stories.

1 June: Kalends of June. Festival of Carna, Roman goddess of doors and locks.

8 June: The old Roman festival of Mens (the mind). This reminds us that we should always act consciously and rationally, and be wary of acting emotionally or under the influence of passion.

9 June: Feast of St Columba, sixth-century Irish monk who founded the famous monastery on the Isle of Iona on the west coast of Scotland. Vestalia, the Roman women's festival of first fruits.

13 June: Feast day of St Anthony of Padua, patron saint of lost things.

15 June: Ides of June. Magna Carta signed in 1215.

21 June: The summer solstice. Midsummer. Day of All Heras.

23 June: Midsummer's Eve or St John's Eve. The night to keep watch with flaming torches.

24 June: St John the Baptist's Day. Official Midsummer's Day. This is the day to dance around bonfires to celebrate the high point of solar light.

28 June: St Peter's Eve.

29 June: Feast day of St Peter and St Paul, martyred during Nero's reign (AD 54−68).

CHAPTER SEVEN

July

Mow Meadow

With my sythe my mede I mawe

– Traditional

IN COMMON WITH many writers who attempt books of advice, I am often accused of failing to live up to my own principles. Readers and friends accuse me of hypocrisy if, for example, they spot me buying bread in the supermarket. I was pondering whether it is really necessary always to set a good example when I came across the following line from Dr Johnson's *Rambler* number 41: '[T]here has often been observed a manifest and striking contrariety between the life of an author and his writings.' I suppose a comparison could be made with the barber who has a bad haircut. But, said Johnson, it is not fair to censure the author for his failings: 'Nothing is more unjust, however common, than to charge with hypocrisy him that expresses zeal for those virtues which he neglects to practise; since he may be sincerely convinced of the advantages of conquering his passions, without having yet obtained the victory.'

So when I express zeal, in this chapter, for the noble scythe and unrelenting mattock, please do not condemn me for sometimes neglecting to use them and reverting to the Strimmer. I really am sincerely convinced of their advantages. If I express zeal for making my own bread, then do not condemn me for sometimes buying it. In my private life, I am neither a Puritan nor a fanatic, and often fail to live up to my own aspirations. In the same way, when praising the old ways, we should not be too hard on ourselves when we use the new, for, after all, we are living in the modern world and it is extremely difficult for most of us to survive without a motor car or, it seems now, a broadband connection.

I have composed the following Latin epigram to express this predicament:

Virtutes etiam non ipse exercitans laudo.

[I praise the virtues while not practising them.]

A better version of this idea was written by Ovid in *Ars Amatoria*:

Monitis sum minor ipse meis.

[I fall short of my own precepts.]

As you will remember from our introduction, this epigram was used by Thomas Fuller in his entry on Thomas Tusser. So the next time someone gleefully points out an inconsistency between your principles and your actions, simply shrug your shoulders and mumble: 'Well, you know, *Monitis sum* . . . and all that.'

But sing the praises of hand tools I must. And, indeed, this year, I can boast that my vegetable patch has not had a single machine on it. Everything has been done by hand. I have clipped the grass paths with a pair of shears and edged them with the spade. I have hoed, weeded, cultivated and manured by hand. Now, I am not saying that the garden will never feel the oil-powered heat of the Strimmer wire but, so far, at least, I have accomplished everything by muscle power alone. So, in our chapter for July, I would like to focus on the mattock and the trusty scythe.

In Praise of the Scythe

In medieval calendars, the images for June and July show happy peasants using the scythe to cut down the hay. Unlike the lonely modern farmer who spends all day (and sometimes all night) alone in a tractor cutting and making hay, the Old World used convivial teams of scythemen to mow the meadows. And hand tools are still commonly used in Old World countries today: I remember my initial shock upon seeing, in Mexico, groups of men cutting the grass by the roadside with sickles. The equivalent in the UK is to see groups of young men by the motorway with Strimmers. (I always imagine that these men are doing some kind of community service as penance for antisocial acts.) The Mexican way at first sight seemed almost absurdly primitive, but then I began to reflect more deeply on this scene, and the fact is that, with a hand tool, the user is given a far greater degree of liberty. The Mexicans were all able to stop for a few moments to wipe their brows and look around them. Without the loud whine of the Strimmer, they could chat to each other. They could sharpen their tools in situ. I also noticed that they were smiling. And while it is difficult to gauge what sort of expression their English Strimmer-wielding contemporaries wear, because they are loaded with protective armour, I doubt very much that they are smiling.

Having used a Strimmer many times myself, I can testify that, by its nature, it does not encourage a cheerful countenance. I would say that it tends to encourage the exact opposite, and that is an attitude of stressful gloom. As is often the case with machinery, the fun is removed from the job and the workman is reduced to a robotic functionary. The noise of the machine bores into your head – it is, literally, boring – and the vibrations pass through your hands into your whole body. The nylon string of the Strimmer tends to get caught up in itself, so you have to take frequent breaks for untangling, and it runs out of petrol quickly. The machine requires a great deal of maintenance, and must be filled with petrol and a measure of the right sort of oil. It is also expensive and breaks down easily. I have two in my barn; the first one broke.

Now compare the scythe. Its first great advantage over the Strimmer is its great beauty. I bought mine from Simon Fairlie, editor of *The Land* magazine and founder of the Tinker's Bubble woodland community in Somerset. The scythes he sells consist of a long curved blade attached to a wooden handle. The blades are hand-forged in Austria by Schröckenfux, established in 1540. The handle has two bits of wood to grab hold of, and the whole seems to have been designed with a wonderful knowledge of the human body: when you pick one up, it feels like the most natural thing in the world. Fairlie cites Ivan Illich's comment in *Tools for Conviviality*, where Illich writes of the need for tools which 'allow men to achieve purposes with energy fully under their control'. To hold a scythe for the first time is rather like holding a gold coin for the first time: it feels right. In the case of the gold coin, the first time you hold one you have the sense of holding real money and not some confusing fiction cooked up by the bankers.

So when you pick up a scythe, you are returned to a sense of harmony between man and technology. Rather like the book, the scythe is a brilliant piece of technology which simply cannot be improved upon. Yes, man tries with his Strimmers and his Kindles, but all rely on oil or electricity, and all are awkward, expensive and just feel wrong.

The action of the scythe is a rhythmic swing from side to side. There are some beautiful videos out there on YouTube which demonstrate the technique. I am a mere amateur and have a lot to learn, but once or twice I have felt that I have swung the scythe correctly, and the experience has been deeply satisfying. Every few minutes, you stop to sharpen the blade. Hanging from your belt is a little brass water-holder, and in it sits your sharpening stone. You can see the little pouch in pictures of medieval scythemen, and indeed in photographs of teams of English meadow mowers (the scythe was still being used right up until the seventies in many parts of England). With your scythe, you can hear the 'fowlis synge' as you work, which is another advantage it holds over the Strimmer.

Come July, my parents-in-law have their own Somerset meadow

mown by the very Simon Fairlie who sold me my scythe. By good fortune, they have a cottage in the closest village to Tinker's Bubble. When those low-impact dwellers first arrived, my parents-in-law, in common with the majority of the villagers, were afraid of Tinker's Bubble, and even campaigned against it, fearing, I suppose, an influx of drug-soaked wasters. But over the years, they have come to recognize that Tinker's Bubble is in fact an Old World settlement. The people living on it are bringing back the old ways, such as using horse-drawn carts, and they make a significant cultural and practical contribution to the community, as well as appearing charming to those who can remember when scything a field was a perfectly normal practice. Tinker's Bubble brings romance to the village.

Now, the other important point to make about muscle power is that it is free, drains no resources and is also health-giving. Scything, walking and cycling create no so-called 'carbon footprint'. They render carbon offsets and expensive visits to the gymnasium completely unnecessary. They promote strength and vitality.

Mr Fairlie recently produced a special edition of *The Land* themed around the issue of muscle power, which he called 'the neglected renewable resource'. He rightly points out that using a hand tool can be a meditative act, and reminds us that teams of mowers with scythes would sing together, which is a beautiful thought. Another advantage of a well-made tool (and the common craft worker's lament is that 'the old tools were better') is that it can be maintained with ease at home and it will last for ever. The problem with modern machinery is that it breaks and needs to be upgraded. You have to buy the new, improved version. It is far cheaper to stick with the hand tool or, in other words, the old, unimprovable version.

Large quantities of people can do amazing things without the help of machinery: *The Land* gives the example of an Amish barn-raising: a team of thirty-five men and boys build and paint a gigantic barn in a single day without the use of power tools. The Amish are indeed an example of an Old World community thriving in the midst of the New World.

Fairlie also includes an excellent article on the contemporary use of horses in agriculture. Again, these need no oil, and of course they produce vast amounts of useful manure. The magazine also contains an account of how the hard-working ox came back to Cuba. In 1992, during the 1990–2000 'special period' when the country was cut off from an oil supply, the government introduced an animal traction strategy. Cuban writer Roberto Sánchez Medina, writing in *The Land*, explains that the Cuban crisis has now eased off as a result of a supply of Venezuelan oil, but that animal traction is still being used, and should be investigated by other countries:

> Mechanization generates a dependence upon external inputs and the market, which has caused, and continues to cause, poverty and loss of land for millions of peasant farmers all over the world. The increasing scarcity of oil and the rising price of fossil fuels will make animal traction an important issue in years to come.

Oxen and horses, unlike oil-powered tractors, are able to produce more oxen and horses, which can be used or sold. When they die, unlike tractors, they rot into the soil and feed the earth.

In the same way, you will still happily be mowing your lawn with your scythe when all the oil has run out. The scythe is perfect. It is Old World technology and simply could not be made better. The scythe will still be in use a thousand years from now, but can we say the same of the Strimmer?

In Praise of the Mattock

Now to the mattock, and a couple of lines from Virgil:

> *Multum adeo, rastris glaebas qui frangit inertis*
> *vimineasque trahit crates, iuvat arva.*

[Much service does he do to the land who with the mattock
breaks up the sluggish clods and drags over it hurdles of osier.]
  – *Georgics*, Book I, ll.94–5

So now when you are breaking those clods, you can say to
yourself, '*Rastris glaebas frango*', meaning, 'I am breaking the clods
with my mattock' or, when your girlfriend asks you what you've
been doing in the garden all morning, simply tell her '*Rastris glaebas
frangabam.*' The combination of gardening and learning Latin is
unbeatable. There is another phrase from the *Georgics* which I love,
and which I have used earlier in this book. I always ponder it when
I am using my mattock, and it is simply '*Rastris adsiduis*' – 'with the
unrelenting mattock'.

Inspired by Virgil, I have written my own Latin couplet about
digging, hoeing and manuring:

> *Rastris adsiduis glaebas frango*
> *herba insecto arvaque iuvo.*

[I break up the clods with mattock and toil, I harry the weeds
and fatten the soil.]

Can I add here, as it were in parenthesis, that I would highly
recommend the study of Latin to anyone who is interested in forging

a connection with the Old World. Not only does it sharpen the brain and therefore make you less easily conned by admen into handing over your hard-earned cash to some appalling scam, it leads you into reading the classics, which are not only beautiful poems but poems with which most of our favourite writers would have been familiar, from Chaucer to Shakespeare to Pope to Coleridge. And just imagine being able to read Virgil's *Georgics*, or parts thereof, in the original!

Now, what exactly is a mattock? Well, it is a sort of hand-held plough. The word is said to derive from the Old English 'maettoc' or 'mattuc', meaning 'club'. It was often used in Middle English and occurs in Palladius. The head has two sides: one is that of a pick-axe, and the other is a wide blade. With a spade, one pushes it with the foot into the ground. With the mattock, a different technique is required. You hold it in the air and let it fall into the ground. You then pull it towards you, and thus the clods are dug. The mattock is particularly useful for turning over new ground. If, for example, you decide to take the sensible decision to take a patch of useless bourgeois lawn and turn it into a productive vegetable patch, then the mattock will fly through it, tearing the grass from the surface. Soon you will have a nice patch of virgin soil, with a pile of turves next to it. The turves can then go upside down in the compost heap.

Oh, I wish dearly that someone had told me about the mattock when I first began gardening. I wrongly put my faith in a contemporary writer on husbandry who advised in his book that you should use your spade like a turf-cutter and clear the ground that way. And so I spent many exhausting afternoons attacking the earth with my spade. The dear and unrelenting mattock, on the other hand, would have sailed through the job with ease.

Some gardeners own a range of mattocks of different sizes. I heard of one gardener returning from Greece, probably the birthplace of this excellent tool, with six mattock heads. Today, the tool is used more widely across the eastern world than in the west, in those areas which are more closely connected to the old ways than the progress-addicted West.

On Making Hay

July is also the month for making hay, that is, cutting and drying grass to store as winter feed for the animals. In the old days, hay-making was a joyous affair, with all the men and boys putting in long days in the sun, drinking ale and cider and indulging in country sports. Nowadays, hay-making is a question of getting the tractors and bailers out and going flat out when the weather is dry. The farmers where I live put in very long days when making hay, because you have to make the most of every ounce of sunshine. And although the process is mechanized, the old joy still remains. You can see the pleasure on the faces of the farmers when the hay-making is complete and their barns are piled high with sweet-smelling bales. No, mechanization has not spoilt the pleasures entirely, but clearly the fun of working in a large team has been lost. Harvest time was also when casual labourers were employed, and it is worth reflecting that, for all the sterling efforts of the trade unions to bring in year-round wages and fixed employment via the invention of the full-time job, something has been lost. Casual day labour suited itinerants and idlers, the masterless men. It also suited farmers who did not want to commit themselves to paying wages all year round. 'I don't like employing people,' says one farmer near me. 'There is too much bureaucratic headache.'

This year we conducted our own hay-making experiment. Alan

and I cut the long grass with a scythe and heaped it up in two long lines, two feet apart. These are called furrows. The idea was that I would turn each furrow over several times a day so that the grass would eventually dry all the way through. Well, I'm afraid I forgot. Then it rained. I waited for a dry day. One came, and I turned the furrows over. But then it rained again. It was clear that I was never going to get this damp grass transformed into hay. So I gave up and piled it next to the compost bins. It seems that you really do have to make hay while the sun shines. One afternoon of procrastination, and all your work is wasted. My animals could have starved. Let us repeat the wisdom of the poet: *labor omnia vicit*. However, in the process, I did catch a glimpse of the pure joy of working with grass and a scythe. The furrows that are produced are actually very beautiful to look at. There are also the delicious fresh scents which fill the air. And you can hear the birds sing and the cattle low. Now here are a few words from John Seymour on hay:

> Good weather is absolutely all important . . . the old-fashioned method was to turn the swathes by hand either with a pitch fork or a wooden rake, according to taste. As you turn them over, fluff them up . . . Then, when you are sure it is dry enough, the old idea was to cock it. Pile it up into little mini-stacks higher than a man and dome-shaped. Let it dry in the cock until the green has really gone out of it . . . when it is dry you can cart it and stack it.

So let us praise the noble scythe and rediscover the joy of making hay, and when our work is done, let us stretch out in the meadows, release Bacchus from his glassy cage, and enjoy the fruits of our labour. Let us re-create this charming scene from the end of Book II of the *Georgics*:

Ipse dies agitat festos fususque per herbam,
ignis ubi in medio et socii cratera coronant,
te libans, Lenaee, vocat pecorisque magistris
velocis iaculi certamina ponit in ulmo,
corporaque agresti nudant prædura palæstrae.

[The master himself keeps holiday, and stretched out on the grass, with a fire in the midst and his comrades wreathing the bowl, offers libation and calls upon you, god of the wine press, and for the keepers of the flock sets up a mark on an elm for the contest of the winged javelin, or they bare their arms for the rustic wrestling bout.]

– *Georgics*, Book II, ll. 527–31

July's Husbandry

So July is about mowing and making hay. It is when the Dogstar rises and, at this time, the grim Hesiod tells you to 'set your slaves to winnowing Demeter's holy grain'. Palladius tells us to sow onions, radish, lettuce, beet and turnips.

Tusser has these lines on making hay:

With tossing and raking and setting on cox,
grass latelie in swathes is hay for an ox:
That done, go and cart it and have it away,
the battel is fought, ye have gotten the day.

In these lines, we can feel the joy of the farmer when the job of hay-making is done. Tusser also gives some tips on how to harvest those broad beans:

Not rent off, but cut off, ripe beane with a knife,
for hindering stalke of hir vegetive life.
So gather the lowest, and leaving the top,
shall teach thee a trick, for to double thy crop.

This is also the time, Tusser says, to harvest hemp for making clothes.

John Evelyn encourages us to apply a weedkiller made from old cigarettes. Whether or not this is an early example of inorganic gardening, I will leave the reader to decide: 'Now (in the driest Season) with *Brine*, *Pot-ashes*, and *Water*, or a decoction of *Tobacco-refuse*, water your gravel-walks, &c. to destroy both *Worms* and *Weeds*, of which it will cure them for some *years*.' Evelyn clearly was also unaware of the importance of the worm in our gardens. Of course he wouldn't have read Darwin on the subject.

The principal job to remember for July is to plant your brassicas, as Cobbett, again in *The English Gardener*, reminds us: 'Plant celery, endive, lettuces, cabbages, leeks, savoys, brocoli, greencale, cauliflowers.' Seymour says similar: 'You may well be engaged in planting out your brassicas. It's not too late. Keep on with the radish and lettuce plantings, of course. Sow a seed bed with spring cabbage.'

Your kale, broccoli and cabbage plants should be planted two feet apart. They should also be protected from the wind, and staked as they grow. I failed in these simple tasks, and the result was very poor growth. I also planted the plants too late, in August or September. I nearly always, in addition, forget to sow a seedbed. Therefore, come planting time, I have no plants. So I go down to the nursery or the market (never to the evil gardening centre) and buy good plants from local growers. The brassica plants will be planted where the beans and early potatoes used to be. Make sure to put a net over them to deter the cabbage butterflies. They lay thousands of eggs, and the caterpillars which hatch from them can be a real pest.

July's Merriment

There was not a huge amount of merriment in July in the Old World, as this was a busy month in the fields. However, July was traditionally the time for apple bobbing. Get a large tub and fill it with water. Bung a load of apples into it. Get everyone to kneel down beside the tub, their hands behind their back. The object is to lean forward and remove an apple with your teeth. Hilarious results ensue.

July's Calendar

10 July: Birthday of John Calvin, 1509, and not a day for celebration in any way at all.

15 July: St Swithin's Day. Swithin was an English monk and Bishop of Winchester. He died in 863. In 971, his bones were transferred to Winchester cathedral. The legend that the weather on St Swithin's Day will determine the conditions over the following forty days has been convincingly proved to be complete hokum.

22 July: Feast day of St Mary Magdalen, patron saint of pharmacists, hairdressers, repentant sinners and prostitutes.

25 July: St James's Day. St James is the patron saint of Spain, and his feast day traditionally marks the start of the oyster season.

27 July: Feast day of St Joseph of Arimathea, who died in AD82 and is commemorated at Glastonbury.

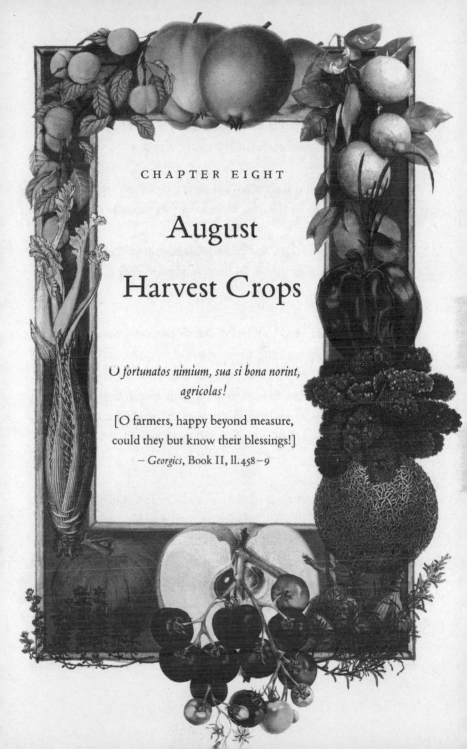

CHAPTER EIGHT

August

Harvest Crops

O fortunatos nimium, sua si bona norint,
agricolas!

[O farmers, happy beyond measure,
could they but know their blessings!]
– *Georgics*, Book II, ll.458–9

IN THE Old World, August was the great month for the harvest, and of course it still is. The medieval calendars show gardeners merrily cutting wheat with the sickle. The Elizabethan ballad 'The Mery Life of the Countriman' quoted by Ronald Hutton in *The Stations of the Sun*, celebrates the romantic pleasures of the harvest:

> When corne is ripe, with tabor and pipe, their sickles they prepare;
> And wagers they lay how muche in a day they meane to cut
>   down there.
> And he that is quickest, and cutteth downe cleanest the corne,
> A garlande trime they make for him, and bravely they bring
>   him home.

The other main crop to harvest at this time of year is the grape. The Roman books on husbandry such as those by Columella and Cato offer endless pages on the proper care of vines and vineyards. Readers, too, were encouraged to grow their own rather than buy in from outside. The stern husbandry guru Varro, writing in 37 BC, attacked what we would call globalization and the retreat from the countryside:

> As therefore in these days practically all the heads of families have sneaked within the walls, abandoning the sickle and the plough, and rather [than] busy their hands . . . in the grain-fields and the vineyards, we hire a man to bring us from Africa and Sardinia the grain with which to fill our stomachs, and the vintage we store comes from the islands of Cos and Chios.

So it is today: we would rather go to the supermarket and drink cans of Stella Artois in front of the television than break the clods in

our allotment with the unrelenting mattock, grow barley and brew
our own beer. We import from elsewhere the things that we could
make or grow ourselves and, like helpless children, follow a vain,
costly, pleasure-seeking path through life, moving from emptiness
to distraction.

Complete self-sufficiency, though, is neither possible nor desirable.
Clearly, there needs to be a mixture of local and global trade. We
love our St Emilion, our pepper, our lemons, our Persian rugs. You
cannot make everything for yourself. Now, this was a debate that
also raged in the early eighteenth century. The *Spectator* magazine
promoted civilized, urban values and teased backwards-looking
rural Tory squires. Addison and Steele, authors of the periodical,
were Whigs – or what we might call modernizers, neophytes,
progressives, liberals – who were very much in love with their
own cleverness. And rather like today's cynics, they delighted in
pointing out inconsistencies in the arguments of their rural-minded
opponents. In the essay 'A Fox-Hunting Gentleman', Addison, on
a ramble through the country, meets a bluff and fiercely anti-Whig
Tory squire:

> As we rode side by side through the town, I was led into the
> characters of all the principal inhabitants whom we met in our
> way. One was a dog, another was a whelp, another a cur, and
> another the son of a bitch, under which several denominations
> were comprehended all that voted on the Whig side.

This sort of character is a perennial: he was also personified in
Nancy Mitford's father, Lord Redesdale, who hated all foreigners,
as well as the bankers and new money. Addison's Tory squire
then goes on to attack the capitalist system: '[H]e expatiated on the

inconveniences of trade, that carried from us the commodities of our country, and made a parcel of upstarts as rich as men of the most ancient families of England.'

You can easily imagine today's Tory duke railing in similar fashion against the massive fortunes made by the hedge-fund men. Addison then employs the stock argument generally used against anti-capitalists, which is that they themselves enjoy the benefits of the system:

After supper, he asked me if I was an admirer of punch; and immediately called for a sneaker. I took this occasion to insinuate the advantages of trade, by observing to him, that water was the only native of England that could be made use of on this occasion: but that the lemons, the brandy, the sugar, and the nutmeg were all foreigners.

At the end of the essay, however, despite Addison's scoffing, you are left with a fondness for the Tory fox-hunter. After all, he has in actual fact shown great kindness and hospitality to Addison and an admirable loathing for capitalism: '[H]e added two or three curses upon the London merchants, not forgetting the directors of the bank.'

Precisely the same battles are fought today. On the one hand, you have your Tory traditionalists who are in fact suspicious of usury and big business, and on the other you have your Liberal progressives who are in bed with the banks. And it occurs to me that all modern politicians, whether left or right, are Whigs, and none is a real Tory, because they all more or less spout Whiggish views. They are all in love with finance, technology, change, reform. My friend Toby Young is one of these. He calls himself a Tory, but in fact he is a Whig: he hates the countryside and is cynical about, for example, anti/globalization protesters. I recently took him to a festival at the house of the environmental activist and aristocrat Hector Christie. We watched various talks which attacked the state and big business. I gave a talk that attacked usury. Toby went to get a burger and noticed that it had been sourced from a big supermarket. 'You can't rant about anti/capitalism and sell crap burgers,' he said. But I defend the Hector Christies of this world, because they are making an effort to improve things. We should not judge them too harshly for small slip/ups. *Monitissum*.

The right balance of global trade and self/sufficiency, both in our everyday lives and as a principle governing national policy, has been debated in Europe for at least two thousand years. But I think that today it would be fair to say that the pendulum has swung too far to the global trade side. Trade has been stolen from the individual and monopolized by the corporation. Instead of making things for ourselves and selling them in the market, which is how things should be done, we work for the corporation, get wages, and then pay other corporations for the things we need. Meanwhile, the rogues of London town who own thousands of shares in these corporations make huge profits out of our passivity and stupidity. We have become too Addisoned, too much like the Roman circus/attending fops criticized by Varro, too Whiggish, too complacent. We need to reawaken the radical Tory within us, the Toryism of, for example, Dr Johnson, who attacked authority and was a vigorous opponent of the eighteenth/century slave trade. The late writer and mystic John Michell called himself a 'radical traditionalist', meaning that he loved the independent spirit of a Cobbett or a Chesterton who praised the 'old liberties', and correctly saw that progressive politics and 'keeping up with the times' are in actual fact tricks to impose a meek acceptance of despotism, the truth, in the words of Rudyard Kipling, 'twisted by knaves to make a trap for fools'.

If we are not to be enslaved by the dubious consolations and distractions of the Brave New World on the one hand – sex, drugs, holidays, plasma screens, football matches – or the despotic neophyte control of the language attempted by governments – Newspeak in Orwell's *Nineteen Eighty-Four* – on the other, then we must look backwards for a way forwards. Novelty by its nature is a friend to the powerful, and when something is trumpeted as 'new' then our warning alarms should start ringing.

Newness, in actual fact, is a cover for two immoral acts: stealing and enslaving. 'New and improved' means 'Throw away that crappy old thing that we sold you last year – embrace our new product!' The latest thing, the cutting edge, the newest discoveries: this is the language of rogues and scoundrels. If, on the other hand, you find a person or a business who loves the old ways – whether they are a tailor, brewer, cheese-maker or farmer – then that is your sign that they value quality over quantity and are more interested in satisfaction than profit. As a rule of thumb, any company that trades its shares on the stock exchange should be avoided. This is because its legal priority is the share price, and that will always be more important than product quality, staff welfare, customer satisfaction or any ethical concerns. The corporation has no conscience. It is only interested in cheering up employees if it makes them more productive workers. It is only interested in ethical issues if signalling some sort of love for the planet will excite investors. Avoid these companies. Instead, use cooperatives and small private ones. There are plenty of these around and, with a little thought, you can quite easily create a life relatively free from the grip of corporate capitalism. A pack of cards, for example, is a lot more fun than a Nintendo Wii and is a tiny fraction of the price.

And when you escape the world of the corporation, you escape the terrible vandalism these people do to the English language. Here, for example, is a bit of blurb from a company that specializes in helping corporations avoid paying tax: 'We specialize solely in facilitating the implementation of sophisticated personal and business asset and income stream restructuring exercises the results of which are significantly tax advantageous consequences for the individuals and businesses who use them.' Or in other words: 'We lie so that you get richer.'

Harvest Time

Here in North Devon, I accept that I am unlikely to be harvesting wheat or grapes in the near future. But, in August, we gather plenty of delicious food from the vegetable garden, and the harvesting of the crops is pure joy. However, it is all too easy to waste food. Many are the times when I have gone to collect a lettuce and found that it has bolted, by which I mean it has sprouted a head of flowers and is now inedible. Indeed, it was a complaint of Cobbett that the vegetable gardens of Kensington were full of bolted lettuces in the summer, the implication being that they were scandalously mismanaged. One gardener I met at a grand household complained that much of his work went in the bin: 'I bring it in,' he said of his lovingly cultivated garden produce. 'They throw it away.' When growing vegetables, we need to develop good habits when it comes to using the food that comes from the garden. This is an art that takes time and experience to master, particularly for those of us who are accustomed to 'running to the markets', to use a phrase from Cobbett, for every little thing.

Peas

We harvest peas all through the summer, and how deliciously sweet and tender they are. I have had great success with Alderman, which grows up to six feet tall. This year we are trying Hatif d'Annonay, Serpette Guilloteau and Telephone. Peas should be harvested as frequently as possible, because the more you pick, the more they grow. The plant tries its best to do its job, which is to produce as many potential new pea plants as possible. If you keep frustrating its efforts by picking pods of all sizes, it will renew its efforts. Peas can be eaten directly from the pod, and children love them. The husk of the pod can be left to rot back into the earth, flung on the compost heap or given to the porkers.

Root Vegetables

Carrot, beetroot, turnip and radish can all be brought into the house during the summer. The turnip is much under-rated. It is easy to grow, delicious, versatile, and has an attractive medieval quality about it. There are a number of varieties to try. When it comes to the beetroot, with its large crinkly seed, try a nice Italian variety such as Sangina. There is a whole world of beetroot husbandry out there, and London restaurants offer beetroot salads using multiple varieties. I predict that the same happy fate awaits the humble turnip: that this excellent root will become fashionable in the metropolitan eateries, and that gardeners will begin to explore unusual varieties. What starts as a backyard project for fun today could turn into a serious restaurant-supply business tomorrow. Carrots are another good-value crop, if you get it right. This year I had my first ever success with them, and one packet of seeds, costing about a quid, has given us two to three months' supply.

Fruit

Now is the time to harvest your gooseberries and blueberries. I haven't bothered with strawberries over the last two years. This is because, come harvest time, they would vanish overnight, prey to the evil slug, which waits under a stone until the humans are asleep, and then, at the precise moment the strawberries ripen, crawls out and spends a good few hours completely destroying the whole crop. Some slugs crawl back under their stones and spend the day in a disgusting strawberry-induced coma, while others simply sleep inside the strawberry itself. My other objection to this over-rated fruit is that the plants occupy the ground all year round, unlike the less selfish fruit or vegetables, which grow and then allow themselves to be eaten, leaving space for new ones. Strawberry plants have to be replaced every three years. They require a good deal of time, cost and effort, and when you consider that you probably only want to eat them four times a year, you have to wonder whether it's worth it, particularly in small gardens. Gooseberries and blueberries, on the other hand, are easy and make excellent eating. Raspberries are well worth growing, as they are much easier than strawberries and the ones you grow are far tastier than the ones in the shops, but, personally, I am not a huge fan of redcurrants and blackcurrants.

Apple trees are miraculous. They are easy to look after, pretty, and each year they offer a heavier crop. The first thing you should do when you move to a new house is plant an apple tree. And when you consider that the cost of an apple tree is the same as the cost of two cheeseburgers then it really is criminal not to plant one, at least. Apple trees should be everywhere. We have two in the front garden. One, a Discovery, was planted by my friends Penny Rimbaud and Eve Libertine, both former members of Crass, the anarchist punk band, and in year one it produced one apple. In year two, we picked five; and in year three, there were thirteen. This year, if the profusion of apple blossom is anything to go by, it looks as if we will have around a hundred apples from it.

There is very little work involved in tending an apple tree – perhaps a little weeding, mulching and pruning – and there are thousands of varieties out there. John Evelyn mentions some wonderful ones, including the Ladies Longing, the Kirkham apple, the John apple, the Seaming apple, the Cushion apple, Golden Mundi, Leathern Coate and Cat's Head. He also grew over 150 varieties of pear. The point of all these different varieties is that they ripen at different times of the year so, with a selection of apples and pears, you can guarantee yourself a steady supply from June to November. The Old World thus had its own way of providing food throughout the year, without the need for electrically powered storage devices.

Onions and Garlic

I have always found onions and garlic easy to grow. Garlic can be jammed in any odd corner and at any time of the year, and it is said to deter pests, so I plant it near the salads. Soon after the stems topple over, the garlic bulbs can be dug up and dried out in the sun on boards or newspaper, or tied up and hung near the oven or fire. They can be stored in bags or in clumps on hooks. I have to say, however, that when it comes to onions, I have followed the advice of Hugh Fearnley-Whittingstall and no longer bother to grow them: we buy onions because they are cheap, we use a lot of them and it would take up too much space to grow them. Also, it has to be said that you'd be hard put to tell the difference between a home-grown and a shop-bought onion.

A Note on WWOOFing

WWOOFing is a wonderful scheme that was invented in the seventies by some idealistic back-to-the-landers. WWOOFing originally stood for 'Working Weekends on Organic Farms'. The idea was that people living in cities would head to the fields at the weekends and work on a farm for free. They would do four hours' work a day, and the farmer – or, more often, amateur smallholder – would give them board and lodging. No money would change hands. The scheme grew, and soon the acronym was changed to stand for 'Willing Workers on Organic Farms'. As a WWOOFer, you sign up to the scheme and stay for a week, two weeks, or longer at a particular farm. You learn skills and get an insight into someone else's way of life. Then the scheme became international: girls from Kiev would turn up at a Welsh smallholding, for example. WWOOFing, people realized, is a fantastically cheap way of seeing the world. Again, the words behind the acronym changed, and now it stands for 'Worldwide Opportunities on Organic Farms'. There are currently five thousand registered WWOOFers in the UK, and around 450 host households.

We have taken advantage of this fantastic free-labour scheme more than once. Most recently, Matt and Laura came to stay for two weeks, and in that time they tackled all the big jobs which I had postponed: they dug the vegetable patch, mulched it, chopped and stacked a huge pile of logs, chopped up a fallen ash branch – and made parsnip wine. If you participate in the scheme, you can end up in some amazing places: Jaz Coleman of the band Killing Joke, for example, takes WWOOFers at his eco-village in the South Pacific. An alternative to the WWOOF scheme is a similar project called HelpX; it offers slightly fuller profiles of both hosts and guests, and is less focused on organic farms.

What the schemes recognize is not only that there are lots of people who relish the idea of going back to the land as a form of holiday from the stresses of urban living but also that, on any smallholding, some extra help, whether in the form of WWOOFers, friends, relations or some form of staff, is essential, particularly if you have young children. To ask a couple to run a smallholding, earn a living, educate their children and enjoy themselves to boot is simply too much. It is a mistake to think that life will become easier if you quit the nine-to-five and embrace country living. You will just find that you are exchanging one stressful situation for another. Help is needed – lots of help! And in return, you can have the pleasure of throwing medieval feasts for your workers, and filling your WWOOFers and HelpXers with good beer.

August's Husbandry

Palladius sows rape and turnip. Tusser recommends that you attend to your saffron plants, and suggests swapping seeds (another Old World practice recommended by modern organic gardeners):

> Good huswifes in sommer will save their own seedes
> against the next yeere, as occasion needes,
> One seede for another, to make an exchange,
> with fellowlie neighbourhood seemeth not strange.

Remember, by the way, to pronounce the final 'e' in Tusser's lines. Tusser also tells us that we should make merry in August:

> In harvest time, harvest folke, servants and all,
> should make all togither good cheere in ther hall:
> And fill out the black boule of bleith to their song,
> and let them be merie all harvest time long.

Here we see that Tusser is insisting on a custom that was already becoming old-fashioned in his day, and that is the medieval approach to celebration, where servants and masters partied together. The separation of servants and masters was a post-Reformation phenomenon and, even in the late-sixteenth century, commentators were complaining that 'the golden age is gone.' I'm afraid I have been unable to gloss 'bleith', but I guess that Tusser is talking about beer, since it was the custom at harvest time to keep the beer flowing for your workers, and they would be given a pint in the morning, a pint at lunchtime and a pint in the evening. This custom persists today, and I am told by WWOOFers that Cider Bill in Wales offers his guests large quantities of cider.

Evelyn tells us to continue sowing in August, and his list includes radish, cabbage, cauliflowers for winter, marigolds, lettuce, carrots, turnips, spinach and onions. Like Virgil, he says we must cut branches: 'Prune off . . . superfluous branches . . . Continue yet to cleanse your *Vines* from exuberant branches that too much hinder the *Sun*.' I have to say that the language Evelyn uses is marvellously rich: the next time I am in my vegetable garden with a visitor, I am going to take the shears and do some chopping, while explaining: 'I'm just going to cleanse these exuberant branches. I find they hinder the sun.' His final tip is an enticing one: 'Make your Summer *Perry* [pear wine] and *Cider*.' We will return to the pleasures and advantages of making your own booze in a later chapter.

Cobbett produces his characteristically lengthy and badly spelt list of jobs, and I am going to reproduce it for the more conscientious among you. The lazy can skip it:

Sow early cabbages in the first week, the last sowing for the year. Red cabbages same time; cauliflower for spring and summer use, about the twenty-first, cress, hardy coss and cabbage lettuces from about the twelfth to the thirtieth . . . Turnips last sowing, Welsh onions first week in the month, Lisbon, Strasburg, and Reading, from the middle to the end of the month . . . planting for winter must not now be delayed, put out as fast as possible, if not enough planted, savoys, cabbages, brocoli, coleworts, celery, &c. Hoe,

and earth up where necessary, weed, and thin young crops, water
and shade where requisite. Gather seeds as they ripen, dry and
store them, dry and house onions, garlic, shalots; dry herbs as
they flower.

The point about seed collection is valid today. The more seeds
you can collect, the less reliant you will be on seeds from elsewhere,
and some seed companies actively encourage you to keep seeds from
your plants. What I try to do is to leave a few plants from each block
or row unharvested, so that they will produce seeds. I then keep these
in brown envelopes for the following year.

Seymour also recommends more sowing of radishes and lettuce.
And, as far as salads go, try hardy ones such as pak choi and Mizuna
so you will get salad leaves in the winter. Think ahead, think ahead!
This has been the hardest lesson for me to learn.

August's Merriment

August is named after Augustus Caesar, the first Roman emperor.
The Anglo-Saxons called it 'Weodmonath', meaning 'vegetation
month'. As Tusser – though not Cobbett or Evelyn – insists, harvest time is also the time to make merry. There should be much
feasting, partying, drinking and dancing. The abundance of the
earth has cheered our hearts, and we should give thanks to Ceres, to
Mother Earth, to God, and to Nature for her fruitfulness.

In Roman times, the harvest was celebrated with a feast for
Ceres, and the custom continued in medieval times under the
name Lammas Day. Lammas means 'loaf mass' and was all about
celebrating the grain harvest by baking fancy loaves with the new
wheat. These loaves were blessed in the church. The medieval
bakers were highly imaginative, and loaves were baked in the shape

of monkeys, elephants and dragons. (Throughout the year, bread baked in the shape of cones, squares, circles, ovals, rectangles and figure eights was used as a teaching aid in geometry lessons.) For the feast, a castle of bread was baked, to be admired during the main courses and eaten at the end of the feast. (Funnily enough, Victoria and I unwittingly re-created this custom when we held a 'Simple Living' course at our home one July. We held a bread-baking class in the kitchen and, without any prompting, the students baked all sorts of creative loaves: plaited ones, giant loaves, loaves in the shape of a rabbit. One baked the face of Winston Churchill. We carried these impressive loaves in a laundry basket to the village hall, the site of the feast we had planned, and put them in the middle of the table, whereupon the assembled party fell upon them with great relish and satisfaction.)

Other medieval delights were gingerbread, currant buns, short-bread, cucumber bread and plum bread. To drink there was Lamb's Wool, a spiced and warmed cider, with baked apples floating frothily on top.

A favourite game was Bringing Home the Bacon, a sort of *Mr and Mrs*-type affair. A mock trial was set up, with several couples competing for the prize. A judge asked a series of 'what if' questions, all based around some sort of domestic disaster and the reactions of the couple to it: 'What if your wife let the fire go out?'; 'What if your husband chased the dog into the banquet hall, which spooked the cat, which leapt into the bowl of cream, which splashed the guest of honour?' The tag to each question would be: 'Would there be no jealousy, joylessness or jangling?' The wife or husband had to use their ingenuity to argue why this sort of negligence in the other would not anger them. The cleverest set of answers won the competition.

At the end of the Lammas Feast, there was a candle-lit procession.

Each person walked in a circle around the hall three times while holding a piece of bread with a candle stuck in it. The following day, everyone ate their bread but saved a quarter of it for a whole year, and then gave it to the birds.

August's Calendar

1 or 2 August: Festival of Ceres, or Lammas Day.

5 August: First day of the oyster season.

10 August: Feast day of St Lawrence, patron saint of cooks.

12 August: William Blake died today, 1827.

15 August: Assumption of the Virgin Mary Day. Today we invoke Mary in her role as the fertile mother, in order to ensure a good grape harvest.

24 August: First day of Mania, the Roman festival. St Bartholomew's Day. He was one of Christ's apostles, supposedly flayed alive and then beheaded. His symbol is a butcher's knife, and he is the patron saint of tanners and leatherworkers. Mania was a Roman festival that celebrated the *manes* (the spirits of their ancestors). London's rowdy Bartholomew Fair (1133–1855) was a continuation of the festival of Mania.

28 August: Feast day of St Augustine, author of the *Confessions* (written AD 397).

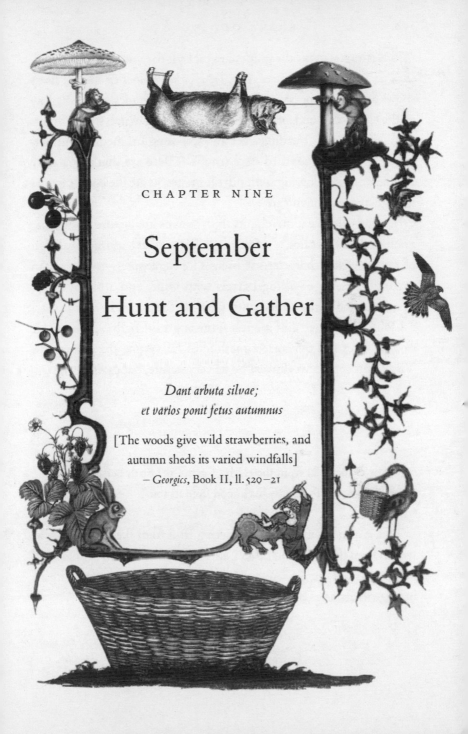

CHAPTER NINE

September

Hunt and Gather

Dant arbuta silvae;
et varios ponit fetus autumnus

[The woods give wild strawberries, and
autumn sheds its varied windfalls]
— *Georgics*, Book II, ll. 520–21

IN SEPTEMBER, the grapes are picked; the wine god is praised. The September scene of *Les Très Riches Heures du Duc de Berry* shows a group of peasants picking and eating grapes in the shadow of the castle of Duc Louis II d'Anjou (a castle which stands to this day). One chap is bending over and exposing his medieval under pants, blue stockings and bare thighs. There are donkeys whose panniers are overflowing with purple grapes, as are the barrels on the back of the ox-drawn cart.

In other calendars, merchants in the towns are pictured weighing grain with their scales, a reference to September's astrological sign of Libra. Other characteristic images for September include a man sowing seeds, a girl filling barrels with wine, and a happy chap, again wearing white underpants, treading the grapes in a large vat.

Columella, Varro and the rest write at great length on the proper care of vines and the correct method of harvesting the grapes. For Virgil, this sort of work was, by its very nature, happy-making:

> *Quibus ipsa, procul discordibus armis,*
> *fundit humo facilem victum iustissima tellus.*

[For farmers, far from the clash of arms, the earth herself, most just, pours forth an easy livelihood from its soil.]

This is also the month for gathering fruit from the hedgerows, as well as from the vines and other cultivated fruit trees and bushes and, it appears from our ancient authorities, the time when young virgins indulge in ecstatic dancing:

> *O ubi campi*
> *Spercheosque et virginibus bacchata Laceonis!*
> *Taygeta!*

[O for those plains, and Spercheus, and Taygetus, where Spartan
girls hold Bacchic rites!]

– *Georgics*, Book II, ll. 486–8

I admit I have not managed to re-create that particular Old
World scene at home, but there is still time. We can, however, quite
easily drink wine, and of course I don't need to remind you of the
importance of wine to Roman culture and the Mediterranean in
general. There are repeated injunctions to drink wine in the eleventh-
century Persian poem *The Rubaiyat of Omar Khayyam*. Christ was a
wine-lover, too: American journalist Barbara Ehrenreich in her
book *Dancing in the Streets*, an excellent study of festivity through
the ages, compares Christ with Bacchus: 'Both were wandering
charismatics who attracted devoted followings . . . both had special
appeal to the poor . . . both are associated with wine: Dionysus first
brought it to mankind; Jesus could make it out of water.'

Wine is, of course, an integral part of the Catholic mass. This
all points to an understanding, in medieval Christianity, of the
importance of pleasure in everyday life, something that was lost
by the Protestants, who were suspicious of sensual pleasure: they
embraced sobriety and forced it on others. The grape, though, is
celebrated in sculpture and art throughout the medieval period,
which itself was heavily influenced – and to a far greater extent
than is commonly thought – by Roman culture. We are taught
that classical culture was 'rediscovered' first in the Renaissance and
then in the eighteenth century, but that, in fact, is pure nonsense.
Latin was the western world's common language, and the medieval
calendars borrowed many of the Roman holidays.

So when we celebrate September as the month of the wine harvest,
we are connecting ourselves in joyous fashion with customs that go
back millennia. The Brave New World will never quite extinguish

them, try as it might. One of the key New World apostles was, of course, Oliver Cromwell, and he is well known for creating an army of well-trained, sober and sombre soldiers, in contrast to the wine-loving, wench-loving, fun-seeking Royalist army.

It is this ancient love of wine that Keats is talking about in his Virgilian ode 'To Autumn', written in undulating pentameters:

> Season of mists and mellow fruitfulness!
> Close bosom-friend of the maturing sun;
> Conspiring with him how to load and bless
> With fruit the vines that round the thatch-eaves run;
> To bend with apples the moss'd cottage-trees,
> And fill all fruit with ripeness to the core;
> To swell the gourd, and plump the hazel shells
> With a sweet kernel; to set budding more,
> And still more, later flowers for the bees,
> Until they think warm days will never cease,
> For summer has o'erbrimm'd their clammy cells.

Wine and the grape connect us to a world of dancing fauns and nymphs. It is the Old World of Mr Tumnus the faun in *The Lion, the Witch and the Wardrobe*, before the White Witch came, with her hatred of the old ways, and banned dancing and cancelled Christmas.

It's not possible, of course, to collect grapes everywhere, and at home in North Devon, we will often long, as Keats does in 'Ode to a Nightingale', for a taste of that Mediterranean warmth. Forgive me for quoting the young poet again, but he is the master of wine-lovers:

O, for a draught of vintage! that hath been
Cooled a long age in the deep-delvèd earth,
Tasting of Flora and the country green,
Dance, and Provençal song, and sunburnt mirth!
O for a beaker full of the warm South!
Full of the true, the blushful Hippocrene,
With beaded bubbles winking at the brim,
And purple-stained mouth;
That I might drink, and leave the world unseen,
And with thee fade away into the forest dim.

How clearly I remember Mr Jacobs, my English teacher, reciting those lines and pointing out that Keats was not drinking sparkling wine but that bubbles do appear at the rim of the glass when you pour your red wine. I now note that Keats was a fan of digging rather than mulching: he approves of 'deep-delvèd earth'. Anyway, luckily for us British, we trade with France, and it is an easy thing to go to the off licence and buy a draught of vintage.

On the Fruits of the Hedgerow

At home, we have our own berry harvest to bring in. I don't know whether the Romans had blackberries, but we are certainly blessed with these gorgeous fruits aplenty in old Blighty. It is a simple matter to walk down a country lane, or even a city lane, and gather a real feast. Each year we bring home baskets of blackberries and other hedgerow fruit, too: elderberries, sloes, hips, haws and apples. With this harvest we make hedgerow jam, of which more later.

Elderberries are particularly satisfying to pick: all you need is a pair of scissors and a basket. All the elderflowers you neglected to pick earlier in the year have by now turned into great sprays of dark-purple berries, and you will soon have a purple-stained basket. The berries can be made into wine or into a sugary syrup. They are the most wonderful gift from heaven, and the elder will grow anywhere: at home it grows alongside the muddy old pond and from cracks in the concrete yard. It grows in hedges, and one year it self-seeded in my vegetable patch. It really does look after itself, and if you don't have elder growing nearby, it would make a lot of sense to plant it. The berries are packed with vitamins A and C, so the syrup is a good cough medicine. I recently tasted an excellent elderberry syrup made by my brother-in-law at Burford. We ate it with ice cream.

Everyone knows the blackberry, but as we tend to under-appreciate what is under our very noses (because it is not advertised on television), it is worth reminding ourselves what a delicious fruit this is. It is far superior in taste to the cultivated raspberry or strawberry, and really one should wonder why on earth we bother working so hard to grow these fruits when a tastier one is on offer for free in great profusion every September. I for one could happily never eat a strawberry again. It is, I repeat, an over-rated fruit. And the blackberry harvest does compensate a little for the inevitable tinge of melancholy that hangs around September, the sense that summer's charms really have fled.

The sloe, the fruit of the blackthorn, is another favourite. These fruits make a gorgeous sight: plump, dark purple and with a sort of cloudy sheen, like a cross between a grape and a plum. Sloe gin is their most famous application, but they have many other uses, making a great addition, as mentioned above, for example, to hedgerow jam.

Hips and haws are the other two gifts of the hedgerow. Hip is the short name for the rosehip, the hard fruit of the wild rose. These little storehouses contain twenty times the vitamin C content of the more famous orange. Haws are the fruit of the hawthorn, and again can be used to make delicious syrups for a steady supply of nutrition throughout the winter.

Our great triumph last year was hedgerow jam. Using a very simple recipe from the must-have cookery book *The Country Kitchen* by Jocasta Innes, we made eight pots of the best jelly I have ever tasted (jelly in the sense of jam without the bits). The whole process was highly enjoyable, from harvesting the fruits, to weighing them, to cooking them. The fruit is drained of its juice, and this juice is then boiled in a large pan with the same amount of sugar. At a certain point – the setting point – the foaming mixture must be taken off the hob and poured into the waiting jam jars, where it should set.

The difficulty is judging just the right moment to pour the jam: oftentimes, I have boiled it for too long, and the result is a jelly that is far too thick and, though it is delicious, hard work to spoon out of the jar. The books tell you to use the 'wrinkle test' or the 'flake test'. In the wrinkle test, you let a drop of the jam fall on to a cold saucer then poke it with your finger. If it wrinkles, the jam is ready. The trouble is, they don't say what 'wrinkles' means. I must have dropped a hundred drops on to a saucer and poked them without having any idea whether it wrinkled or not. It was the same with the absurd 'flake test'. In this one, you are told to put your wooden spoon into the boiling mixture. Then lift it out and let the jam run off. If it forms a flake, it is ready. But how do you define a flake, for heaven's sake? It's completely impossible to tell, for a beginner. By the time you have done innumerable flake and wrinkle tests, you think, Bugger this, and take it off the heat anyway, and it is either too runny or too thick.

No: forget the tests – buy a jam thermometer. This will tell you precisely when the jam is ready and you will have no more problems. I resisted buying one at first, because it didn't seem very

Old World. But when you are an unschooled amateur, you really do need one. I don't doubt that after a few years' experience, the flake or wrinkle test will be sufficient. But, really, shame on the textbooks for imposing the misery of the flake and wrinkle on thousands of first-time jam-makers!

One thing to do is to get your children involved in jam-making. With any luck, they will pick it up, and will not, like us members of the helpless generation, need to relearn with great toil those Old World skills that the New World has tried to do away with as it chases growth, targets, efficiency and the bottom line.

It is not an exaggeration to say that my hedgerow jam was the best jam ever made by a human being. As you eat it with toast, you can physically feel it doing you good: in that jam is stored all the sun- and rain-power, all the cosmic energy, of a whole year. We have to live with less sun in the winter, which is why we need to eat it in bottle form through the medium of the hedgerow fruit.

In gathering wild food, we get a glimpse of our own pre-agricultural past, and of the collective joy of gathering, because collecting berries is so often done in chatty, convivial groups. The little wounds one receives while gathering are somehow enlivening: the New World has tried to banish pain, but in the Old World we get little stings and scratches, and we deal with them cheerfully. We later admire our scratched and 'purple-stainèd' hands: these are real hands, hands that have done more than tap at a keyboard, hands that have done some real work. These hands have lived.

On Hunting

September is the month when, as well as gathering, we start to hunt. And by 'hunting', I'm not talking about the apparently very enjoyable but surely rather silly sport of fox-hunting, or the even sillier sport of paying vast sums of money to shoot pheasants which are then thrown away – I'm talking about the more ancient art of catching animals for eating. This is often called poaching, because it tends to involve catching animals that are living on someone else's land, and therefore, in these enclosed times, do not belong to you. In the Old World, of course, there were vast areas of common land, where we all had the right to graze our animals, collect firewood and set traps. That has all now changed and there are no commonly shared areas, unless you count parks and National Trust and National Parks land. So the hunter must either poach or get permission from the landowner if he or she wants to hunt animals. For example, because I live in a rented house, I am not allowed to shoot pheasants that walk across my garden because, by law, they belong to my landlord.

Now, there is one kind of hunting which it is very easy to get permission for, and that is ferreting, which is a huge pleasure and was a popular sport in medieval Europe.

It was Brian the Potter who introduced us to the pleasures and joys of ferrets. Brian called one day and said that he had some ferret babies (kits) to give away, and would we like some. I asked the family, and the response was a unanimous 'yes'. We visited the babies a few times for some lessons in handling them. The first misconception people hold about ferrets is that they bite you. This is not true of ferrets who have been properly handled from a young age. They can be taught not to bite. It is true that one of the ferrets bit Delilah when he was young, but now they would never dream of doing such a thing. (And if they do try, just tap their nose.) From Brian's, then, we came home with two ferrets, a boy and a girl (a hob and a jill). The children named them Twister and Whisper, and they have grown into the most charming small pets we have ever had.

They are far more fun than a rabbit. Set loose in the kitchen, they will dash about, and jump, and play with the dog. They are perennially curious creatures. They sniff everything and explore the whole room, carefully examining everything in it. You can put them on the kitchen table and let them run through cardboard tubes. They love climbing and leaping, and will climb up the wire parts of their cage, or 'court', which is the nice name for a large ferret house. Ferrets sleep for something like twenty hours a day, so if you leave them for a while in the kitchen, they will soon tire and find a little corner in which to snuggle up and sleep. Like many animals, they curl up into a circle.

The really great thing about ferrets, though, is that they are so useful. They catch food for you. The principle of ferreting is this: you find a rabbit warren early one morning. You peg specially made nets called purse nets over each of the holes. Then you lift one of the nets and send the ferrets down into the rabbit holes. The frightened bunnies make a bid for freedom, dash through a hole and straight into a net. They then tumble across the meadow in this net bag. You pick up the rabbit and humanely dispatch it. Then you gut it, take it home with any others you have caught, skin it and put it in a pie.

Ferrets are made for this job. They resemble, in the words of the critic Nick Lezard, a 'draught excluder with legs'. They are like furry tubes and, truly a friend to man, have other practical uses: for example, to lay cables in underground pipes. Experienced ones are used to control rats. It is strange that in that curious country, the United States of America, which is both sentimental and brutal, to hunt rabbits using ferrets is banned, but all sorts of cruelties and indignities are imposed on pigs, sheep and cows in order to keep the population overfed. This is the land of Bambi and McDonald's.

When we acquired our ferrets, I bought a book called *Ferrets for Dummies* from the pet shop, without realizing that it was an

American guide to ferret-keeping. I nearly threw it across the room in disgust when I read the following passage. And to make things even more patronizing, there was a little tick in front of each of the bullet points. Just look at the absurd anthropomorphism that is going on here:

- It's illegal.
- Your ferret can get lost, maybe even for good.
- It's cold, dark and scary down those rabbit burrows (to me, anyway).
- Your ferret would prefer to be cuddled up with you in a safe, warm house.
- Your ferret can drown in water-filled burrows.
- Hey, what did a rabbit ever do to you?

It's hard to know where to start, but here you have all that is wrong with contemporary Brave New World culture and the muddled thinking that goes with it: the fear of adventure, the privileging of safety over really living, the fear of messy nature. Then there is the author's fluffy, anaemic prose style. The 'cold, dark and scary' bit about rabbit burrows is wrong in a thousand ways. The burrows are in actual fact cosy and warm, to a rabbit, and therefore presumably also to a ferret. The author tries to evade this issue by writing 'to me anyway', but this is ridiculous, since she has clearly never been in a rabbit hole. The point about being in a safe home is pure Brave New World, and the whole thing actually denies the ferret its reason for existence: they like working, they love going down holes, they are hunters and that is the whole point of a ferret. Finally, the Disneyesque sentiment behind her last point is insane: you might as well ask what a chicken, pig or cow ever did to you.

The fact that ferrets are good pets is a bonus. It is also true that rabbits make good eating and are a pest, so it makes double sense to hunt them. I have learned that squeamish Americans have their ferrets' anal glands removed so they don't smell. Therefore the American ferret is not allowed to be a ferret, and that is a great crime against them. If I may stretch a point, it rather reminds me of the paradox of eighteenth-century America, which declared itself the land of the free but was the world's foremost user of slaves. It is a contradiction that Dr Johnson, tooth and nail an opponent of the eighteenth-century slave trade, succinctly points out in his pamphlet 'Taxation No Tyranny' in 1775: 'How is it that we hear the loudest yelps for liberty among the drivers of negroes?'

Most countries, however, are fortunate in that ordinary Old World activities such as ferreting, which combine pleasure with utility, are not banned by law, and so we can still pursue them. As for hunting foxes, it seems to me to be a complete waste of time, but I would not ban it. Hunters tell me of the pure joy to be found in riding at speed in a group through beautiful countryside. When hunting, you are connected to nature and the landscape at a far more profound level than when you just look at it through your car's windscreen. And as far as banning things goes, the curious thing about the hunting ban in the UK is that it has made hunting more popular than ever. It is like the War on Drugs: it has the precise opposite effect to the one intended. It simply gives drugs lots of free publicity and sharpens up the dealers, and therefore leads to a widening of the drugs market.

There are other Old World hunting methods which bring you into direct communion with the earth and with animals. Falconry is clearly one, and I would dearly love to learn about this one day. I have held a hawk on my gloved hand at a country fair and peered at him, and they are noble creatures indeed. There is something very beautiful about man working with animals, whether it be horses, oxen, ferrets, hawks or dogs.

On shooting pheasants – unless they are wandering around your land – I say little. Again, to pay large sums of money to blast out of the air pheasants which will only be thrown away later seems the height of folly and waste. However, I have been beating once or twice with our black Labrador, and that was extremely enjoyable. You get paid, and it is a nice walk through the countryside, but with a purpose. Last year we went beating on the Duke of Somerset's estate, and we saw a white deer bound through the wood. Victoria regularly takes our dog off to work at a local shoot and returns with pheasants, duck and woodcock, which we pluck, gut and roast.

When the better sort use their skill to catch and kill animals as a sort of elegant diversion and status symbol, it is called hunting (the first thing the *nouveau riche* stock jobber does on getting some money is to put the Barbour on and go on a pheasant shoot or join a hunt). When hunting is done by the poor in order to get food, it is called poaching. In the eighteenth century, when there was far less common ground than in pre-Reformation days for the poor to use for hunting, poachers would be severely punished:

> They hang the man and flog the woman
> Who steals the goose from off the common
> But let the greater villain loose
> That steals the common from the goose.

As this well-known and oft-quoted anti-Enclosure rhyme relates, the common people were denied access to the land by rich landowners, who themselves were fired up by the New World ideology coming from writers such as Adam Smith and Malthus. We urgently need, worldwide, a 'common land' movement, to create areas of land that can be used, for free, by all communities, for recreation, grazing and growing fuel. This is something that councils could easily do, but instead they spend millions on creating sterile paved areas with silly water features and baffling bits of modern art such as you might see, for example, outside Birmingham New Street station. This is because we have all, more or less, been conditioned by the Brave New World to want to be seen to be keeping up with the times.

So let us poach to our heart's content. If you do not want to poach, then simply ask permission from a landowner to go ferreting. This permission will often be freely given: we ask our landlord for permission and he always says yes. Hawking is also an ancient pursuit that is within reach of ordinary people, and you will find local clubs which will help you get started.

I should also mention fishing. Clearly, here is an ancient form of hunting which can still be practised on a small scale. Like ferreting, fishing does two important things. It connects you with the landscape, making you a part of it rather than a mere spectator. And it also provides food. So, it is an anti-capitalist activity.

The great book about fishing is of course Izaak Walton's *The Compleat Angler* from 1653. It is probably the most political guide to angling ever written, being essentially an anti-Puritan tract. It is also, charmingly, against scoffing. Since most of us have a friend who is a scoffer, someone who pours scorn on your various projects and enterprises, then I think this passage from Walton may be useful:

It is an easy thing to scoff at any art or recreation; a little wit mixed with ill nature, confidence, and malice, will do it; but though they often venture boldly, yet they are often caught, even in their own trap, according to that of Lucian, the father of the family of scoffers:

Lucian, well skilled in scoffing, this hath writ:
Friend, that's your folly, which you think your wit:
This you vent oft, void both of wit and fear,
Meaning another, when yourself you jeer.

Yes, how true that is: the scoffer only makes himself look contemptible in the eyes of the assembled company. We should commit those last three lines to heart, and recite them the next time a friend scoffs at our innocent recreations. We can also condemn, as Walton does, 'serious and grave men':

Men that are taken to be grave, because nature hath made them of a sour complexion; money-getting men, men that spend all their time, first in getting, and next, in anxious care to keep it; men that are condemned to be rich, and then always busy and discontented. for these poor rich-men, we Anglers pity them perfectly.

So writes Walton of that new breed of hard-working, po-faced men of business. It is very true that hunting, and indeed gathering, is in itself an attack on the world of 'money-getting'. Hunting and gathering remove us from the world of commerce. When we hunt and gather, we neither work nor spend. Hunting and gathering are of no service at all to the economy and its growth, which is why you will not find them encouraged or taught by the institutions of the state. Indeed, the state may even be actively hostile to them: we have seen how ferreting is banned in America, and the UK government recently tried to ban hunting with dogs. To a Republican statesman, hunting and gathering are, in a sense, deeply traitorous, since they remove us from two economically useful activities: working and shopping. Avatars of the New World are therefore hostile towards hunting and gathering. But they tend to dress this hostility up as an apparent concern for animal welfare. Luckily, the Old World spirit is ever ready to return to the surface, and all over the world, lately, we have seen a renewal of interest in both hunting and gathering as useful, satisfying and merely sensible pursuits.

In London's Richmond Park, keepers have been dismayed to find that the Poles, far better schooled in the arts of foraging than we Brits, have been collecting chestnuts in the autumn. They have put signs up telling people to stop it at once. This brings to mind two chestnut stories from left-wing historian Peter Linebaugh's *Magna Carta Manifesto*. Linebaugh reports that, in 1803, political activist Thomas Spence was threatened with arrest when caught gathering chestnuts on the Duke of Portland's land. The nuts, he said, 'are the spontaneous gifts of nature ordained alike for the sustenance of Man and Beast, that choose to gather them, and therefore they are common'. This seems to me to be a good line of defence. Perhaps the Poles could make use of it. And, in 1826, the owner of Hatfield Forest in Epping made the following complaint about local chestnut-gatherers:

> . . . as soon as the nuts get ripe . . . the idle and disorderly Men and Women of bad Character . . . come . . . in large parties to gather Nuts or under pretence of gathering Nuts to loiter about in Crowds . . . and in the Evening take Beer and Spirits and Drink in the Forest which affords them an opportunity for all sorts of Debauchery.

Who would have thought that gathering nuts would be seen as such a subversive, dangerous and licentious activity? I think all freedom seekers owe it to themselves to get out into the woods, forests and hedgerows, and gather nuts while ye may.

Notes from Gilbert White

No study of husbandry in calendar form could be complete without a reference to Revd Gilbert White, author of the charming book of observations of the natural world *The Natural History of Selborne*. The book is written in the form of a series of letters, and White has two nice observations as far as September goes:

> Weasels prey on moles, as appears by their being sometimes caught in mole-traps . . .
>
> Many birds, which become silent about Midsummer, re-assume their notes again in September, as the thrush, blackbird, woodlark, willow-wren, etc.

This was written on 2 September 1774. White also tells a good story about how a farmer exacted cruel and humiliating revenge on a bird of prey which had been stealing his hens:

> A neighbouring gentleman one summer had lost most of his chickens by a sparrow-hawk, that came gliding down between a faggot pile and the end of his house to the place where the coops stood. The owner, inwardly vexed to see his flock thus diminishing, hung a setting-net adroitly between the pile and the house, into which the caitiff [the offending bird] dashed and was entangled. Resentment suggested the law of retaliation; he therefore clipped the hawk's wings, cut off his talons, and, fixing a cork on his bill, threw him down among the brood-hens. Imagination cannot paint the scene that ensued; the expressions that fear, rage, and revenge inspired, were new, or at least such as had been unnoticed before: the exasperated matrons upbraided, they execrated, they insulted, they triumphed. In a word, they

never desisted from buffeting their adversary till they had torn him in an hundred pieces.

A Short Note on Wood

Do you have enough dry wood to last through the winter? Should you order some wood now so that you will have a good dry pile in twelve months' time? September is the month to make sure that this is sorted out.

September's Husbandry

We mentioned earlier that, for the Roman farmer, September was all about the grape harvest, and he very definitely looked to the moon for help in timing the harvest. Grapes for drying, said Columella, should be picked when the moon is waning, while Pliny writes that it 'helps greatly if one picks the grapes *crescente luna*'. Cato advises that you bear in mind the moon when cutting wood: 'All timber to be cut and all stamps grubbed when the moon is waning . . . it should not be cut except from the twentieth to the thirtieth day.'

For Palladius, September, when the moon (Phebus) is waning, is the time to manure your land:

> Thi landes dounge,
> In hilles thicke, in feldes thynne it thrave,
> In wanyng of Phebus be thai to flonge [flung, i.e. spread]

Palladius suggests that you sow peas, and also lupine as a green manure. Sow cress, dill, radishes, parsnips, lettuces, beet, coriander and turnip. When harvesting grapes to keep, choose those which are neither too ripe nor too sour, those which look like bright, hard gems.

Tusser comes out with the following sententious saw:

> Who goeth a borrowing,
> goeth a sorrowing.
> Few lends (but fooles)
> their working tooles.

And, actually, this injunction not to lend your tools is good advice. I once borrowed a spade from our landlord to shovel some snow. I returned it, leaving it in the entrance to one of his sheds. Three weeks later, he knocked on the door and asked for the spade back, with some heat, as it had apparently vanished. We did find the thing in the end, but not before a bit of uncomfortable argy-bargy. Tusser goes on to list what he calls 'husbandlie furniture'— in other words, the tools and other bits of hardware that are needed. September is a good time to inspect and tidy your tools, to clean and mend them. In Tusser's list he includes 'brush sithe and grasse sithe, with rifle to stand', and 'shovel, pickax, and mattock, with bottle and bag'.

Tusser is in favour of going by the moon when gathering fruit: 'The Moone in the wane, gather fruit for to last.' And, as far as bees go, now is the time to gather the honey:

> Place hive in good ayer, set southly and warme,
> and take in due season wax, honie, and swarme.

He says also that you should plant your strawberry plot, and plant gooseberries and raspberries. If you have pigs, then give them apples and acorns:

> Some prowleth for acornes, to fat up their swine,
> for corne and for apples, and al that is thine.

I like the use of the word 'prowleth' for 'gather', with its suggestion of something a little furtive. Now is the time also to make planks, to be ready in March: 'Now sawe out thy timber, for boord and for pale.'

Evelyn counsels sowing and planting when we are approaching a full moon, as the Romans did, and harvesting while it wanes. As if growing fruit and vegetables weren't difficult enough, without having to worry about the position of the moon to boot. However, he tells us not to worry overmuch about it, and quotes Columella: '*In hac autem Ruris disciplina non desideratur ejusmodi scrupulositas*' (But in this country, such minute exactness is not required).

Evelyn tells us to gather our apples, pears and plums. He says we should sow lettuce, radish, spinach, parsnips, cauliflowers, cab/bages, onions and artichokes. He says also that we ought to plant '*Straw-berries* out of the Woods'– a little Virgilian touch there. Evelyn also remarks that '*Cider-making* continues', and reminds us that now is the time to plant your tulip and daffodil bulbs. Last year, for the first time, I remembered to do this and spring was rendered joyful and colourful as a result. He also warns: 'Cats will eat, and destroy your *Marum-Syriacum* if they come at it, therefore guard it with a *Furs*, or *Holy-branch*.'

September's Merriment

September's principal occasion for merriment was Michaelmas. This was an important feast for medieval Christians. Medieval mer/riment historian Madeleine Cosman tells us that it was celebrated with three Gs: glove, goose and ginger. In the towns, a gigantic glove, ten feet high, was hoisted up by means of a pole on to the roof of a tall building, and this was the sign for the Michaelmas Fair. Merchants local and foreign would descend on the town, and the marketplace would be filled with glassware, jewellery, wines, saddles, swords, tapestries, pitchers, platters, cheeses, vegetables and ponies. The booths and stalls were arranged around the edge of a field or in rows in a hall. There were entertainers and sweet-sellers. This is the kind of fair we should bring back today. I have just had a chat with the landlord of our local pub about putting on a market once a month. The cost per stall would be very low, and it would be a chance for local people to sell their wares. I, for example, could sell books, eggs and excess vegetables from the garden, and maybe honey and jams. Visitors would love it, and it would provide an outlet for produce and other wares, thereby encouraging locals to grow and make stuff at home.

The Michaelmas feast traditionally features roast goose. Skilful cooks would re-feather the bird after cooking, so it would come to the table as if alive, and decorated with the fruits and flowers of the season. In Norfolk, biscuits showing a man riding on a goose would be baked. These were called 'Tatty on a goose'. To accompany the goose, there is a special emphasis on ginger products. Ginger beer and ginger wine are served, as well as gingerbread, ginger snaps and ginger cake. Perhaps ginger was important because it was considered good for stomach and chest illnesses.

Michaelmas wakes and revels continued into the nineteenth century. The Bunbury Wake of 1808 boasted the following amusements:

> . . . pony and donkey-racing; wheelbarrow, bag, cock and pig racing; archery, singlestick, quoits, cricket, football, wrestling, bull and badger baiting, dog-fighting, goose-riding, bumble-puppy . . . dipping, mumbling, jawing, grinning, whistling, jumping, jingling, skenning, smoking, stalling, knitting, bobbing, bowling, throwing, dancing, snuff-taking, pudding-eating . . .

Such rumbustious Georgian village revels were undermined by the later Temperance movement and the growing concern over cruelty to animals. Observers were often horrified, too, by the drinking and the violence. But still make sure that you throw a big feast at some point in September, and hold a Michaelmas fair in your area. Eat goose. Dance a caper and eat sweetmeats.

September's Calendar

1 September: Kalends and the Feast of St Giles, patron saint of the
disabled.

13 September: The Ides of September. A big feast was held in Rome,
and no political business was to be carried out; there was no voting.
The festival Lectisternium was held, in honour of Jupiter, Juno and
Minerva. So this would be a good date to throw a feast in your nearest
village hall.

21 September: St Matthew's Day.

23 September: Autumnal equinox. The nights from now are longer than
the days.

29 September: Michaelmas. St Michael is the chief of the angels. The
equivalent pagan figure is Gwynn ap Nudd, lord of the underworld.

CHAPTER TEN

October

Brew Beer

Nunc te, Bacche, canam

[Now I sing of you, O Bacchus]
— *Georgics*, Book II, l. 2

BEER and wine gladden the hearts of men. I sing their praises, and indeed I don't know how I would live without them. They are truly gifts from the gods. They cure our sorrows; they make life bearable. In this it seems that Virgil would concur, and here are the lusty lines that open the second book of the *Georgics*:

> *Huc, pater o Lenaee (tuis hic omnia plena*
> *muneribus, tibi pampineo gravidus autumno*
> *floret ager, spumat plenis vindemia labris),*
> *huc, pater o Lenaee, veni nudataque musto*
> *tingue novo mecum dereptis crura cothurnis.*

[Come, Father of the Winepress: yours are the gifts that abound all around; for you blossoms the field teeming with the harvest of the vine, and the vintage foams in the brimming vats. Come, Father of the Winepress, strip off your buskins and with me plunge your naked legs in the new must.]

Ah, those were the days! When we stripped off our buskins and plunged our naked legs in the new must (that is, the unstrained grape juice)! And, with any luck, performed Bacchic rites with Sabine maidens. What glorious sensuality! Truly husbandry is the noblest and most pleasure-giving of all the arts, and wine and beer are rightly put at the centre of the thrifty household by all our great authorities on husbandry, from Columella to Seymour. Indeed, the first thing the first wine grower did was get drunk:

Noah, a tiller of the soil, was the first to plant the vine. He drank some of the wine, and while he was drunk, lay uncovered in his tent.

It would seem to be a very wise idea to learn how to make your own booze, as not only will the quality be good but it will save you a fortune. Healthy, too: Noah lived to be 950. Roman and Greek households made their own wine. Socrates discusses the subject in the *Oeconomicus* of Xenophon, and Cato's *De Agricultura* offers a number of recipes for wine. Socrates, I should add, is no libertine, and indeed counsels against fleeting pleasures such as 'gambling and consorting with bad companions'. He says that such pursuits are 'really pains concealed beneath a thin veneer of pleasures'. And Columella goes into great detail on how to make wine. What the recipes and guidelines appear to have in common is that they do not use yeast: the grape juice ferments naturally, and then, as now, the magic ingredient in wine-making is time. Columella argues that the best wine is the simplest:

We regard as the best wine any kind which can keep without any preservative, nor should anything at all be mixed with it by which its natural savour would be obscured; for that wine is most excellent which has given pleasure by its own natural quality.

However, Columella also writes that a nice sweet wine can be made by adding crushed iris:

The following is the way to make sweet wine. Gather the grapes and spread them out in the sun for three days; on the fourth day at noon tread the grapes while still warm; remove the must from the untrodden grapes, that is the must which has flowed into the must-vat before it has been squeezed into the wine press and, when it has ceased to ferment, add well-crushed iris, but not more than an ounce of it to fifty sextarii [a sextarius was roughly one pint] and pour off the wine after straining it free from dregs. This wine will be pleasant to the taste and will keep in good state and is wholesome for the body.

While Columella does mention the joys of drinking 'foaming beakers of Pelusian beer', you will search in vain for beer recipes in the Greek and Roman farming books. Indeed, it was common for beer to be despised by the Greeks and Romans as a barbarian's drink (even though beer-making goes back to the civilized Sumerians and Egyptians). Beer deadened the intellect whereas wine enlivened it. Tacitus mentions beer as a favourite of the bellicose Germans, and Pliny writes disapprovingly of beer-drinking in France and Spain:

> The natives who inhabit the west of Europe have a liquid with which they intoxicate themselves, made from corn and water . . . so exquisite is the cunning of mankind in gratifying their vicious appetites that they have thus invented a method to make water itself produce intoxication.

Roman historians also mention that the Britons in the south at the time of the invasion brewed ale from barley and wheat. William of Malmesbury informs us that the English at the time of Henry II were addicted to drinking, and that the monasteries were world famous for their ales. Beer, then, was a central part of English life in the Middle Ages, and indeed it still is. The central difference between medieval beer and today's is that medieval beer was not flavoured with hops. In fact, beer writer Stephen Harrod Buhner suggests that hops were deliberately introduced for their soporific effect on the workers: hopped beer ensured that they went to sleep early, whereas pre-hop beers were more energizing and led to late-night revels and mystical communion. Hops were introduced to England from Flanders in 1525. Certainly, hopped beer was very common by

Tusser's time. He includes directions on keeping a hop-yard in the ideal small farm.

The medievals continued the tradition of wine-making in October, and calendar scenes for October show men pressing grapes with their feet and making barrels. Sometimes more advanced technology is on show: the Flemish 'Golf' Book of Hours shows a group of workmen busy pressing the wine using a giant press with a screw while noblemen with swords at their side sip the juice. This machine-made wine, though – the *vin de presse* – was always considered inferior to the wine made by foot – the *vin de goutte*. A picture of the wine market at Bruges shows a giant man-powered crane lifting barrels on and off waiting boats, and this image was produced, one imagines, partly to show off to the world what advanced technology Flanders had invented.

The *Kalender of Shepherdes* celebrates October as the month to make booze or, as the medieval phrase had it, 'all maner wyne to presse and claryfy':

> Among the other October I hyght
> Frende unto vynteners naturally
> And in my tyme Bachus is redy dyght
> All maner wyne to presse and claryfy
> Of which is sacred as we se dayly
> The blyssed body of Cryst in flesshe and blode
> Whiche is our hope/refeccyon/and fode.

And here we see the rather wonderful link between the sensual pleasure of wine and the worship of Christ. There seems no contradiction for this medieval Christian between drinking deep of Bacchus and religious devotion.

Now, the most ancient of all fermented drinks is probably mead, and that simply means wine made from honey. I understand from anthropologists that hunter-gatherers would have got drunk on honey wine. The simplest way to make mead is to mix honey with water and then just leave it. The yeasts in the air will come along and the honey water will begin to ferment. Your wine will start to bubble. Magically, intoxicating alcohol is formed under your very eyes. Buhner says that mead-making sprang up all over the world in far-flung cultures which would have had no method of communicating with each other:

> What seems clear is that human knowledge of fermentation arose independently throughout human cultures, that each culture attributed its appearance to divine intervention, and that its use is intimately bound up with our development as a species.

As in so many other areas of life, the simple process of making wine, and the slightly more complex process of making beer, has been taken away from us by big business. Most of us would not dream of making our own booze. But to do so is liberating and could save you money. I recently met a gent at the bar at a festival. He sported a generous moustache, a top hat and a blue velvet jacket. He was clearly, then, a free man. He expressed shock at the high prices the bar was charging and commented that he didn't generally pay for booze, as he made it himself. He said that the beer he made was easily the equal of a good ale made by a small brewery. And the cost was tiny: 'How does five pence a pint sound to you?' he said. Wine-making, he said, is even easier. And, furthermore, he said he made his own spirits, and that excited me, because this is illegal: the state wants to hang on to the tax it charges on strong booze. However, we should, I suppose, rejoice that it is not illegal to make your own beer and wine.

Probably the most persuasive writer when it comes to beer and its manufacture in the home is William Cobbett. He felt that good strong beer kept the English labourer healthy and happy, and that everyone should learn how to make it, because, he wrote, 'competence is the foundation of happiness.' Cobbett wanted labouring families to stop drinking tea, which he viewed as 'an enfeebler of the frame', and get back into drinking good old English beer made at home. In his time, which was around 1820, Cobbett writes that the people:

> . . . still drink beer, but in general it is the brewing of common brewers, and in public houses, of which the common brewers have become the owners, and have thus, by the aid of paper money, obtained a monopoly in the supplying of the great body of people with one of those things which, to the hard-working man, is almost a necessary of life.

Motivated by these thoughts, Cobbett set down precise instructions for brewing beer at home in *Cottage Economy*.

One English drink which is as great as beer, and far easier to make, and which is curiously neglected by Cobbett, is cider. John Evelyn tells his gardeners to make cider, as well as perry. As with all wines, the preparation process is quite simple, and the key ingredients are the magic of fermentation and time. The word 'cider' derives very simply from the Latin *sicera*, meaning strong drink. Like beer, its production has been monopolized by a few gigantic companies making a very poor product indeed. But making your own cider and perry is romantic and easy. The names of the old varieties are often very pretty, and I'd like to list here the apple varieties that were recommended as particularly good for cider production in the Herefordshire area by a committee invented for the purpose in

1899: Old Foxwhelp, Cherry Pearmain, Cowarne Red, Dymock Red, Eggleton Styre, Kingston Black, Skyrme's Kernel, Spreading Redstreak, Cherry Norman, Royal Wilding, Handsome Norman and Strawberry Norman. A 1910 article on cider recommends the following apple varieties in Devon: Hangdowns, Fair Maid of Devon, Woodbine, Duck's Bill, Bottle Stopper, Golden Ball and, of course, the wonderful Slack-my-Girdle. Those names alone should be sufficient inducement to start making cider.

For those taking their first steps in the world of husbandry, then the simplest booze to make would be cider or wine, and good wine can be made from elderberries or parsnips.

My Own Attempts to Make Booze

Sloe Gin

The easiest booze to make, since it is not really 'making' booze at all, is sloe gin. Collect a load of sloes from the hedgerows and mix them with a bottle of gin and lots of sugar in a demijohn. Leave until Christmas, or the following Christmas, and you have a delicious flavoured spirit. It can also be made with vodka. (Can I say here that I think the demijohn is a thing of beauty. These satisfyingly shaped glass bottles hold, typically, one gallon or five litres of liquid, although there are bigger sizes. Sitting in the corner of the kitchen, they make a pleasant sight, and the knowledge that they contain a delicious intoxicating liquid only adds to the pleasure.)

Beer

I was determined to make beer, both because, until relatively recently, most households in Blighty did make their own, and also because I stood to save lots of money. But I was put off by Cobbett's instructions in *Cottage Economy*. Even his list of equipment is daunting, although it is fascinating because it reveals that home brewing (like home baking) was in earlier times done on a far larger scale than it is today. This is presumably because households were more populous:

FIRST: a copper that will contain forty gallons at least; for, though there be but thirty-six gallons of small beer, there must be space for the hops, and for the liquor that goes off in steam. SECOND: a mashing tub, to contain sixty gallons . . . THIRD: an underbuck or shallow tub to go under the mash-tub, for the wort to run into when drawn from the grains. FOURTH: a tun-tub, that will contain thirty gallons, to put the ale into work, the mash-tub, as we shall see, serving as a tun-tub for the small beer. Besides these, a couple of coolers, shallow tubs, which may be the heads of wine-butts, or some such things, about a foot deep, or if you have four it may be as well, in order to effect the cooling more quickly.

Well, it seemed to me that a better idea would be to go down to the homebrew shop and buy one of those kits, and this I did. The principle of these kits seems to be that you pour a can of gloop into a big bucket and mix it with water and yeast. You then leave it for ten days in a warm place then siphon the mixture into bottles and leave them for a few weeks. At the end of this process, you should have forty bottles of delicious beer at a cost of a third of the retail price. This is the theory.

The practice was rather different. The mixing of the gloop with water and yeast seemed to go off without incident. The mixture bubbled and frothed, and it smelt faintly of beer. But the siphoning process was hell. First, being of unscientific mind, I had failed to realize that the bucket being siphoned from must be placed on a higher level than the bottles being siphoned to. So this process occasioned much spitting and cursing, during which I had the time to taste the beer that I had made. It was a watery concoction with a vague hint of yeast. But I told myself that this was not the final product, so I should be patient. Eventually, I got the hang of siphoning, and can report that it is good fun. The problem was that there was now beer all over the floor. Next came the process of capping the forty bottles. I had bought forty flat bottle-tops and a capper for the purpose. You hit the capper with a hammer, and the bottle-top gradually closes around the neck. Now maybe I was doing it wrong, but each bottle-top seemed to require about forty blows with the hammer. After a while, I became impatient and hit the capper harder. This smashed the bottle, sending a shard of glass into my hand and a bottle's worth of beer all over the table and the floor. I was now covered in sweat, blood and beer, and I still had a lot of capping to go. Still, it would all be worth it when I drank my own homebrew. When the job was finally finished, I put the bottles into a crate and stored them in the dairy, thinking all the time of that line from Edward Lear's 'The Jumblies':

> And they bought a Pig, and some green Jack-daws
> And a lovely Monkey with lollipop paws
> And forty bottles of Ring-Bo-Ree.

Maybe I should call my beer Ring-Bo-Ree rather than a more conventional name like Tom's Stout or Hodgkinson's Old Head Banger. As I put my head on the pillow that night, I calculated that my total financial saving was £11.60. Would it be worth the pain and the misery? No. When I opened the bottles two weeks later, the resulting froth was just fizzy yeast water. Just drinkable, but only just. I decided at that point that some things are best left to the experts and went back to buying my Cotleigh Barn Owl with great joy. Two years later, after the memory of the horrors had receded, I had a second attempt at making beer from a kit, and I'm afraid that, again, the result was pretty foul. Really, my lesson is that kits are best avoided, and instead I should take advice from an expert. Book learning and kits don't always cut it. They fill you with hope by telling you that it's easy, and then depress you mightily when you find out that it isn't.

Wine

I, too, can now attest that, far easier than beer-making, is wine-making. The principle in wine-making is that the juice is squeezed from the fruit or vegetable and mixed with water, sugar and yeast (or nothing at all). It is left to ferment in a tub then transferred to demijohns, where it continues to ferment, and where the sediment settles. Finally, the clear wine is transferred to wine bottles and left for six months or a year.

Proper grape wine is still made on a small scale without machinery in French households. One of the freshest and most delicious red wines I have tasted was made by my literary agent Cat and her French partner Bernard in Provence. And they make the wine in true Virgilian manner, stripping off their buskins and crushing the grapes with their feet. Bernard calls it *vin de garage*, and here is roughly how they do it, according to Cat:

Bernard says the best method of picking grapes is by hand, and the best way to crush them is with your feet (feet are supple and you can feel the grapes with your toes). Then, with nothing else added, the juice is put in a great big wooden barrel and left until fermentation starts (approximately two to four days). After that, you get back into the barrel, totally naked this time, and turn everything over.

And you continue to do this twice a day, morning and evening, until the fermentation is finished – approximately two weeks or so. Then you leave it for two or three months to macerate, sniffing it every day to check it smells *franchement* [good], and hoping it's not turned to vinegar. Then you let the juice out of the bottom of the barrel and press the rest in your *pressoir*. Then you put it in your Marie-Jeanne [great big glass bottle], leave it until the spring and then put it in bottles in summer. There are various things that need doing in the meantime, such as airing the wine, etc., but that's roughly it. Ready to drink after a year. Very delicious!

Now, I'm not saying that we should all start making wine in this manner. Clearly, Bernard is an expert, and although the process may seem simple, he is drawing on years and possibly generations of experience. What is fascinating, though, is that the Old World belief in the superiority of handmade wine with no preservatives held by Columella and the medievals persists to this day.

For the English husbandman, I think it is better to buy your grape wine, and make your own wine from parsnips or elderberries. These two wines are considered the best by John Seymour and Jocasta Innes, our most excellent authorities. We followed the recipe in Jocasta's *Country Kitchen* book and most of the work was done by WWOOFers. Laura and Matt came to stay with us under the scheme, and they got lots done. They scrubbed and peeled eight pounds of parsnips from the garden then boiled them up with a gallon of water. After this, the mixture was allowed to drip through a jelly bag into a big plastic fermenting bucket. This parsnip juice was mixed with lemon juice, tepid water, sugar and yeast. The resulting must was left for ten days in the bucket to ferment. Each day, I stirred the bubbling, frothy mixture. We then poured it into demijohns which were fitted with airlocks. The wine is now sitting in the kitchen. It is nearly clear, and when it is completely clear, we will siphon it into bottles and store it somewhere cool for six months. In this way, we will have made about twelve litres – sixteen bottles – of very cheap and we hope very delicious parsnip wine.

Cider

I have not yet made cider, but my friend and fellow husbandman Gavin Pretor-Pinney, he of the clouds and waves books, has done. It is not just a matter of hurling a few apples into a cider press. There is a lot of work involved, and he says that you should gather a large group of friends together, because this will lighten the load and because cider-making is customarily a communal activity. Gavin says that the UK apple-preserving society Common Ground is to be commended for its work on apples and orchards, and for introducing an Apple Day to the UK in October. Gavin mentions a few of the delightfully named varieties of cider apple, such as Wear and Tear, Sheep's Nose and Poor Man's Profit. Gavin followed the instructions in *Real Cider Making on a Small Scale* by Michael J. Pooley and John Lomax. He made his cider in October, opened it in February and says it was delicious.

Another great husbandman, Graham Burnett, has also made cider with great success. He says the palaver comes in preparing the apples to be juiced but that, after that, the process is simplicity itself: 'You just leave it!' he says. You do, however, really need a cider press. Graham bought one and says that it was money well spent, since now he can make his own booze.

A Final Cautionary Note

Now, let us remember that country life is not free of worry. There are many tasks to carry out, things can easily go wrong, and you may find that the new stresses are equivalent to the kind of stress that nine-to-five work might bring. This is not a new observation. There is a wonderful essay by Dr Johnson, *Rambler* number 51, entitled 'The Employments of a Housewife in the Country'. The essay purports to be written by a young lady of fashion called Cornelia. She goes to visit her aunt in the countryside and is surprised that, 'instead of the leisure and tranquility which a rural life always promises', she finds 'a confused wildness of care and a tumultuous hurry of diligence'.

Cornelia goes to bed early because the household has to rise early 'to make cheesecakes'. In her bedroom are 'large sieves of leaves and flowers that covered two-thirds of the floor, for they intended to distil them when they were dry, and they had no other room that so conveniently received the rising sun'. Cornelia discovers that her aunt, whom she christens Lady Bustle, is obsessed by 'pickles and conserves'. And Cornelia notices that her aunt's creative country life seems as full of care as the city life:

> While her artificial wines are fermenting, her spirits are disturbed with the utmost restlessness and anxiety. Her sweetmeats are not always bright, and the maid sometimes forgets the just proportion of salt and pepper, when venison is to be baked. Her conserves mould, her wines sour, and pickles mother [oxidize]; and, like all the rest of mankind, she is every day mortified with the defeat of her schemes and the disappointment of her hopes.

October's Husbandry

Varro advises that the following operations be carried out at this time of year: 'Planting of lilies and crocuses . . . from the beginning of the west wind to the rising of Arcturus, it is proper to transplant from the nursery wild thyme . . . dig new ditches, clear old ones, prune vineyards and orchards.'

Palladius advises dunging your land. He also writes many lines on vine and olive husbandry, including the direction to put six pounds of goat's dung on every olive tree. This is the time also to transplant the leeks: 'Nowe leek ysave in veer transplanted be.' If you forget to 'ysave' your leeks earlier in the year, you can cheat by buying little leek plants from the nursery, or scrounging them from a better organized local gardener.

For Tusser, October is very much the month for sowing wheat, but, he writes, sometimes you should wait until Hallowe'en:

> Greene rie in September when timely thou hast,
> October for wheat saving calleth as fast.
> If weather will suffer, this counsell I give,
> Leave sowing of wheat before Hallowmas eve.

Dead cattle should be burned or buried and not allowed to rot, for:

> Such pestilent smell of a carrenly thing,
> to cattle and people great peril may bring.

At home we have found that the ferrets have been useful when it comes to dead animals: they love flesh, and so if we find dead chickens or mice or rats, we chuck them into the ferret cage.

Sloes, the fruit of the blackthorn, should be gathered for their medical properties:

> By thend of October, go gather up sloes,
> have them in a readiness plenty of thoes,

And keep them in bedstraw, or still on the bow,
to staie both the flixe of thyself and thy cow.

A nineteenth-century commentator, Mavor, adds: 'They are an excellent and cheap remedy for laxity of the bowels, in men and cattle, if judiciously used.'

Evelyn tells us to make booze: 'Make *Winter Cider*, and *Perry*' and also tells us to have a good tidy-up:

It will now be good to Beat, Roll, and Mow *Carpet-walks*, and *Camomile*; for now the ground is supple, and it will even all inequalities. Finish your last *Weeding* &c. . . .

Sweep, and cleanse your *Walks*, and all other places from *Autumnal leaves* fallen, lest the *Worms* draw them into their holes, and foul your *Gardens* &c.

Cobbett is as busy as ever, at least in his supervision of his team of gardeners:

Sow a few mazagan beans, cress, white coss lettuces in frames for spring planting, and plant the principal crop of cabbages for spring, lettuces, coleworts, celery . . . finish taking up and housing potatoes, the same of carrots, salsafy, sorzenara, shelter seedling cauliflowers from frost, or they will be *black-shanked* . . .

Transplant young fruit trees; plant stocks of all kinds as soon as the sap is down. Apples and pears, and all winter-keeping fruit, must not be delayed gathering beyond this month.

For October, Seymour has only one instruction: 'Sow your broad beans.' He adds: 'Most books recommend sowing them in spring –

we never do. Sow them in the spring and the aphids will eat them. Sow them in October and you will have fine, healthy plants that will laugh at the aphids and give you a heavy crop.'

In my experience, it doesn't seem to make much difference either way: some years I have sown broad beans in October or November, and some years in February or March. Still, it can't be a bad idea to sow in October, because that means one less job in the spring. I am generally lazy and wait till March, but my slackness should not excuse yours.

October's Merriment

As this is the month that signals our entrance into winter, it is a time for light and warmth, hence the bonfires. Trick-or-treating is related to the earlier custom of 'souling'. Children would walk from door to door, singing and begging for soul cakes. (Now, of course, Hallowe'en is another opportunity for unscrupulous merchants to make money from selling plastic tat.) Here is a souling rhyme that you can all chant together:

> Souling, souling, for soul cakes we go,
> One for Peter, one for Paul,
> Three for him who made us all.
> If you haven't got a cake, an apple will do,
> If you haven't got an apple, give a pear or two.
> If you haven't got a pear then God bless you.

Flames are the order of the day, as Madeleine Cosman writes in *Medieval Holidays and Festivals*: 'Flames are thought to welcome good spirits and prevent evil ones from coming near, so every table has a

Jack O' Lantern.' In the old days, a turnip or squash would have been used for the lantern. Now, of course, the pumpkin does the job.

One game is to re-create the court of King Crispin, who is the patron saint of cordwainers, shoemakers who work with the finest leather (the word is derived from 'cordovan', leather produced in Córdoba, Spain). One guest dresses up as a king while the others wear purple baldrics, each with a small gold boot painted on it.

The day to throw a feast is, then, 31 October. Go souling early on, break out the cider, perry and beer, play some games and sing some songs. Worship the worthy apple, the grape of Britain. End with a procession, with each guest holding a candle stuck in a shiny apple. Bow to King Crispin, and leave your candles burning to scare away evil spirits, pray for the dead and cheer your good souls.

October's Calendar

11 October: Meditrinalia, Roman feast day, a harvest thanksgiving.

25 October: Feast day of St Crispin, as mentioned in Shakespeare's *Henry V.*

31 October: Hallowe'en, the evening before All Hallows Day, which is when we remember the dead. Hallowe'en marked the end of the year in the ancient Celtic calendar and was marked by the feast of Samhain, or summer's end. The departure of summer is echoed in the Roman myth of Astrae, goddess of October. Daughter of Zeus, she lived on the earth among the humans during the Golden Age, but she retreated to the upper world when civilization began to degenerate.

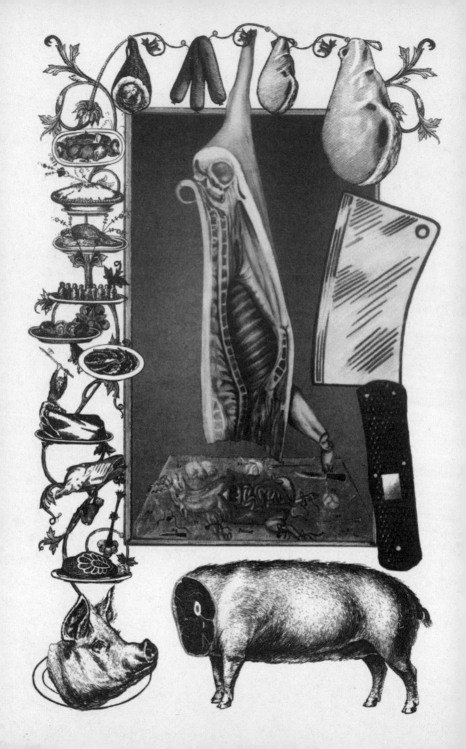

CHAPTER ELEVEN

November

Kill Pig

At Martynesmasse I kylle my swine

– Medieval verse (traditional)

ALL THE authorities are agreed: November is the month for killing the pig. The images for November in the medieval calendars abound with porkers. The Vienna calendar of 837 shows a man wearing a delightful blue smock thrusting some sort of lance into a pig's face. In the illustration for November in the frescoes in San Isidoro in León, Spain, from around 1130, a jolly peasant has grabbed a pig by its ear and is about to knock it on the head with a hammer. There is a cloister boss (that is, a sort of ornamental stud) in Pamplona cathedral, built in the fourteenth century, which shows a woman holding an axe with which she is about to strike poor piggy down. *Les Très Riches Heures du Duc de Berry* spares us the killing scene, and instead November's image features a swineherd knocking acorns out of oak trees for a group of hungry hogs. The Bedford Hours of 1425 shows a bearded peasant with red hood, blue tunic and white apron about to bring a gigantic hammer down on the head of an unsuspecting pig. The hammer blow or the strike from the axe stuns the pig, after which its throat is cut.

Other calendars offer scenes of pigs being butchered. Flemish calendars of a more urbane nature show city-based pig markets in November. And paintings by Brueghel commonly depict peasants cutting a pig's throat and collecting the blood to make blood pudding. Bede called November 'blod-monath' (blood month).

The poets write of pigs. For the wonderful John Clare in his *Shepherd's Calendar*, first published in 1827, as well as November being the month of mist and the 'melancholy crow', pigs are also given a mention:

> The hog starts round the stye and champs the straw
> And bolts about as if a dog was bye.

Pig-killing was going on in Ancient Greece and Rome as well. Varro tells us that pigs were sacrificed on all sorts of occasions: 'Pigs are sacrificed at the initial rites of Ceres . . . [and] when a treaty is made, a pig is killed . . . at the beginning of the marriage rites of ancient kings and eminent personages in Etruria, the bride and groom, in the ceremonies which united them, first sacrificed a pig.'

Varro tells a fascinating tale about a very fat pig: 'I recall that I went to look at a sow which was so fat that not only could she not rise to her feet, but actually a shrew-mouse had eaten a hole in her flesh, built her nest, and borne her young.'

Now that *is* fat.

Why Keep Pigs?

Cobbett, our favourite liberty-loving Englishman, was of course a great supporter of the backyard pig for the cottager. Already, in 1820, as a result of industrialization, people were giving up the age-old practice of pig-keeping, which was why Cobbett felt that it was his duty to reskill the people. As he writes in *Cottage Economy*:

A couple of flitches [salted and cured sides of hog] of bacon are worth fifty thousand Methodist sermons and religious tracts. The sight of them upon the rack tends more to keep a man from poaching and stealing than whole volumes of penal statutes, though assisted by the terrors of the hulks and the gibbet. They are great softeners of the temper, and promoters of domestic harmony.

Be careful, though, warns Cobbett. The Methodist parson, a type for whom Cobbett reserved a particular loathing, will pay a surprise visit at pig-killing time, and you will feel honour-bound to give him some of your best bacon: 'Upon what, then, do these modern saints, these evangelical gentlemen, found their claim to live on the labour of others?'

The technique was to buy a three, or four-month-old pig in March. In those days, this would have cost fifteen shillings; today it will be something like £30. The pig should be fed on milk and scraps, apples and acorns, so the cost of keeping it should be pretty low. Hogs produce useful manure, too.

The unromantic Cobbett does not write of the pleasures of the pig, his happy countenance and affectionate and amusing ways. And neither does John Seymour, who nevertheless has very good advice on feeding and killing, and makes the following useful remarks on pigs and waste:

> Always keep a pig bucket in the scullery. When we have a pigless period we don't know what to do. What do we do with all that lovely greasy rich washing up water? Criminal to throw it down the sink. What do we do with the celery tips, the potato peelings, the carrot tops, the waste food? Out in the garden what do we do with the pea and bean haulms, the sweet corn tops, the scythed nettles, the pulled out weeds?

When killing time comes, it is more humane, writes Seymour, to kill the pig at home with a .22 rifle than to send it to the abattoir: 'The .22 is by far the kindest way to kill a pig. One moment he is happily eating – the next moment he is in Heaven.'

My Own Pig-keeping Experiences

Well, it was with all this in mind – the traditional importance of the pig to the smallholder's life, the fun of keeping them, the cost savings, the delicious meat, the animal-welfare issue – that Victoria and I embarked on our first and (thus far) only pig-keeping adventure. Read on and be warned: do not make the mistakes I made.

In April one year we bought two young male pigs from a neighbour. They were saddlebacks, the black pig with a white stripe round the middle. Young pigs are today called weaners; in earlier times, as noted above, they were called 'gruntlings', as in the following lines from 1686:

> But come, my *gruntling*, when thou art full fed,
> Forth to the butcher's stall thou must be led.

At first our gruntlings went unnamed, because we had been warned that we would become attached to them if they were named, and therefore it would be traumatic to kill them (this turned out not to be the case). We later named them Gnasher and Rasher, the names coming from my son Arthur's *Beano* comic.

The pigs lived on a bit of spare ground at the back of our neighbour's house, which she kindly let us use. This was an area about thirty feet square, overgrown with thistles and nettles, and with a lean-to outhouse open at one end. The space was perfect.

The pigs ate a mixture of bought-in food and scraps from the kitchen and garden. Pigs will eat virtually anything, hence their role as rubbishmen in the medieval cities. In Siena in the thirteenth century, for example, citizens competed for the contract to be the rubbishman, and keep pigs and their manure into the bargain. A 1296 document says that the highest bidder will be able to keep 'a sow and four piglets so that they can gather and eat all the spilled cereal'.

I have now discovered that under UK law pigs must not be given any catering waste, and that includes any food that has even passed through the kitchen. Our government says that this new law is needed as a protection against foot-and-mouth disease. Whether or not this is really true, and indeed the science appears to be fairly poor, as it is well known that porcine species cannot catch foot-and-mouth, it has the effect of making pig-keeping into more of a professional than an amateur affair.

So, instead of giving your pig all your waste food, which is one of the primary purposes of having one, under this silly law, you have to buy food for it. Pig nuts, as the bought-in dried food is known, are all very well, but they must be so boring for the pigs: what's for dinner? Pig nuts. What's for lunch? Pig nuts again. And the effort you have made to remove yourself from the system a little bit, by using waste creatively and usefully and contributing to your own supply of food rather than just buying everything you need, is thwarted yet again.

Upon being placed in their new home, Gnasher and Rasher diligently set about eating it: soon there were paths through the nettles and thistles, and after a month the overgrown yard had been converted into a well-dug and manured mudpatch. In fact, pigs can be used very effectively to clear new ground for vegetable growing.

The pigs were delightful creatures and very easy to look after. We fed them once in the morning and once in the evening. We used an old butler's sink for their water, since they would turn over anything less heavy than that with their mighty snouts. What the pigs loved more than anything else was being scratched and, after being fed, they would sit down on their back legs, like a dog, while we scratched their backs (while surreptitiously trying to ascertain how much fat was on the meat).

When feeding your pigs, the aim is to create meat with a certain amount of fat on it. The pig in Cobbett's day would probably have had two to four inches of fat, whereas the preference today, with our anti-fat prejudices, is for half an inch or less. Victoria and I like fatty bacon, so when October came around, with just a few weeks to go until killing time, we started to feed our pigs up. We gave them, for example, about two hundred apples from a tree on our landlord's land. We gave them as many acorns as we could find. Every day, they drank all the water I carried from the stream that runs by our house. 'They'll be good eating, I expect,' our landlord said. They were certainly well-fed pigs, they had a varied diet, and our landlord was right: they gave us excellent meat: sweet and tender, and with plenty of tasty fat.

Here is a little rhyme I wrote about the pigs:

> Our gruntlings ate a patch of weeds and greens.
> And every acorn carried back from walks,
> The shells of peas, old turnip tops and beans,
> One hundred apples and potato stalks.
> They drank the fresh cold water which I brought
> They snorted, dug and slept but could not talk,
> We scratched their bristly backs and watched them snort.
> Their fun-filled lives resulted in great pork.

Yes, I know it's not quite Keats or Virgil, but it's a start. And it does scan and rhyme fairly well: just look at those iambic pentameters and the A/B A/B rhyme scheme.

We bought two pigs partly, of course, because we would get more meat that way, but partly also because animals like company.

A Digression on the Innate Sociability of Beasts

On our smallholding in North Devon, we have noticed that if animals have no creature of their own species with whom to socialize, then they will hang out with other animals. For example, when the pony escapes, she will be found three fields away, happily grazing in the middle of a group of cows. During the time we had our pigs, our chickens were being picked off by the fox, who came each afternoon at four o'clock and brazenly carried away an egg-layer in his mouth. Finally, we were left with one solitary chicken, a lovely young cockerel, a Dorking, who had been born on the farm. With no chickens to consort with, he would instead go and sit on the gate to the pigs' area, just to be near another warm-blooded creature. It was a touching sight. But then, alas, Mr Fox took him away as well.

The inter-species sociability of animals was a phenomenon noted by Gilbert White in *The Natural History of Selborne*. In a letter written on 15 August 1775, he writes of the 'wonderful sociality' in the 'brute creation', and tells the following rather beautiful and touching tale:

Even great disparity of kind and size does not always prevent social advances and mutual fellowship. For a very intelligent and observant person has assured me that, in the former part of his life, keeping but one horse, he happened also on a time to have but one solitary hen. These two incongruous animals spent much of their time together in a lonely orchard, where they saw no creature but each other. By degrees an apparent regard began to take place between these two sequestered individuals. The fowl would approach the quadruped with notes of complacency, rubbing herself gently against his legs; while the horse would look down with satisfaction, and move with the greatest caution and circumspection, lest he should trample on his diminutive companion. Thus, by mutual good offices, each seemed to console the vacant hours of the other.

It was, as Groucho Marx might have said, nothing serious, a poultry affair.

At one stage, we had two semi-wild rabbits living in the yard. They were pet bunnies who had escaped but still lived around the house. Before dark, I would go out to feed the hens. When I threw out their feed, not only the hens but also the rabbits and the pony would come over and share the feast. Such harmony between species was a delight to see.

Back to the Pigs

Come November, then, it was killing time for the pigs. Persuaded by John Seymour that the humane (and cheaper) way to kill them was at home, we asked a local slaughterman, Peter, to come round. This he did, with our neighbour Paul, who had sold us the weaners.

We drove the pigs into a trailer. Peter brought out a powerful pistol and, while stroking the pigs and chatting to them, put a bullet into their brains. They fell soundlessly to the floor, with just a couple of spasms. It is difficult to describe one's feelings on the killing of such a large sentient creature. It is not a pleasant experience. I felt a huge gratitude towards the pigs. There was a tinge of sadness, to be sure, but this was offset by the knowledge that our pigs had suffered far less than any pig which goes through the normal channels of intensive piggery followed by the slaughterhouse.

The next step was to tie those mighty beasts up by their ankles and cut their throats. This we did, and Victoria, in true medieval style, collected the pigs' blood, which we had to stir and make into blood sausages that very evening. I also made two gigantic liver pâtés that evening.

We cut the heads off, and Peter and Paul eviscerated the animals.

To collect the guts, we used two of those excellent large buckets that are made from old tyres, a very good use for otherwise landfill-destined rubber. I then buried the guts in the vegetable patch. We put two big hooks in the ceiling of the dairy and hung the headless pigs from them. There they stayed for a couple of days. The children spent the killing day with a friend. Delilah had cried when I showed her a dead rat, saying, 'I care for all animals, even rats.' So we thought it best to keep the children away.

Now came the most difficult part of the process – or at least difficult because I made it difficult out of a mixture of stupidity and bad advice. How to remove the bristles? Unlike commercial pigs, our nice rare-breed pigs had thick black bristles growing out of them. They were beautiful in a way, but of course had to be removed. Cobbett did this by burning them off. Seymour scalded his pigs to remove the bristles; in the slaughterhouse, the pigs are dipped into a boiling-hot bath.

Our first attempt was with a wallpaper steamer. The idea here was that the steamer would loosen the bristles, which could then be scraped off with a sharp knife. I did this for about two hours but only managed to de-hair a very small patch of pig. Then I tried using the blowtorch. This created a hell of a stink and was also very slow going. By the following day, I had only removed a tiny fraction of the bristles. I tried lighting them with a match, but this method was not very efficient either. (It was freezing cold in that dairy, by the way.) Next, I got a packet of Bic razors and spent a few hours shaving the pigs.

At this time, we had a Polish woman who came in to help with cleaning once a week. As you might know, the Poles are in general infinitely more capable and practical than us flabby, disempowered Brits, who can barely change a light bulb without calling 'a man' in, let alone process a pig. Well, she witnessed my attempts to debristle the hogs, came into the dairy when it stank of burnt pig hair, saw the puddles of water caused by the steamer and the piles of used disposable razors clogged with black stubble, and she later said to Victoria: 'It make me so sad to see Tom with the pig hairs. My parents, they just throw boiling water over the pig, and the hairs, they come out.' It appeared that either the burning or the scalding approach took only two minutes, whereas I must have been working in this stinking, freezing-cold dairy for about three days, and the pigs were still looking unshaven.

Finally, the pigs were bald enough to butcher. My friend Simon, an excellent chef, came round the next day with some sharp knives and a book on cutting up pigs. We got to work. We set up a giant trestle table in the dairy and, with the book propped open in front of us, started to divide the first pig into joints. Simon knew just what to do, and we worked happily with me as his assistant, and cut up the hams, hands, trotters, hocks, enjoying the experience of filling the house with excellent meat, as Cobbett describes in *Cottage Economy*: 'Souse, griskins, blade-bones, thigh-bones, spare-ribs, chines, belly-piece, cheeks, all coming into use one after the other.' Still, it did take us two days.

Later, Simon said that he'd found out that the mobile butcher charged a tenner and took just forty minutes to joint the meat. Since then, I have seen a proper butcher do it, and he does it with great speed and efficiency. Again, it is a silly mistake for the apprentice husbandman to try to do everything himself. It is far better to hire a professional, who will take an hour to do what takes you two days.

We filled the freezer with joints. I calculated that, at market rates, we had produced about £1,000 worth of the finest organic pig meat you could hope for. My friend the intellectual pig farmer John Mitchinson came to stay for a weekend and brought his sausage-making machine, and we made a range of sausages, using leeks, rosemary and other herbs in the mix. We also made twenty chorizos using smoked paprika and fennel (these turned out to be completely inedible). We bought Jane Grigson's classic book on charcuterie, and John commented that it seemed strange to him that more butchers didn't go in for charcuterie and make delicious hams and sausages. We sank our hams into a rich brine made of real ale and juniper berries, where they remained for two months. We then took it to Victoria's family for Christmas. We laid bacon in salt and put it in wooden boxes. It was quite different from commercial bacon: it was sweeter and more solid tasting. However, it was far too salty. We had salted it for too long. The ribs, on the other hand, tasted fantastic. We made a terrible error, though, and somehow left the freezer switched off all weekend, so the frozen joints became unfrozen. You cannot, of course, refreeze meat, so we distributed the cuts to friends and neighbours.

While the experience had its joyful moments, we definitely took on too much. The helpless city dweller cannot hope to become a farmer overnight. It takes years. And, therefore, all apprentice smallholders need as much help as they can get. Still, I was filled with satisfaction: we had created our own top-quality meat and the whole process had been achieved in the most humane way possible. Our youngest son, Henry, was sad that the pigs had died. But his brother Arthur argued: 'They wouldn't have even existed if we weren't going to kill them!' The pigs did have the best life and best death possible for a gruntling destined to become a porker.

The Authorities Take a Dim View

I was so enthused about the whole pig-keeping experience that, when a newspaper asked whether I would like to contribute a restaurant review, I decided to write about Simon's restaurant, really as an excuse to boast about the pigs. I told the whole story: how we had had them killed at home, and had butchered and processed them ourselves, and how wonderful the whole thing had been. Here we were, living the old English cottager's life as championed by Cobbett! The piece appeared on Sunday two weeks later. Then, the following morning, as I was drinking my tea at the kitchen table, Victoria glanced through the kitchen window and said: 'That man looks like he is about to tell us off.'

I looked up and saw a man with a clipboard closing the garden gate and walking up the path to our front door. He was about sixty, and was wearing a Barbour over a dark office suit. I opened the front door.

'Mr Hodgkinson?'

'Yes. Come in.'

He sat down at the kitchen table and got out his clipboard. On it was a photocopy of my newspaper article, with various chunks highlighted in fluorescent yellow. The man explained that he had come from our local environmental health department. He had read my article and would like to ask us a few questions.

'Have your children eaten any of this meat?'

'No,' said Victoria. 'They didn't like it,' immediately realizing that she had blundered.

The man told us that it was against the law to kill pigs at home. His department had, he said, successfully prosecuted people for this crime.

'I thought we just weren't allowed to sell it,' I countered.

'In our view,' said the pig inspector, 'giving the meat to other people, including friends, neighbours and children, is the same as putting it on the market. The pigs should be killed at the abattoir so we can check that the meat is safe before it is presented for human consumption.'

He said that if I had killed the pig, then I was legally permitted to eat it, but no one else, which is clearly ridiculous.

'But surely our way is more humane?' I said.

'It may be, and I accept that the meat tastes better because there is less adrenalin in it. But we can't have untrained people killing pigs at home. They might do it wrong.'

The fact that a trained chef had processed our pigs, and that he would have spotted immediately if the meat had been diseased, seemed to cut no ice. 'Leave it to the professionals and experts,' seemed to be the message. 'We can't have ordinary people killing pigs at home.'

At this point I became angry.

'Why are you wasting time and money pursuing us when, every day, pigs and chickens live and die in the most appalling conditions? Go and close the people who do that down. We acted humanely.'

I was wondering whether I should have claimed that I was a pre-Reformation Christian, and that my religion stated that I must kill pigs at home. For PC reasons, the ministry cannot condemn killing a pig by bleeding, for example, because that is the Muslim way. Maybe I could play the religious card?

As far as I'm concerned, the real reason why centralized states are against people killing pigs at home is commercial. The health and safety argument is a cover. One of the state's primary roles is to serve large business interests. The religion of growth does not like it when people remove themselves from the system and practise a little self-sufficiency, and its high priests do their best to put you off doing it, with bureaucracy, rules and cost. The practice of cottage pig husbandry, such a central feature of the household economy for so many thousands of years, and still an important feature in some parts of the world today, removes the family from a commercial transaction which contributes to GDP and economic growth. It shrinks the market for pork. A knock-on effect of this is that small abattoirs everywhere are closing down because they cannot afford the full-time veterinary and other costs imposed by the ministry. These costs can only be borne by large slaughterhouses. As a consequence, animals travel along the motorway for hundreds of miles to be killed in gigantic killing factories, clearly an absurd state of affairs. Killing pigs at home, or locally, is sensible. It is an ancient practice. It saves money. It produces a far higher quality product than the dominant system, and it is far kinder to the pig. Therefore we should campaign for the restoration of this very basic old liberty. Smash the system!

The hassle didn't stop there. The man then went round to Simon's restaurant and inspected it, causing a whole lot of stress. He also ticked off our neighbour, Paul, who had helped kill the pig. Although the inspector himself was a bit of a weak character, a little like Mole in *The Wind in the Willows*, there was a faintly threatening tone to his questions. This sort of thing of course is not exactly new: Flora Thompson in *Lark Rise to Candleford* says that 'men from the ministry' would sometimes appear to inspect the backyard pigs.

Keeping a pig has always been a way for the poor man to experience plenty once a year: at pig-killing time, there is an abundance of bacon and pork, with enough to feast on and to give away to the neighbours. Writes Flora Thompson, the pig was a central feature of the household: 'Men callers on Sunday afternoons came, not to see the family, but the pig, and would lounge with its owner against the pigsty door for an hour, scratching piggy's back and praising his points or turning up their own noses in criticism.' A travelling pig killer would be employed: 'The next thing was to engage the travelling pork butcher, or pig-sticker, and, as he was a thatcher by day, he always had to kill after dark, the scene being lighted with lanterns and the fire of burning straw which at a later stage of the proceedings was to singe off the bristles of the victim.'

In *Lark Rise to Candleford*, the killing of the pig would lead to an outbreak of hospitality, as had been the custom for centuries: 'The next day, when the carcass had been cut up, joints of pork were distributed to those neighbours who had sent similar ones at their own pig-killing. Small plates of fry and other oddments were sent to others as a pure compliment, and no one who happened to be ill or down on his luck on these occasions was ever forgotten.'

It is curious that we did exactly the same thing with our pig joints, but quite unself-consciously. Clearly, we were simply following a very natural and very ancient custom, an almost instinctive one but one which has been all but destroyed by the state. It is not completely dead: our farrier keeps pigs, and so do a handful of local smallholders. But they are in a minority, and you can see why: the authorities make it so very difficult for you. What's the point of going through all that hassle, and possibly breaking the law, when you can just pop down to the supermarket? Going back to freedom can be hard and depressing work.

What we need is a new form of licence for a travelling slaughterman and butcher. He or she would go on a course in order that the authorities can be satisfied that he can recognize diseased meat. Then he could happily go round the country killing pigs for husbandmen and reassuring the state that the pork on these remote farms is perfectly safe. The alternative is, of course, for the cottager to kill the pigs at home in secret: after all, how would they find out? Most people are not so stupid as to boast about their pig-killing experiences in a national newspaper. But of course the 'ignore the law' route is not really satisfactory, as it transforms perfectly honourable and responsible people into outlaws. I have set up a little website to gather support on this issue. It is called thislittlepiggie stayedathome.org.

The intrusions by bustling officialdom did not end with the visit from the council man. Other agencies got on my back. I received a letter from David Statham, Director of Enforcement from the Food Standards Agency, the motto of which is 'Safer food, better business.' He expressed his concern that people might copy 'the practices described in your article', as if I had been enthusing about the joys of child sacrifice. Then, a few months later, I had a telephone call from another bureaucrat. She asked what I had done with the entrails of the pigs.

'I can't remember,' I replied. 'I think I threw them away.' In fact, I had buried them in the vegetable patch. I had burned the bones in a giant, crackling, primal bone-fire. That was probably illegal as well. I had stood there throwing the bones on it as the sun set, feeling mighty pagan. I put the skulls on the top of the fire and went to bed. In the morning, I looked out of the window and saw a pig skull sitting on the grass: it had rolled off the fire in the night.

'Well,' said the bureaucrat. 'They should have been collected and taken to a registered incineration facility.'

Yes, I thought. More jobs for the boys. More forms, more driving, more motorway traffic. More spending all round. More growth. I would have had to pay for this service. The costs of the slaughterhouse and the entrails incineration would all cut into the money we were trying to save by keeping our own pigs. No wonder smallholders are put off.

The other thing I noticed over the pig-killing episode was how queasy friends were about the whole thing. In Huxley's *Brave New World* the people are conditioned to hate nature and to be squeamish. A squeamish population is clearly good for GDP and growth, because the people will tend to buy nice clean products wrapped in plastic from the supermarket rather than facing death and blood themselves. And so it is in our society. 'Oh, I couldn't do that,' meat-eating friends would say about our killing experience. They would refuse the meat. But they are happy to buy little pork chops from the sanitized capitalist food outlets. They will eat disgusting bacon from abused pigs but not delicious bacon from a happy pig. Either be a vegetarian, or don't, but don't get on your moral high horse. This squeamishness, in my view, is merely a sign of the most abject submission to state conditioning.

Now, having read the documents sent to me by Mr Statham, which offer a description and interpretation of the legislation surrounding this issue, I've found a paragraph which seems to indicate, in fact, that I have not broken any law. Although the document states: 'It is not . . . lawful for the farmer to supply privately killed meat to the rest of his household,' it also says that this law is only applicable to those species which carry foot-and-mouth disease, i.e. sheep, cows and goats. Pigs, or 'porcine species', are exempt: 'Porcine species, poultry, farmed game species and rabbits are not under SRM [Specified Risk Material] controls and may be supplied by a farmer to the rest of his household.'

It seems, then, that by their own admission, the authorities are wrong, and that you *can* kill your pigs at home, and you can supply the meat to the rest of your household. Just don't sell the meat, and don't report your experiences in wide-distribution media outlets. The best advice really would be to try to get a handle on the law before you go in for pig-keeping. The laws often change, for one thing, and they are certainly open to interpretation. But having closely reviewed the documents, I would say that you are safe to kill, butcher and eat your pigs at home. But you need to get someone in who knows what they are doing.

The Advantages of Keeping Pigs

Well, the advantages are manifold. The meat is better; the pigs are happier; your pork and bacon are far cheaper. You remove yourself from complicity with the really horrifying industrial pig-keeping world, where pigs are kept indoors in tiny cages. The pigs eat all the rubbish and produce manure. They clear ground. They are charming creatures. The whole process is enjoyable, and it is not a burdensome amount of work. Pig husbandry is easier than cow or sheep husbandry. 'Keeping pigs is simplicity itself,' says one farmer neighbour. I would recommend anyone try it who has a bit of land to spare. My friend John shares the job with a neighbour in his village. This means that there is cover when one of you is away or ill. The other great thing is that you can do less or more pig-keeping at different times. To buy weaners, raise them and have them killed is actually only a six- to nine-month commitment. It could very conceivably be done in a suburban garden. Just make sure you are aware of the laws before embarking on pig-keeping.

November's Husbandry

This is the month to cover your vegetable beds with a nice thick layer of old manure and straw. I tend to forget and neglect the garden till March, when I dig and manure it. But this year I am resolved to do things properly. One great advantage of keeping hens is that you have an endless supply of litter which you can spread on the vegetable patch. I throw huge amounts of straw around in the henhouse, and then once a month or so shovel a load of it into the wheelbarrow and dump it either on the compost heap or straight on to the vegetable beds.

Palladius tells us to sow wheat and beans: 'November wol with whete & far be sowe,' he writes, and:

> . . . benes unto great felicitee
> Right fatte or dounged lande thai loveth best.

Wheat would be an excellent money-saving crop to grow: at the time of writing, its price on the commodities market is shooting up. Sow also African and common garlic: 'This Moone Ulpike and Garlic is to sow.' They should be planted four inches apart and, if you want big bulbs, tread down the stalk: 'But forto hede hem greet trede downe the stele.' Plant plums, peaches and pears. Clean the beehives.

Tusser delights in November as pig-killing time:

> At Hallontide, slaughter time entereth in,
> and then doth the husbandman's feasting begin:
> From thence unto Shroftide kill now and then some,
> their offal for houshold the better will come.

Tusser, like Palladius, advises the sowing of garlic and beans. And, he writes, you should dig, manure and mulch the garden:

> If garden requier it, now trench it ye may,
> one trench not a yard from another go lay:
> Which being well-filled with muck by and by,
> go cover with mould for a season to ly.

Sweep your chimneys in order to avoid chimney fires:

The chimney all sootie would now be made cleene,
for fear of mischances, too oftimes seene:
Old chimney and sootie, if fier once take,
by burning and breaking, some mischeefe may make.

Clean your composting loos and bury the muck to fertilize the soil:

Foule privies are now to be clensed and fide
let night be appointed such baggage to hide:
Which buried in garden, in trenches alowe,
shall make very many things better to growe.

This is an idea that is coming back: I have just returned from the Glastonbury music festival, and this year there were more composting loos than ever before. A composting-loo expert gave a talk where he said that all you need is a bucket with a loo seat on it. The human waste – or 'remains of human feasts', as Columella described it – is mixed with organic matter such as woodchips or leaves. Once a week, the bucket is carried to the compost heap, the contents dumped and carefully covered with straw. A year later, it is ready to dig into your garden. Indeed, composting loos were used without any trace of eco-self-consciousness by the residents of Exmoor, where I live, until fairly recently. Families in the thirties would have a dung heap out the back, where all the kitchen and animal waste would go. Ted Lethaby of Exmoor remembers the lavatory arrangements: 'The toilet was up the garden, up the steps at the back of the house, and it was a bucket too. When it was full, it was chucked on to the dung heap as well.' This demonstrates once again that cutting-edge environmental ideas in fact tend to belong to the Old World.

John Evelyn is in a tidying mood: '*Sweep*, and cleanse your *Garden-walks*, and all other places, from *Autumnal* leaves, the last time.' These leaves can be spread over your vegetable patch as a mulch, or put into black plastic sacks to turn into compost. Evelyn recommends watering your plants with 'water mingled with a little *Sheeps*, or *Cow-dung*'. (Again, this is an idea that is often suggested in gardening books as if it were a new innovation.) Like our earlier authorities, Evelyn also suggests sowing beans.

Cobbett in *The English Gardener* is a little more ambitious and also repeats the customary advice: '*Sow* early peas, leeks, beans, radishes . . . Thin lettuces sown last month in frames, sift fine dry mould among them to strengthen them . . . Attend to the grass lawns and verges, sweep up leaves . . . Dig, trench and manure vacant land.'

Seymour gives no directions for the vegetable garden beyond 'muck-carting, digging or ploughing, cleaning up and feasting', and that I think sums up November's principal jobs excellently. This year, as I mentioned earlier, we got two WWOOFers in to spread manure over my vegetable patch.

November's Merriment

The principal party for November is of course Bonfire Night. While Thomas Hardy and other folklorists believed that the custom of November fires pre-dates the bungled attempt to blow up the Houses of Parliament on 5 November 1605, recent scholarship has shown this to be untrue. Ronald Hutton writes: 'There is absolutely no trace of late autumn or early winter bonfires in medieval or Tudor England.' Bonfire Night is a decidedly Protestant invention, he writes, a creation of the New World, and was invented by the MP Sir Edward Montagu in 1606. It has sometimes become excessively rowdy, and it still is a riotous occasion in the Sussex town of Lewes.

There really was, however, much feasting in the Old World on 11 November, or St Martin's Day. Generally, this would be an opportunity for a pork-based meal.

November's Calendar

5 November: Bonfire Night.

25 November: Feast day of St Catherine. Tricks are played. 'Catherine Wheel' was the name given to the rings of fire created by fire jugglers as they twirled their torches (the wagon-wheel chandelier in the medieval feasting hall was also called a Catherine Wheel), after St Catherine of Alexandria, the learned saint who died in the fourth century. She is the patron saint of lawyers, wheelwrights, rope-makers and carpenters, and is particularly revered as a guardian of women, being patron saint also of lace-makers, spinners, unmarried women and female students. The activities around her feast day are called 'Cathernings' so, in November, it is a-Catherning we will go.

CHAPTER TWELVE

December

Feast

Hiems Ignava colono

[Winter is the farmer's lazy time]
– *Georgics*, Book I, l. 299

WINTER is the most feared season in the medieval calendar. One description of a themed fifteenth-century feast has winter as a man 'with his grey locks, feeble and old, sitting on cold, hard stone, niggard in heart, and heavy of cheer'. Therefore it was absolutely imperative to fight the bad weather by making the household warm, cosy and joyful. Calendar scenes for December will often feature cheering images such as bakers taking fresh bread out of the oven, or a chicken being roasted over a roaring fire. In order to keep the dark and the cold out, it was of critical importance to keep a goodly blaze going in the grate.

This is true of the Hodgkinson homestead: living in a house without central heating, we rely completely on the wood-burning stove to keep us warm in winter. Our Exmoor winters can be harsh, and we keep ourselves snug and cheerful with the wood-burner. Just one day without the fire – perhaps I am too lazy to light it – will cast a chilly gloom over the household. The fire keeps winter out.

In the medieval calendars, December is often shown as the month of feasting. A common image is of a nobleman sitting at a trestle table, a companion on either side, and a range of dishes and goblets of wine set before him. In the calendar at San Isidoro, a man is enjoying a feast while warming his feet by a blazing fire. The January illustration in *Les Très Riches Heures* shows the duke enjoying a sumptuous feast while various hangers-on try to curry his favour. The tables generally seem to be covered with white tablecloths, which is always a smart touch. I think a clean white tablecloth is a very simple way to elevate the soul. Feasts and festivals, then, make the hardships that the natural world throws at us easier to bear.

On Christmas, Greatest Feast of the Year

Now the greatest festival of the whole year is of course Christmas. The important thing to remember about Christmas is that, before the Reformation, it really did last twelve days. That was twelve days during which no work was permitted. The fields would be empty and the shops would be shut (our own recently abolished Sunday-trading laws were a relic of the old custom of setting aside certain days for feasting and not for commerce). The feasts were theatrical and lavish, but the food was dainty, in a tapas style, as this typical menu, listing both food and entertainment, from Madeleine Cosman in *Medieval Holidays and Festivals* shows:

Course one: Fruytes melior. Plum, quince, apple plus pear with rosemary, basil and rue in a pastry tart. Instrumental music with lute, viol, Krummhorn, bell and drum.

Course two: St Johns' Urcheon [or 'bread']. Chopped meat formed into the shape of a hedgehog, wrapped in carob pastry. Merlin the magician.

Course three: Almondyn Ayroun. Almond omelette with currants, honey and saffron. Juggler with balls and daggers.

Course four: Saumon Rosted. Roasted salmon in onion and wine sauce. Minstrel's songs.

Course five: Fruytes Royal Rice. Artichoke filled with blueberry rice. Singers of ballads and street cries.

Course six: Aigredouncy. Honey-glazed sliced chicken rolled with mustard, rosemary and pine nut. Dancers perform lively *galliards* and stately *pavanes*.

Course seven: Herb cake. Mood music to represent the four humours.

Course eight: Cheese. Songs for the four temperaments.

Course nine: Dukkes Wynges. Roasted chicken and pheasant
    wings. Sword magic.
Course ten: Elderberry divination cakes. Small crullers in funny
    shapes. Sir Gawain and the Green Knight play.
Course eleven: Circletes y Roundels. Almond spice cakes on
    roundels, platters with words or poems written on them, to be
    sung by guests. Fire juggler.
Course twelve: Parade of the Subtleties. Ceremonial carving
    and eating of sugar and pastry sculptures. Musical instruments
    honouring the season or a special guest. Shawms [loud horns]
    signal the end of the feast.

The food would be eaten with fingers and a knife, the effeminate
fork having yet to be invented. The medievals had finger bowls
filled with scented water with which to wash their hands between
courses. Is it so difficult to imagine re-creating such a feast today, in
the village hall?

A further feature of the Christmas feast would be illusion foods.
We mentioned the hedgehog previously. Birds were another centre-
piece: partridges, pheasants and peacocks would be brought to
the table having been roasted and re-feathered, so that they looked
almost alive. Sometimes their claws and beaks would be painted
with gold. And delicate dishes such as a pie filled with twenty-four
blackbirds, which flew out of the hall when it was opened, really
were set before a king. There was a sense of drama around food
which has nearly (but not completely) vanished in today's utilitarian
times. These days, the only occasion when we tend to let rip as far as
theatrical feasting goes is at weddings. But, before the Reformation,
this sort of playfulness at mealtimes was more common.

Colour was a hugely important part of the medieval feast, and
food dyes were made simply by boiling up leaves with water: red

rose petals for red dye; dandelion for yellow; mint, parsley or spinach for green; violets for lavender.

A Time to Suspend Toil and Play Games

One appealing feature of December is that it seems generally not to be a hard-working month, as the quote from Virgil opening this chapter testifies. There is no work to be done in the fields from now until the middle of January or even February. Christmas is for staying in and for playing games. For Chesterton, in his essay *The Spirit of Christmas* (1929), it was the festival not for hustle and bustle, but to be at home:

> The Christmas season is domestic; and for that reason most people now prepare for it by struggling in tramcars, standing in queues, rushing away in trains, crowding despairingly into tea-shops, and wondering when or whether they will ever get home . . . Now the old and healthy idea of such winter festivals was this; that people being shut in and besieged by the weather were driven back on their own resources.

Chesterton says that it should be a fun-filled but also a creative time of year:

> Christmas might be creative. We are told, even by those who praise it most, that it is chiefly valuable for keeping up ancient customs or old-fashioned games. It is indeed valuable for both those admirable purposes. But in the sense of which I am now speaking it might once more be possible to turn the truth the other way round. It is not so much old things as new things that a real Christmas might create. It might, for instance, create new games,

if people really were driven to invent their own games. Most of the old games began with the use of very ordinary tools or furniture.

This past Christmas, I was sent an excellent book called *Parlour Games for Modern Families*. Written by two Australian journalists, it contains the rules for over a hundred games: card games, word games, pencil and paper games – all costing practically nothing. This has been a great boon, and we loved playing consequences, pontoon, wink murder, and the children particularly enjoyed Mad Scientist, a blindfold game in which the players have morsels of food thrust into their mouths and have to identify what they are eating. I wrote about the book in a newspaper, and it shot to that paper's number-one spot, where it stayed for three weeks. Clearly there is a thirst out there for the old ways.

Astrologically speaking, in December we are in the sign of Sagittarius, which is often shown as a hunting centaur, and there is a lovely picture of a centaur in the Bedford Hours of 1425. He is wearing a red jacket with enormously wide sleeves, lined with white, and his wrists are wrapped in green. One other winter image in a fresco at the Castello del Buonconsiglio in Trento, northern Italy, shows some elegantly dressed lords and ladies pelting snowballs at each other's faces while a poacher with dogs returns from a hunt, a rabbit slung over his back. The emphasis is on keeping warm and eating well.

Our traditional medieval poem of the seasons ends with the couplet:

> At Martynesmasse I kill my swine
> And at Christmas I drynke red wyne.

In the pagan calendar, too, December was a month for the sensual pleasures and for making merry. The first day of the Roman Saturnalia, a decadent festival when slaves became equal with their masters, was 17 December. It was a sort of licensed blow-out. Indeed, the midwinter festival seems to be a common feature of many cultures and religions – pagan, Jewish, Mithraic and Christian – which pegged their feasts around the winter solstice.

Today, Christmas is still the most merry and indeed the most medieval time of year. (I think it is significant that my New World mother does not 'do' Christmas, considering it to be a waste of time and money. She would rather get on with some important work.) When we sit around a table enjoying Christmas dinner, with its dressing up, games, wine and songs, devoting ourselves to play and pleasure, we are afforded a little insight into life in the Middle Ages, that passionate, beauty-filled age. Christmas is decidedly on the side of the flesh, in contrast to Lent, which is all about the spirit. It is also all about light, emerging as it does from the pagan celebration of the birthday of the sun. In *Saturnalia*, Lucian writes about the custom at parties of electing one of the assembled company temporary 'king'. This king gives silly orders, 'telling one man to shout out something disgraceful about himself, another to dance naked, pick up the flute girl and carry her three times around the room'. In this sense, wearing antler horns, falling over and photocopying your naked behind at the office party is very much in the true spirit of Christmas, and the Malvolios who would sneer at such vulgar activities during the season are missing the point.

Soon after the early Christian Church established 25 December, the winter solstice, as the date for the feast of Christmas, other feasts sprang up: the 26th was for Stephen, the first Christian martyr; the 27th for John the Evangelist; and the 28th for the Massacre of the Holy Innocents by Herod. At the other end was 6 January, the feast of the Epiphany. And so it was that in 567, the Council of Tours declared the whole twelve days a festival. Originally, the more ascetically minded members of the council persuaded the rest to keep three days in the middle as a fast, but soon they gave up on that idea. It was clear that the people were intent on keeping New Year's Eve as an occasion for revelry as well. The Twelve Days of Christmas became the most important festival of the year in the colder North European countries. It was a brilliant idea: the revelry was guilt free because it simultaneously celebrated Christ's birth, and so pleasure and piety were happily married.

Nearly one hundred years later, the custom of the long holiday at Christmas persists, despite the best efforts of the Puritans and the Commonwealth to abolish it. It is common practice these days for people to arrange their holidays in such a way that we do no work between 23 December and 2 or 3 January, giving a ten-day break. The 2 or 3 January would have been considered too early to return to work by the medievals, in the days before those two enemies of nature, central heating and electric lighting, came along and extended the working day and the working season. Therefore I propose the following strategy for those of you who would like to celebrate Christmas in the old – and by 'old', I mean pre-1535 – way. Simply tell your boss that you cannot return to work till Plough Monday, and say that this is for religious reasons. If pressed, inform him or her that your religion is 'pre-Reformation Christian'. Surely in our politically correct age the boss will have to respect the fact that it is against your deeply held religious convictions to perform any sort of work before the Feast of the Epiphany.

Christmas was the time for hospitality, and right into the Tudor age the grand houses were expected to throw open their doors and provide a feast for the tenants. The villeins would bring gifts of produce from the farm. This custom was noted by Tusser:

At Christmas be merie and thankfull withal,
and feast they poore neighbors, the great with the small.

One common custom at Christmas was the 'wassail'. This means 'your health' in old English, and thus approximates to our custom of saying 'Cheers' when about to start drinking. A bowl full of punch would be passed from guest to guest, shouts of 'wassail' and 'drinkhail' accompanying the boozing. Ronald Hutton quotes the following account of an elaborate wassail and feast from 1555. Into the room came 'twelve wessels with maidens singing, with their wessels; and after came the chief wives singing with their wessels; and the gentlewoman had ordained a great table of banquet, desserts of spices and fruit, as marmalade, gingerbread, jelly, comfit, sugar plate and diverse others'.

Wassailing also referred to the custom of wandering from house to house begging for treats, rather in the fashion of the song 'We Wish You a Merry Christmas', which includes the lines 'Bring us some figgy pudding' and 'We won't go until we get some.' It was also of course a time of gift-giving: Tusser says that at Christmas people 'gave many gifts'.

Christmas in Decline

These sorts of lavish Christmases continued through the religious upheavals of the sixteenth and seventeenth centuries. In the 1640s, Sir Humphrey Mildmay of Danbury in Essex hired a fool for New Year's Day and played dice, card and board games most evenings. By 1702, though, such hospitality was in decline, as Poor Robin's Almanac noted:

But now landlords and tenants too
In making feasts are very slow;
One in an age, or near so far,
Or one perhaps each blazing star;
The cook now and the butler too
Have little or nothing for to do.

The reforming Scots were the first to try to abolish Christmas as a papist feast. In Aberdeen in 1573, a church court tried fourteen women for 'playing, dancing and singing of filthy carols on Yull Day at even'. In 1593, the nobles of Elgin banned all 'profane pastime . . . viz, footballing through town, snowballing, singing of carols, or other profane songs, guising, piping, violing and dancing'.

During the dark days of the Commonwealth, Christmas was again attacked. In 1643, Parliament went into work as usual on 25 December, and many of the London churches were closed. In January 1645, Christmas was abolished by law. The ban led to outbreaks of violence, which turned into Royalist uprisings at Canterbury. The idea of 'rioting for Christmas' may seem odd to us, but it really did happen. The effect of the Puritan ban was actually to drive Christmas underground and make outlaws of those who celebrated it. The feast returned with the Restoration in 1660. The Protestant reformers had failed to ban Christmas.

Light and Greenery

One obvious winter task is to decorate the house. There is a tendency today to scoff at those households who cover the outside of their home with complex arrangements of coloured lights and glowing Father Christmases, but what they are doing is merely a modern continuation of what Christmas was always about, a celebration of light at the turning point of winter. When the nights are short, we need to make our own light, whether with candles, gas or electricity, and I think that to brighten up a house in this joyful way is actually life-affirming, and a far better use of the light bulb than keeping the machines working all night, which was its original purpose.

A more refined version of this modern custom, and one which I notice has returned lately, probably as a result of a recommendation in one of those 'beautiful homes' magazines, is the Tudor habit of putting a lighted candle in each window, and this clearly has a cost advantage over fairy lights. There is no point, either, in wasting money on artificial Christmas decorations when holly and ivy are available free or very cheaply. Fill the house with holly and ivy and you will create a thorough and intense Christmas vibe. The idea here is to celebrate life at the most lifeless season of the year, hence the arrival of the evergreens in the house.

How cheap and easy it would be to re-create the medieval Christmas. Instead of burdening Mother with the cooking, the guests (or villeins) should all bring a dish. Take as much time off work as possible! Switch off the television and computer and play bridge, backgammon and chess instead. At the court of Charles II, Twelfth Night was a night for gambling. Stage Christmas plays. A Mummers' play re-enacting the battle between St George and the dragon was put on by the North Devon Mummers at my local pub last Christmas. The players followed up the performance with a set of drinking songs. The pub was packed and we made merry, children and all. A Puritan observer in 1643 would have been horrified by the spectacle of such old-fashioned, superstitious and popish merriment. But it is truly wonderful that these old ways persist and that they are spontaneously organized by the people and not the result of some horrific plan cooked up by central government or local councils.

Governments are generally suspicious of merriment, and it was not long ago that the UK government cracked down on raves in fields, again driving merry-makers underground. In the case of rave, with its ecstatic dancing, almost religious in nature, the movement was later effectively destroyed by being commodified and sold to tourists as a uniquely British attraction via the conduit of the Ministry of Sound and other money-grubbing operations. Rave was also overtaken by the wet, narcissistic and apolitical Britpop scene, which was far more attractive to governments, rock'n'roll having been thoroughly and effectively commodified already.

There are signs, though, that music-making is returning to its pre-Industrial past. It became a 'product' in the fifties, and the following five decades saw great fortunes made by popular troubadours, and even greater fortunes by the owners of the record companies. Today, music is returning to the pubs, and the proliferation of music festivals shows that live music is more popular than ever. And, indeed, the big record companies have noticed this: HMV, for example, has invested in live-music venues and shares in the profits of the Glastonbury Festival.

Such festivals, though, are costly blow-outs for the punters and big money-makers for the owners. Sadly, it is very difficult to sustain a free festival, because of the bureaucracy and general form-filling involved. Free festivals do not contribute to GDP, and therefore are not generally encouraged. For the past few years, I have helped out at a local free festival in North Devon. The festival is completely volunteer-run, and by careful planning, for eight years we have been able to put on a fabulous free party at low cost. The funds are raised through an auction, through the bar, by selling sites for stalls in the market, and by local businesses advertising in the programme. This year, though, there was trouble. There were fights and hard-drug dealers. The result of this is that our festival has become high

risk. That means that to run it next year we would have to spend
£40,000 on extra policing. Since our total budget is £30,000, this is
just not viable. I have heard similar stories about other festivals: one
Saturday-night fight, of the sort that happens every weekend in every
market town across Blighty, can cost you £40,000. So now what
do we do? We have considered going down the commercial route
and charging for tickets. But that ruins the point of the free festival.
And it would mean that we had submitted to the commodification
of merriment.

A Time for Singing and Games

One Christmas custom that I have introduced is the ukulele sing-
along. Each Yuletide, at the in-laws', I take my ukulele and we sing
old carols, as well as pop hits such as 'Merry Xmas (Everybody's
Having Fun)' by the inimitable Slade. It's a wonderful feeling:
rather than listening to the experts on television, we amateurs make
our own racket. So it is that at Christmas every sense is indulged: the
eyes are delighted by the candles and the decorations; the nose by the
delicious smells of food cooking; the ears by (mostly) sweet music;
the mouth by the feast with its beer and wine; and our sense of touch
by hugging and kissing each other.

Kisses were a central feature of the Old World. Lords and ladies
were encouraged to kiss their servants as a mark both of reverence
and humility. On Maundy Thursday, the well-to-do were asked to
kiss the feet of the poor, and on Good Friday people kissed the cross.
Indeed, medieval folk seemed to be kissing each other – and holy
relics – non-stop. In his excellent study *The Senses in Late Medieval
England*, C.M. Woolgar observes: 'When two people kissed, their
"spirits", that is their breath, mixed and were joined, from which
a sweetness of the mind was born: it bound together the minds of

those kissing, so it was a threefold kiss – physical, spiritual and intellectual.'

In the rich sensual world of the Middle Ages, and particularly in the later period, kissing was heavy with symbolic significance. It was later frowned upon by the proto-Puritan Lollards and then the unsensual Puritans. But again, the custom persists, and in recent years I have noticed a new readiness amongst male friends to hug and kiss each other. I think English men are more likely to express affection for each other physically than they were twenty years ago. And this is not a new relaxation of formality: it is a return to the Old World ease – a Catholic or continental habit that has returned to Blighty, which, it seems, swings perpetually from its inner Malvolio to its inner Sir Toby Belch.

Another feature of the old Christmases was dancing, and again it is a great shame that today, instead of dancing ourselves, we tend to watch other people doing so on television, on shows such as *Strictly Come Dancing*. The existence of these shows, though even just as spectators – and the continuing success of musical theatre – demonstrates that we still love dancing, despite the best efforts of the Puritans to wipe it out. Clearly, we need to bring back dancing lessons, and the sort of dancing where we actually dance with each other rather than bobbing up and down on the spot, which is the custom in the modern disco. My own dance moves were picked up from watching other people during the rave years. But how dearly I would love to do the galliard with my Lady!

Read now the beautiful description of Christmas at Camelot, as it appears in *Sir Gawain and the Green Knight*, that great and very alliterative poem of the late fourteenth century. What is particularly striking is that Christmas is celebrated in a huge gang. It's like a commune of lords and ladies:

This king lay at Camelot one Christmastide
With loyal lords, liegemen peerless
Members rightly reckoned of the Round Table,
In splendid celebration, seemly and carefree.
There tussling in tournament time and again
Jousted in jollity these gentle knights,
Then in court carnival song catches and danced;
For there the feasting flowed for fully fifteen days
With all the meat and merry-making men could devise,
Gladly ringing glee, glorious to hear
Debonair rejoicing by day, dancing at night!
All was happiness in the height in halls and chambers
For lords and their ladies, delectable joy.
With all delights on earth they housed there together,
The most renowned knights acknowledging Christ,
The loveliest ladies to live in all time,
And the comeliest king ever to keep court.
For this goodly gathering was in its golden age
Far famed,
Well graced by God's good will,
With its mettlesome king acclaimed:
So hardy a host on hill
Could not with ease be named.

Let me conclude with some more remarks from Chesterton, for
whom Christmas was a time to retreat from the busy New World.
For him, Christmas was all about freedom:

But let there be one night when things grow luminous from within: and one day when men seek for all that is buried in themselves;
and discover, where she is indeed hidden, behind locked gates

and shuttered windows, and doors thrice barred and bolted, the spirit of liberty.

December's Booze

We have given a few hints on how Christmas was celebrated in the old days. Now here is a recipe for making the popular medieval drink, spiced ale. Note that this is a modern version: as mentioned earlier, hops began to be used to flavour beer only in the very late Middle Ages. Before that, ale was made from a variety of ingredients.

1 gallon ale
Sugar, nutmeg, cinnamon, ginger
12 small apples, peeled with cores removed
Cream, salt

Heat ¾ of the beer, but do not boil. In a separate pot, mix ¼ of the beer, apples, sugar, nutmeg, cinnamon and ginger. Boil. Mix both into large serving bowl. Whip cream and add to mixture or separately to each glass.
Be merry.

December's Husbandry

Sadly, the pages for December were torn out of the manuscript of Palladius that was used for the medieval translation, presumably by a medieval thief who wanted to take the tips back to his own house. But we do have this winter scene from Virgil:

Et quidam seros hiberni ad luminis ignes
pervigilat ferroque faces inspicat acuto;
interea longum cantu solata laborem
arguto coniunx percurrit pectine telas.

[One I know spends wakeful hours by the late blaze of a winter
fire, and with sharp knife prints torches; his wife the while solaces
with song her long toil, runs the shrill shuttle through the web.]
   – *Georgics*, Book I, ll. 291–4

Or, as the contemporary poet might write:

> One there is I know
> Who sits up late in winter and watches telly,
> Generally a DVD box set of *The Wire*, while his wife,
> Humming tunes from *Mamma Mia* to herself,
> Moves mouse and updates her Twitter and Facebook page.

(Shouldn't we be doing something useful and enriching rather
than Twittering our lives away? When you Twitter and go on
Facebook, you are merely increasing the value of Twitter and
Facebook, who make profits from the time you spend on their
programmes by selling advertising space on them. As you waste
your time, you make profits for someone else.)

Although Virgil mentions a few light tasks for the winter months,
he is clear on the main purpose of the season, which is to party:

Hiems ignava colono.
frigoribus parto agricolae plerumque fruuntur
mutuaque inter se laeti convivia curant.
invitat genialis hiems curasque resolvit.

[Winter is the farmer's lazy time: when it's cold outside farmers
enjoy their gains and give themselves to mutual entertainment.
Genial winter plays host and charms away their worries.]

— *Georgics*, Book I, ll. 299–302

The medieval phrase was 'winter's rest'. And at home, we
experienced exactly this in the winter of 09/10. In January, we were
snowed in for ten days, and the children could not get to school.
As a result, work was suspended and instead we concentrated on
playing games, keeping our wood fire blazing, watching films,
cooking and doing a bit of extra Latin grammar. Snow brought a
cessation of toil, it stopped the wheels of commerce turning, and for
that we thanked it.

Tusser, like Virgil, recommends that the good husbandman
sharpen his tools during those long December nights: 'Get grind-
stone and whetstone, for toole that is dulle.'

Today's Old Worlder will sharpen his scythe blade – so superior
to the Strimmer. Protect your strawberries from the frost, adds
Tusser, with a good mulch:

> If frost doe continue, take this for a lawe,
> the strawberies looke to be covered with strawe.

To ensure that your bees survive the winter, as today, you need to
feed them:

> Go looke to thy bees, if the hive be too light,
> set water and honie, with rosemarie dight.
> Which set in a dish ful of sticks in the hive,
> from danger of famine yee save them alive.

For Tusser again, Christmas is the time for great feasts, for hospitality, and for the relaxation of class boundaries:

> At Christmas we banquet, the rich with the poore,
> who then (but the miser) but openeth [h]is doore?
> At Christmas of Christ many Carols we sing,
> and give many gifts in the joy of that King.

Tusser repeats the now familiar theme of the hardness of winter, and therefore the necessity of neighbourliness and charity, particularly towards the old and the weak (and I'm happy to say that this custom persists today):

> At Christmas the hardnes of Winter doth rage,
> a griper of all things and specially age:
> Then lightly poore people, the yoong with the old,
> be sorest oppressed with hunger and cold.

> At Christmas by labour is little to get,
> that wanting, the poorest in danger are set.
> What season then better, of all the whole yeere,
> thy needie poore neighbour to comfort and cheere?

As to what to eat, Tusser offers the following tips:

> Good bread and good drinke, a good fier in the hall,
> brawne, pudding and souse, and good mustard withall.

> Beefe, mutton and porke, shred pies of the best,
> pig, veale, goose and capon, and turkey well dressed;

Cheese, apples and nuts, joly Carols to heare,
as then in the countrie is counted good cheare.

Note that the carols of those days were 'joly' and not the gloomy
dirges of today. It was presumably these 'joly' carols which were
denounced by Puritan reformers as profane.

John Evelyn does not mention merry-making in his *Kalendarium*
but sticks closely to his brief, which is the work to be done in the
garden. Clearly, by the seventeenth century, merriment had ebbed
away from the centre of life, and the gardening guidebooks were
more strictly practical. Like the others, Evelyn repeats the perennial
advice that you should continue to dig and dung. He also says that a
few sowings can be made: 'Sow for *early Beans*, and *Pease*, but take
heed of the *Frosts*; therefore surest to defer it till after *Christmas*, unless
the *Winter* promise very moderate.'

This reminds us that, in the Old World, in the pear orchard –
as well as, as we have seen, in the apple orchard – a succession of
different varieties, ripening at different times, was used in order to
provide fresh fruit over the longest possible period. And they had the
most delectable names: 'The Squib-pear, Spindle-pear, Doyonere,
Virgin, Gascogne-Bergomot, Scarlet-pear, Stopple-pear . . . '

Evelyn is also thinking about his irrigation systems, and decides
to cover his water pipes in some Old World lagging: 'Look to your
*Fountain-Pipe*s, and cover them with fresh and *warm Litter* out of the
Stable, a good *thickness*, lest the *Frost* cracks them.'

Well, if only we had listened to Evelyn in our first year in the
farmhouse. For our unlagged pipes did indeed freeze. It took a lot
of work with the blowtorch to unfreeze them, work which was
carried out – did I mention this sad event before? – by the local
village rogue, who took advantage of our city-bred helplessness and
charged us a small fortune for this little job.

Cobbett's entry for December is by far the shortest of all the months, so while, like Evelyn, he does not actively tell you to have a good time, clearly there is less work to do and therefore more time for japes and conviviality. But just for the record, he does advise that you:

[S]ow radishes on heat, or on warm borders . . . cover peas and beans . . . Hedge, ditch, and drain as wanted, dig, trench, and manure vacant land . . . FLOWER GARDEN – Nothing can be usefully sown or planted [huzzah!]; protect tender shrubs and plants by matting them, or straw, cover bulbs from frost.

Chucking some straw around always seems like a good idea, from many points of view. All gardeners would do well to buy themselves one or two small bales each year. As well as being useful for the compost heap, for litter and for mulch, straw looks very beautiful, especially in its bale form when the sun hits it.

John Seymour gives no instructions for December beyond the injunction to cart muck and dig and tidy up, and, of course, to feast. And, while we are on the subject of Seymour, I have heard from more than one well-placed source that Seymour himself was not quite as effective a smallholder as he presented himself to be. His talent, like Tusser's, was perhaps more in the communication of the thing than in the actual doing of it. Furthermore, he sent many idealistic young families out into the wilds chasing the silly and impossible dream of 'self-sufficiency'. Many returned to the cities three years later, chastened and hungry. Matt Holland of Lower Shore Farm in Swindon, an excellent set-up which runs courses on poultry, vegetables and other aspects of smallholding, says that he far prefers the word 'resourcefulness'. So do not feel guilty when you buy stuff: why bother going to all the trouble of growing and storing maincrop potatoes, for example, when good sackfuls can be bought so cheaply?

December's Merriment

Clearly, the principal feast of the season is Christmas, and really we should give ourselves up to the full twelve days of merry-making.

December's Calendar

10 December: Lux Mundi. A French festival to celebrate the goddess
Liberty.

17 December: First day of Saturnalia.

21 December: Winter solstice.

24 December: Fast day.

25 December: Christmas Day.

26 December: Feast of St Stephen.

27 December: Feast of St John the Evangelist.

28 December: Feast of the Holy Innocents.

31 December: Hogmanay, the feast of Hogmagog.

Dramatis Personae

Here are short biographies of the great authorities on husbandry, in chronological order.

HESIOD is known as the father of Greek didactic poetry. He probably lived in the eighth century BC. He was born at Ascar, near Mount Helicon. His poem *Works and Days* is a sort of shepherds' calendar. The first third argues against idleness and praises hard work. The second gives various rules on husbandry, and the third is a religious calendar of the months.

XENOPHON (430–354 BC) was a wealthy Athenian and a friend of Socrates. He fought on behalf of the Persian king Cyrus in 401 BC, and then led the Greeks back to the coast. He joined the Spartans and was exiled from Athens in 394 BC. He was given an estate by the Spartans, where he lived for years, writing, hunting and educating his sons. He is the author of *Anabasis*, an account of his homeward march. He is also the author of four books featuring Socrates: *Memorabilia*, *Apology*, *Symposium* and *Oeconomicus*, which gives advice on household management.

CATO (234–149 BC). Marcus Porcius Cato was a Roman statesman and soldier. He was the first important writer in Latin prose. Most of his works are lost, but we have *De Agricultura*, a terse guide to farming which includes many recipes.

VARRO, MARCUS TERENTIUS (116–27 BC) was a renowned man of learning. He was a man of affairs, an antiquarian, historian, philologist, student of science, agriculturist and poet. He lived to be ninety years old. He wrote seventy works, but only one complete work survives, and that is *De Re Rustica*, his farming and gardening manual.

VIRGIL (Publius Vergilius Maro) was born on 15 October 70 BC near Mantua and educated at Cremona, Milan and Rome. Like his friend Horace, he came from the yeoman class. After studying rhetoric, he studied philosophy with Siro the Epicurean. He was supposedly shy, and slow in speech. He wrote in perfect hexameters. His pastoral poems, the *Eclogues*, were finished in Rome and published in 37 BC. He spent the next seven years writing his great didactic farming poem, *The Georgics*. He then wrote the *Aeneid*. In 19 BC he set out for Athens with the plan to spend three years polishing the poem. But he was taken ill on the journey, and died at the age of fifty.

COLUMELLA (Lucius Junius Moderatus Columella) was born near the beginning of the first century of our era. He was a native of Spain, but went to live in Rome. He lived during the time of Pliny the Elder and Seneca. He owned various farms in Italy. He is known for his *De Re Rustica*, a systematic treatise on agricultural affairs with advice on everything from soil management to beekeeping, and *De Arboribus*, about vines, olives and other trees.

PLINY THE ELDER, Gaius Plinius Secundus (AD 23–79), pursued a military career in Germany and an administrative one in Gaul and Spain under the emperor Vespasian. Many of his works are lost, but his great 37-volume *Naturalis Historia* survives.

PALLADIUS, Rutilius Taurus Aemilianus, was a Roman writer of the fifth century AD. His poem *De Re Rustica* was written in fourteen books and was largely derived from Columella and the rest. It was, however, a favourite of the medievals, who translated it.

THOMAS TUSSER (1524–80) was an East Anglian farmer whose rhyming guide to husbandry, *A Hundreth Goode Pointes of Husbandrie*, later expanded to *Five Hundreth Pointes*, was a Tudor best-seller. He was an excellent chorister when a boy. He had a hellish time at Eton and then went to Trinity Hall, Cambridge, which he loved. On leaving Cambridge, he spent ten years as court musician at the service of William, First Baron Paget of Beaudesart. He then farmed in Suffolk, and wrote his *Hundreth Good Pointes*. Later he became a singer at Norwich cathedral, and then a farmer again. Although Thomas Fuller said he farmed to 'no profit', Tusser did in fact leave a small estate in Cambridgeshire in his will, suggesting that he was not altogether a failure.

JOHN EVELYN (1620–1706) was a famous diarist. He lived with his grandmother near Lewes, Sussex, when a boy. He went to Balliol College, Oxford, and left without taking a degree. He fought in Holland and returned in the autumn of 1641 to find England on the brink of civil war. He travelled in France and Italy. Under the Commonwealth, he spent his time gardening at Sayes Court at Deptford. Later, the gardens were wrecked by a tenant, Peter the Great, who made it one of his amusements to ride in a wheelbarrow along a thick holly hedge planted by Evelyn. Evelyn was one of the promoters of the Royal Society and had various jobs at the court of Charles II. His book *Sylva* was a plea to replant the forests which were being torn down for fuel for the glass factories and iron furnaces. The preface to the book asserted that he really had induced landowners to plant millions of trees. His work on gardening, *Directions for the Gardiner*, was never published in his lifetime.

WILLIAM COBBETT (1763–1835) was a radical writer, autodidact, reformer and politician. The son of a small farmer, he grew up near Guildford. He had a boring job as a clerk at the age of seventeen but left it to go to Chatham with the intention of joining the army. While waiting there he read huge piles of books and learned by heart Lowth's *English Grammar*. He moved to the United States in 1792. In 1796, he set up in Philadelphia as a bookseller and publisher of his own works. He moved back to England in 1800, having been fined for various libels (these fines would dog him all his life). He got himself in debt and wrote a guide to English grammar which sold ten thousand copies in a month. Back in England, he farmed at Botley in Hampshire. He wrote a weekly paper entitled *Cobbett's Register*, which sold over seventy thousand copies a week and was the *Private Eye* of its day. His husbandry guidebook, *Cottage Economy*, was published in 1829, and *The English Gardener* in 1833. He became MP for Oldham later in life.

JOHN SEYMOUR (1914–2004) was a writer and smallholder. He travelled when young in Africa and then lived on a houseboat and various farms in England. His husbandry guidebook, *Self-Sufficiency*, was published by Faber & Faber in 1970 and, in 1974, the young publishers Dorling Kindersley released an illustrated version, *The Complete Guide to Self-Sufficiency*. The book was a big hit. Seymour also made radio and TV programmes, and started a self-sufficiency school in Ireland. He was arrested in 1999 for damaging GM crops.

Bibliography

A list of the books I read and consulted while writing this one.

Bacon, Francis, 'On Gardens', collected in *A Century of English Essays*
    (London: Dent, 1929)
Biddick, Kathleen, *The Other Economy: Pastoral Husbandry on a Medieval*
    Estate (London: University of California Press, 1989)
Buhner, Stephen Harrod, *Sacred and Herbal Healing Beers*
    (Boulder: Siris Books, 1998)
Butler, Colin, *The World of the Honey Bee* (London: Collins, 1959)
Campbell, Susan, *A History of Kitchen Gardening*
    (London: Frances Lincoln, 2005)
Cato and Varro, *De Re Rustica*, trans. W. D. Hooper & H. B. Ash
    (London: William Heinemann Ltd, 1979)
Chaucer, Geoffrey, *The Canterbury Tales*, ed. A. C. Cawley
    (London: Dent, 1984)
Chesterton, G. K., *Fancies Versus Fads* (London: Methuen, 1923)
— *The Thing* (London: Sheed & Ward, 1931)
Clare, John, *The Shepherd's Calendar*
    (Oxford: Oxford University Press, 1973)
Cobbett, William, *Cottage Economy*, (Oxford: Oxford University Press,
    1980)
— *The English Gardener* (Oxford: Oxford University Press, 1979)

Columella, *On Agriculture*, Books I–IV, trans. Harrison Boyd Ash
    (London: Harvard University Press, 2001)
— *On Agriculture*, Books V–IX, trans. E. S. Forster & Edward H.
    Heffner (London: Harvard University Press, 1968)
— *On Agriculture*, Books X–XII, *Trees*, trans. E. S. Forster & Edward
    H. Heffner (London: Harvard University Press, 2001)
Cowper, William, *The Task* (London: Routledge, 1875)
Darwin, Charles, *The Formation of Vegetable Mould through the Action of*
    Worms with Observations on their Habits
    (London: Faber & Faber, 1945)
Duffy, Eamon, *The Stripping of the Altars: Traditional Religion in England*
    1400–1580 (New Haven & London: Yale University Press, 1992)
Ehrenreich, Barbara, *Dancing in the Streets: A History of Collective Joy*
    (New York: Metropolitan Books, 2007)
Evans, Jeremy, *The Complete Guide to Beekeeping*
    (West Ashling: Bees & Things, 2005)
Evelyn, John, *Directions for the Gardiner and Other Horticultural Advice*, ed.
    Maggie Campbell-Culver (Oxford: Oxford University Press, 2009)
Fearnley-Whittingstall, Hugh, *The River Cottage Cookbook*
    (London: HarperCollins, 2001)
Fergusson, Rosalind, *Chambers' Book of Days: A Miscellany of Popular*
    Antiquities in Connection with the Calendar (Edinburgh: Chambers
    Harrap, 2005)
Fukuoka, Masanobu, *The One-Straw Revolution*
    (Mapusa, Goa: Other India Press, 2005)
Fuller, Thomas, *The Worthies of England*
    (London: George Allen & Unwin Ltd, 1952)
Gimpel, Jean, *The Medieval Machine: The Industrial Revolution of the Middle*
    Ages (London: Futura Publications Ltd, 1974)
Goodchild, Claude and Thompson, Alan, *Keeping Poultry and Rabbits*
    on Scraps (London: Penguin, 2008)
Glover, T. R., *Virgil* (London: Methuen, 1942)
Grigson, Jane, *Charcuterie and French Pork Cookery*
    (London: Penguin, 1969)

Henisch, Bridget Ann, *The Medieval Calendar Year*
(Pennsylvania: Pennsylvania State University Press, 2002)

Holmes, Richard, *Coleridge: Early Visions*
(London: HarperCollins, 1998)

Hutton, Ronald, *Stations of the Sun: A History of the Ritual Year in Britain*
(Oxford: Oxford University Press, 1996)

Huxley, Aldous, *Brave New World* (London: Penguin, 1935)

Innes, Jocasta, *The Country Kitchen* (London: Frances Lincoln, 2003)

Irving, Miles, *The Forager Handbook: A Guide to the Edible Plants of Britain*
(London: Ebury, 2009)

Johnson, Samuel, *The Works of Samuel Johnson, LL.D., A New Edition in
Twelve Volumes* (London: 1823)

Jones, Myfanwy and Tsintziras, Spiri, *Parlour Games for Modern Families*
(London: Penguin, 2009)

Katz, Sandor Ellix, *Wild Fermentation: The Flavour, Nutrition and Craft
of Live-Culture Foods* (White River Junction, Vermont: Chelsea
Green, 2003)

Landsberg, Sylvia, *The Medieval Garden*
(London: British Museum Press, 1998)

Larkcom, Joy, *Grow Your Own Vegetables*
(London: Frances Lincoln, 2002)

Linebaugh, Peter, *The Magna Carta Manifesto: Liberties and Commons for
All* (Berkeley: University of California Press, 2008)

Logsdon, Gene, *The Contrary Farmer*
(Post Mills, Vermont: Chelsea Green, 1970)

Longnon, Jean and Cazelles, Raymond (introduction), *Les Très Riches
Heures du Duc de Berry* (London: Thames & Hudson, 1993)

Massingham, H. J., *The English Countryman: A Study of the English
Tradition* (London: B. T. Batsford, 1943)

McKay, James, *The Complete Guide to Ferrets*
(Shrewsbury: Swan Hill Press, 2004)

Niall, Ian, *The New Poacher's Handbook* (London: Heinemann, 1960)

Orwell, George, *The Road to Wigan Pier* (London: Penguin, 1962)
— *Diaries* (London: Harvill Secker, 2009)

Ovid, *Fasti*, trans. Sir James George Frazer
    (London: William Heinemann Ltd, 1959)

Palladius, *On Husbondrie*, ed. Revd Barton Lodge MA
    (London: N. Trübner & Co, 1873)

Pennick, Nigel, *The Pagan Book of Days: A Guide to the Festivals,*
    Traditions and Sacred Days of the Year (Rochester, Vermont: Destiny
    Books, 2001)

Phoebus, Gaston, *The Hunting Book* (London: Regent Books, 1984)

Pliny, *Naturalis Historia* (London: William Heinemann Ltd, 1971)

Ramsay, David, *Unforgotten Exmoor: Words and Pictures from a Vanished Era*
    (Porlock: Rare Books & Berry, 2009)

Rhys, Ernest (introduction), *A Century of English Essays, Ranging from*
    Caxton to R. L. Stevenson to the Writers of Our Own Time
    (London: J. M. Dent & Sons Ltd, 1929)

Schramm, Ken, *The Compleat Meadmaker*
    (Boulder: Brewers Publications, 2003)

Seymour, John and Sally, *Self-Sufficiency: The Science and Art of Producing*
    and Preserving Your Own Food (London: Faber & Faber, 1970)

Singer, Andrew, *Backyard Poultry Book* (Bridport: Prism Press, 1988)

Sommer, H. Oskar (ed.) *The Kalender of Shepherdes: The Edition of Paris*
    1503 in Photographic Facsimile (London: Kegan Paul, Trench,
    Trübner & Co., 1892)

Spenser, Edmund, *The Faerie Queene*, ed. Thomas P. Roche Jr
    (London: Penguin, 1984)

Steiner, Rudolf, *Bees*
    (Great Barrington, MA: Anthroposophic Press, 1998)
  — *Agriculture Course: The Birth of the Biodynamic Method*
    (Forest Row: Rudolf Steiner Press, 2008)

Stone, Brian (trans.), *Sir Gawain and the Green Knight*
    (London: Penguin, 1964)

Thomas, Dirk, *The Harrowsmith Guide to Wood Heat*
    (Charlotte, Vermont: Camden House Publishing, Inc., 1992)

Thompson, Flora, *Lark Rise to Candleford*
    (Oxford: Oxford University Press, 1965)

Thompson, Laura, *Life in a Cold Climate: Nancy Mitford*
 (London: Headline Review, 2004)

Tusser, Thomas, *Five Hundred Points of Good Husbandry*
 (Oxford: Oxford University Press, 1984)

Virgil, *The Eclogues, The Georgics, The Aeneid* I–VI, trans.
 H. R. Fairclough (London: Harvard University Press, 2006)

Voltaire, *Candide* (Paris: Bordas, 1982)

Walton, Izaak, *The Compleat Angler* (London: J. M. Dent & Sons, 1953)

Waring, Adrian and Claire, *Teach Yourself Beekeeping*
 (London: Hodder Headline, 2006)

Wender, Dorothea (trans.), *Hesiod and Theognis* (London: Penguin, 1973)

White, Revd Gilbert, *The Natural History of Selborne Vol. 1*
 (London: Cassell, 1887)

Whitley, Andrew, *Bread Matters: The State of Modern Bread and a Definitive
 Guide to Baking Your Own* (London: Fourth Estate, 2006)

Whitlock, Ralph, *A Calendar of Country Customs*
 (London: B. T. Batsford Ltd, 1978)

Woolgar, C. M., *The Senses in Late Medieval England*
 (New Haven & London: Yale University Press, 2006)

Xenophon, *Memorabilia, Oeconomicus, Symposium, Apology*, trans.
 E. C. Marchant & O. J. Todd (London: Harvard University Press,
 1923)

TOM HODGKINSON

HOW TO BE FREE

MODERN LIFE IS ABSURD. HOW CAN WE BE FREE?

If you've ever wondered why you bother to go to work, or why so much of consumer culture is crap, then this book is for you. Looking to history, literature and philosophy for inspiration, Tom Hodgkinson provides a joyful blueprint for a simpler and freer way of life. Filled with practical tips as well as inspiring reflections, here you can learn how to throw off the shackles of anxiety, bureaucracy, debt, governments, housework, supermarkets, waste and much else besides.

Are you ready to be free? Read this book and find out.

'One of the most provocatively entertaining, creatively subversive and, frankly, essential manifestoes of this or any moment' *Time Out*

'As a follow-up to his charming *How to be Idle*, Tom Hodgkinson offers nothing less than a manifesto of resistance to the modern world' *Guardian*

'An inspiring collection for those of us who yearn to cast off our corporate and consumer shackles' *Psychologies*

TOM HODGKINSON

HOW TO BE IDLE

Society today extols the virtues of efficiency and frowns upon laziness, but as Oscar Wilde once said: doing nothing is hard work. As modern life grows more and more demanding, the loafers of this world can feel the odds stacking against them. But help is at hand! From Tom Hodgkinson, editor of *The Idler*, comes an antidote to the work-obsessed culture that puts so many obstacles between ourselves and our dreams. Learn how to reclaim your right to sleep in, skive off, lunch at leisure, have a hangover and take time out; and how to let the day slip past you in the best possible way. The message is clear: in so doing, you'll be taking control of your life.

Are you ready to be idle? Read this book and find out.

'A superb, life-enhancing celebration of idleness. A book to be enjoyed at leisure and to change lives' *Sunday Times*

'So stuffed with wisdom and so studded with good jokes that I raced through it like a speed freak' *Independent on Sunday*

TOM HODGKINSON

THE IDLE PARENT

Modern life is wrecking childhood. Why can't we just leave our kids alone?

If you've ever wondered why so many of today's children are unhappy, spoilt, stressed and selfish, then the answers and the remedy are to be found in *The Idle Parent*. Tom Hodgkinson wants us to leave our kids be, to give them the space and time to grow into self-reliant, confident, inquisitive, happy and free people. Full of practical tips on what to do and (more importantly) what not to do, Tom will not only help your kids to be happier but will also help you, their parents, live happier and more fulfilled lives.

'Wise, practical, funny, personal, it will make you a much better parent' **Oliver James**

'An inspiring book, genuinely subversive. Time to put away "silly adult things" and embrace childhood in all its messy glory' *London Lite*

'A recipe for bright, happy people with need of neither television nor shrink. Who could ask for more?' *Evening Standard*

He just wanted a decent book to read ...

Not too much to ask, is it? It was in 1935 when Allen Lane, Managing Director of Bodley Head Publishers, stood on a platform at Exeter railway station looking for something good to read on his journey back to London. His choice was limited to popular magazines and poor-quality paperbacks – the same choice faced every day by the vast majority of readers, few of whom could afford hardbacks. Lane's disappointment and subsequent anger at the range of books generally available led him to found a company – and change the world.

'We believed in the existence in this country of a vast reading public for intelligent books at a low price, and staked everything on it'
Sir Allen Lane, 1902–1970, founder of Penguin Books

The quality paperback had arrived – and not just in bookshops. Lane was adamant that his Penguins should appear in chain stores and tobacconists, and should cost no more than a packet of cigarettes.

Reading habits (and cigarette prices) have changed since 1935, but Penguin still believes in publishing the best books for everybody to enjoy. We still believe that good design costs no more than bad design, and we still believe that quality books published passionately and responsibly make the world a better place.

So wherever you see the little bird – whether it's on a piece of prize-winning literary fiction or a celebrity autobiography, political tour de force or historical masterpiece, a serial-killer thriller, reference book, world classic or a piece of pure escapism – you can bet that it represents the very best that the genre has to offer.

Whatever you like to read – trust Penguin.